MW01088061

Thinking about God

JPS
ESSENTIAL
JUDAISM
SERIES

University of Nebraska Press
Lincoln

Thinking about God

Jewish Views

RABBI KARI H. TULING

The Jewish Publication Society
Philadelphia

© 2020 by Kari H. Tuling

All rights reserved. Published by the University of
Nebraska Press as a Jewish Publication Society book.

Manufactured in the United States of America.

Library of Congress Cataloging-in-Publication Data
Names: Tuling, Kari H., author.
Title: Thinking about God: Jewish views / Rabbi
Kari H. Tuling.
Description: Lincoln: University of Nebraska Press,
[2020] | Series: JPS essential Judaism | Includes
bibliographical references and index.
Identifiers: LCCN 2019042781
ISBN 9780827613010 (paperback)
ISBN 9780827618466 (epub)
ISBN 9780827618473 (mobi)
ISBN 9780827618480 (pdf)
Subjects: LCSH: God (Judaism) | Bible. Old
Testament—Criticism, interpretation, etc. |
Rabbinical literature—History and criticism.
Classification: LCC BM610 .T85 2020 |
DDC 296.3/11—dc23
LC record available at https://lccn.loc.gov/2019042781

Set in Merope by Mikala R. Kolander.

For Carol and Gerald, my parents

For Ben, my son

For Tom, my love

Contents

PART 2.
Does God Have a Personality — or Is God an Impersonal Force?

PART 3.
Does God Redeem — or Might God Not Redeem?

PART 4.

Is God a Covenantal Partner and Lawgiver — or Might These Roles Be Rethought in the Modern Age?

Acknowledgments

This book has its origins in a course called "Jewish God Concepts" I taught for the Department of Jewish Studies at the University of Cincinnati. I am grateful to the department for its support during those years.

I would like to thank Rabbi Barry Schwartz, director of The Jewish Publication Society (JPS), for suggesting that I write this book on the basis of that course's syllabus, and for shaping the book's structure and content. His input has pushed me to reconsider and rework major portions of this book in multiple ways, and the work has benefited greatly as a result. I am also deeply thankful to Joy Weinberg, the JPS managing editor, for her careful reading and astute editing. Her vision of what the book should accomplish and her understanding of the reader's perspective has made it much more effective as a pedagogical tool. Together, their thoughtful and insightful critique at each step of the process has been nothing short of transformative, in the best sense of that word. I also express my deep appreciation to the University of Nebraska Press team for working with me to bring this book to fruition. It has been a wonderful experience.

I would also like to thank Barbara Wolff, the artist who produced the wonderful work, "To Him That Made the Great Lights," a detail of which graces the front cover. I encourage you to visit her website, artofbarbarawolff.com, to appreciate the full image as well as the range and depth of her artwork.

Thank you to the Memorial Foundation for Jewish Culture for their financial support during the writing of my unpublished dissertation, *Between Maimonides and Kant: Hermann Cohen's Religion of Reason*. Significant portions of the dissertation appear in this book. I also offer thanks to my dissertation readers, Barry Kogan and Michael Meyer, as well as the faculty and library staff of the Hebrew Union College—Jewish Institute of Religion.

I also greatly appreciate the members of my congregation, Kol Haverim in Glastonbury, Connecticut, for their ongoing enthusiasm for this project, and for their willingness to read the work-in-progress. Thank you to my lay leadership team as well as the Kol Haverim staff for their support.

My deepest thanks, of course, go to my immediate family: my parents Gerald and Carol, my son Ben, and my husband Tom. You make everything possible. Your unwavering belief in the value of this book and of the work I do has given me much strength. I love you.

Introduction

Why should we care about theology? What difference, really, does it make if we think of God as a bearded gentleman or as an invisible force? Why should it matter whether someone thinks this or that event is the will of God?

Theology defines what is possible in our lives. To give an example: If you believe in miracles, then miracles can happen in your life. And if you do not, then they cannot. This is not a form of magical thinking but a statement about the role of belief. Our conceptions shape the contours of our world. So your decision as to whether or not miracles are possible determines whether or not events will qualify as miracles for you. Your theology, in other words, sets limits—expansive or restrictive—of what is possible in your world.

It is very common, in fact, for a person's theology to change over time. In the book of Genesis, for example, we see Joseph's theological self-understanding evolve. In his arrogant youth, Joseph's brothers throw him in a pit and then sell him as a slave to Egyptians, but by the time his brothers arrive in Egypt years later desperate for food, Joseph is vizier, second in command only to Pharaoh. He could have them killed, of course, or imprisoned. Instead, he decides to test them, to determine whether they would abandon another brother as callously as they had abandoned him. After a couple of ruses, he is satisfied that they have changed and reveals himself to them, weeping:

Then Joseph said to his brothers, "Come forward to me." And when they came forward, he said, "I am your brother Joseph, he whom you sold into Egypt. Now, do not be distressed or reproach yourselves because you sold me hither; it was to save life that God sent me ahead of you. It is now two years that there has been famine in the land, and there are still five years to come in which there shall be no yield from tilling. God has sent me ahead of you to ensure your survival on earth, and to save your lives in an extraordinary deliverance. So, it was not you who sent me here, but God—who has made me a father to Pharaoh, lord of all his household, and ruler over the whole land of Egypt. (Gen. 45:4–8)[1]

Joseph's optimism here seems to be a useful choice. He finds a way to forgive his brothers for their brutal treatment of him. But still there is a problem: we are left with that canard, "It was God's will." If we accept that the good things that happen are God's will, do we not have to accept that of the bad as well?

We see, rather, that Joseph's understanding of God changes as he grows older. One might say his theology improves. As the story continues, we learn that there is still a current of mistrust between Joseph and his brothers. Many years later, after their father dies, the brothers appear before Joseph and beg for their lives. Convinced he has been waiting for this moment before exacting his revenge, they make up a story in the hope that Joseph will be moved to have mercy on them. But Joseph tells them: What you had intended for evil, God transformed into good. The jealousy that led you to sell me into slavery ultimately became the catalyst for saving a population from starvation. And on this basis, he forgives them.

This is a more nuanced theology than what we saw earlier. Notice that he does not say it was God's will. Notice also that he does not argue that things had to happen this way. Nor does he pretend that his brothers' motives were pure, or that their actions were any less destructive than they actually were. Rather, Joseph has created a theology that allows him to heal and forgive, by assuming that God has transformed all the negatives into something positive.

Defining Theologies

If I were to ask you to define your own theology, would you know how to answer? Whenever I have asked this question of students in my classes, the *theists* (persons who believe that God exists) in the group usually speak in experiential terms: they articulate times they felt God was near to them. The *atheists* (persons who believe there is no God) usually speak in material terms: they suggest that science explains all we know, and there is no room for the metaphysical in this universe. Some claim that belief in God is a form of "magical thinking."

After that initial conversation, however, things get more difficult to articulate. There is more to define than the simple binary of "does God exist/not exist?" There are quite a few options, actually. *Animism* is the idea that all things in the world, including objects like rocks and stones, are alive in some way, possibly inhabited by demigods. *Dualism* is the idea that two powers are at work in the universe, usually opposed to one another. *Monolatry* is the belief in one god who has power above all other gods that are worshiped. *Monotheism* is the worship of a single god or god-concept rather than a collection of gods. *Pantheism*, the idea that God is present in all things, and *panentheism*, the idea that all things are part of God, are yet other possibilities.

Judaism is considered to be *monotheistic*. It is possible, however, that the Hebrew Bible shows traces of *monolatry*, possibly as remnants of earlier thought. We see examples in the text, such as in the Song of the Sea, which reads: "Who is like You among the celestials / Who is like You, majestic in holiness, / Awesome in splendor, working wonders!" (Exod. 15:11). The "celestials" here may be angels, but they also may be other gods.

There is yet another dimension to consider: is the presence of God close to us, or very far? *Immanence* is the idea that God is experienced as being very near and personal to us; *transcendence*, on the other hand, is the idea that God serves as the distant, commanding, and awesome power. Some god-concepts include both; others favor one over the other.

Mysticism puts the emphasis on the *immanence* of God. In this spiritual orientation, one attempts to achieve union or communion with God by going beyond the boundaries of time or space, either through specific ritual practices or through the study of specific texts, particularly those that disclose a hidden meaning. One of the forms of medieval Jewish mysticism is the *Kabbalah*. The word means "that which is received," referring to the how these texts were conveyed, as a tradition, by mouth from a learned master to a student. *Hasidism*, another mystical movement, was started by the Baal Shem Tov in eighteenth-century Poland. A healer and charismatic spiritual leader, he taught his followers to be joyous and wholehearted in their worship.

By contrast, *rationalism* — theologically speaking, the analysis of the evidence for God and faith on the basis of empirical results — puts the emphasis on the *transcendence* of God. The preeminent rationalist in the Jewish tradition is Moses Maimonides, the twelfth-century polymath who was an original and subtle thinker in the fields of Jewish law, philosophy, and medicine. In the modern and postmodern era, rationalist thinkers include the German-Jewish professor and philosopher Hermann Cohen from the liberal/Reform stream of Judaism, and the American scholar and rabbi Joseph Soloveitchik from the traditional/Orthodox world.

A few more concepts may be helpful as we get started. *Providence* is the idea that God takes care of us, seeing to it that our lives unfold according to plan. If you believe there is no *free will*, you may believe that God takes care of all the details of life. If so, that would mean we live in a *deterministic* universe, where everything is preordained. However, it is more common to believe that we do have free will. Yet another option is *limited determinism*, which is the idea that God controls some things but not others.

My Theological Journey

Personally, I have not always found it possible to believe in God. It's a strange confession from a rabbi, I suppose, given that I have made my living as a representative of God, but it is quite true. I grew up, as many of us do, with a basic sense of God as a king or father-figure, but once I reached young adulthood, I had deep problems with that god-concept. I would call myself an atheist simply because I could not conceive of a god worthy of worship. As a college student, I posted quotes about atheism on my dorm-room bulletin board. Nothing religious made any kind of sense to me.

What changed my life, however—what put me on this path first as a Jewish seeker and ultimately as a rabbi—was a book of Jewish theology. I was in an adult b'nai mitzvah course at the time. One day, as I advocated my very rationalist point of view about God, Rabbi Allen Krause (now of blessed memory) observed that I agreed with Maimonides. So, on a business trip in Boston, when I saw a book about Maimonides written by Abraham Joshua Heschel, I picked it up to read on the airplane.

I really liked the book; when I saw another one of Heschel's books, I bought that one too. I believe that the second book I picked up was *God in Search of Man*, but I am not entirely certain; it could have been *Man's Quest for God* or *Man Is Not Alone*, for I devoured several of his theological works in rapid succession. I read everything Heschel wrote with "God" or "man" in the title within the span of weeks. It is still a bit of a blur: I dove deep, rarely surfacing between books.

What I found so persuasive in Heschel's work was the idea that the path to God is through wonder. Heschel pointed to our sense of awe at the everyday, such as the sight of scarlet and orange leaves in the fall, or the sound of a small child's giggle, or the delicate taste of a ripe peach. He vividly evoked our feeling of radical amazement in those moments when we stand before the ocean or see the valleys stretch out below us from a mountaintop. These, he said, are the first steps toward appreciation of the Divine, because they point to a realm beyond our understanding, a realm in which we feel a kinship with the world around us. There's a lipstick mark in my copy of *God in Search of Man* from when I was so overwhelmed by this idea of radical amazement that I let the book drop from my hands. I was thinking then of the experience of being in deep forest, where it is both so very quiet—absent the noise of people and traffic—yet also so wholly alive with sounds—the presence of the trees, the birds, and the wind.

Furthermore, Heschel explained that the very purpose of worship was to become aware of those moments in which we are no longer locked within the confines of our own needs and desires, but rather united with the whole of life. In prayer, we are attempting to rise above ourselves, to transcend what we are capable of doing alone, to seek that which is more meaningful than our passing existence. Prayer also allows us to voice that sheer gratitude we feel just to be alive. That "aha!" moment I experienced when I let the book fall, recalling that feeling of being in deep forest surrounded by the world—it was named *gratitude*!

Ultimately, it was profoundly moving for me to encounter a deeply religious person who was also spiritually honest. In the place of neat answers and tidy constructs, Heschel asked searching questions. Two examples: "What formula could explain and solve the enigma of the very fact of thinking?"[2] and, what if "the feeling of awe" that we experience in the presence of nature is actually a "misunderstanding of an ordinary fact"?[3] Heschel demanded truthful answers. As he wrote in response to the first question, "The most incomprehensible fact is the fact that we comprehend at all,"[4] and in response to the second: "In asserting that the ineffable is spiritually real, independent of our perception, we do not endow a mere idea with existence, just as I do not do so in asserting, 'This is an ocean', when I am carried away by its waves. The ineffable is there before we form an idea of it."[5] In the context of his prose, I met a genuinely pious Jew who could pray, really pray, even in the wake of tragedy, even in the wake of great pain, even as a refugee who barely escaped from Europe and could do nothing to save his mother and three sisters from being killed in the Holocaust. I imitated him, as best I could, in little steps.

I did not start out knowing how to pray. At the time, I did not yet know Hebrew or the mechanics of prayer. I was still deeply alienated from God. But the attempt to imitate Heschel, his life, and his way of prayer was what led me to this life, where I am now, a rabbi, a profoundly committed Jew, a human being whose heart is open to sensing and celebrating the Divine in my life. In these ways, prayer has changed my life radically.

Of course, sometimes we feel more grateful than at other times. Some years after my ordination, I was invited to speak at my son's Jewish day school about prayer. I was recovering from ankle surgery and—thinking the kids might be curious about my bright purple cast—I decided to speak about *Asher Yatzar*, the prayer thanking God for our ability to stand before God and pray. As the prayer explains, if one of our tiny openings were to shut—or one of our closed places were to open—we would not be able to stand. As I told the assembled students, I now understood more precisely what that prayer meant: a small set of ligaments maybe a centimeter long had been able to sweep me off of my feet.

In the days leading up to the ankle surgery I had fretted a lot; I was worried about it. My husband mused on the fact that while I now believed that God created the whole world and everything in it, it appeared I was deeply concerned that God was not sufficiently involved in the details. I laughed at the thought of such a contradiction and then said, yes, exactly: chaos is built into the system. The surgical outcome—and more generally, what would happen in my life over the next week—was wholly unpredictable, at least at some level.

In fact, these days I have the sense that built into the chaos of the cosmos is a kind of Divine delight in our endless human ability to surprise, to create whole new possibilities out of the materials we have been given.

But if God does experience surprise, wouldn't there also be surprises that would be much less welcome to God? Think, for example, of what God demands of us in the Bible. We are to be just, to act uprightly. We are commanded: Love your neighbor as yourself. Do not stand idle while your neighbor bleeds. If you see your enemy struggling to keep a load from falling, help. Do not put a stumbling block before the blind. Keep honest weights and measures. Do not oppress the stranger, the orphan, the widow—or anyone else who is vulnerable, for that matter. What happens when we choose badly? What happens when we hurt others, either in malice or by mistake?

It seems to me that affirming the existence of God also means affirming that justice is demanded of us, even in the face of a chaotic world. The fact that we cannot be certain of a particular outcome in advance does not mean that there is no God, or that God has no concern for us, or that God is not all-powerful, or that we are free to behave as we please, consequences be damned. There are indeed consequences.

Please do not ask me to explain them to you, though, in some kind of neat phrase that sums up why such things happen. In fact, as far as I am concerned, any theology that can confidently explain why children get cancer is a monstrosity. As I see it, chaos is built into the system, and sometimes truly hideous things happen to perfectly good people. Affirming that there is moral coherence in the world, that the world makes sense at a deep level, is not the same thing as affirming that all the loose ends will tie up neatly. So it is that I can pray intently for healing, and maybe even intensely feel the positive energy generated by those prayers, but I cannot make a deal with God to live to see my great-grandchildren, or to guarantee that my own child comes to no harm.

What I can do, and did, is to write this book — a book I never would have imagined writing when I was a young adult, and the very book I wish had been available to me at the start of my own Jewish journey. I wrote it in the hope that it might help you, the reader, understand what I then did not yet know: in the Jewish tradition there are many diverse, often contradictory, and entirely sophisticated ways to think about God.

About This Book

Based on a course I developed for the University of Cincinnati, *Thinking about God: Jewish Views* unfolds as a series of topical questions about the nature of God.

Many books on Jewish theology introduce readers to major thinkers or theologies, sometimes dividing Jewish theology into discrete historical periods. Yet, I would argue, the project of Jewish theology is not moved forward solely by the work of this or that idiosyncratic thinker, and works organized strictly chronologically make it difficult to fully acknowledge the intertextual nature of evolving god-concepts. The Bible, for example, is not from a single period in a long history; it is also a living document, still present and relevant to the conversation that unfolds now. So, too, are all the other texts, regardless of timing. A Jewish theologian today will respond to the full tapestry of Jewish thought — all of it, biblical to postmodern — all at once. Thus this work uniquely addresses these realities, in three ways: (1) it is organized topically, (2) it covers the full span of Jewish history, and (3) it takes an intertextual approach by highlighting the interplay between texts over time and how the later texts participate in the ongoing process of Jewish commentary.

Four parts—"Is God the Creator and Source of All Being—Including Evil?," "Does God Have a Personality—or Is God an Impersonal Force?," "Does God Redeem—or Might God Not Redeem?," and "Is God a Covenantal Partner and Lawgiver—or Might These Roles Be Rethought in the Modern Age?"—offer different contexts for thinking about the nature of God. Every chapter opens with three questions, the first of which seeks to identify how a particular theological conundrum has been understood by different strands of Jewish tradition from biblical times to the present. We begin with the Hebrew Bible: "A Biblical View." In every chapter, each of the subsequent sections—"From the Liturgy," "A Rabbinic View," "A Medieval View," "A Modern View" (always more than one)—responds directly or indirectly to the biblical text. Then, after a summary of the views presented, the second two questions appear to flesh out the larger questions at hand.

Chapter 1, "What Does It Mean to Say That God Created the World?," addresses how different strands of Jewish tradition through the ages have understood God's Creation of the world, along with the meaning of the seven-day Creation narrative and the intended role of humanity. In looking at explanations of God's rationale for Creation over the course of some two thousand years, we see considerable disparities. Bachya Ibn Pakuda, a Jewish philosopher from eleventh-century Spain, sought to establish that each thing in the world has its cause, in a chain of causes that goes all the way back to God, who in turn precedes Creation as its first and only cause. But in the rabbinic view, the Torah itself served as the blueprint for the Creation of the world. The modern thinker Rabbi Lawrence

Kushner similarly made use of this rabbinic text to suggest that the biblical seven-day Creation story is not taken to be historical—it is not expected to convey in scientific terms precisely how the world came to exist. However, it is taken to be true—as it addresses the deep structure of reality and God's relation to it.

Chapter 2, "How Does Evil Exist in a World with a Good God?," considers how different strands of Jewish tradition have addressed the apparent contradiction implied by the coexistence of evil with a good and all-powerful God. Choosing to embrace—rather than spurn—the shadow side of our psyche, the ancient Rabbis concluded that some of our baser yearnings—such as our desire to be something in the world—serve to motivate our highest achievements. On the other hand, Maimonides suggested that our highest calling is the contemplation of God, and we must regulate our appetites to stay focused on that goal. In the modern period, the German philosopher Hermann Cohen argued that just as the introduction of sin in the Adam and Eve story is indicative of moral development within the Hebrew Bible, we, too, can also grow in moral maturity, by maintaining awareness of the correlation between what God demands of us (the highest ideal of what is good) and what we are able to accomplish.

Chapter 3, "Is God Like a Person?," evaluates the variety of Jewish answers to the question of God's physical form, along with the questions of what is to be gained when we think of God as a person and how imagining a personal God is different from imagining God as an impersonal force. In the Rabbis' view, God does not live in the world the same way other beings do; rather, the world exists *within* God. On the other hand, Maimonides argued that God does not have a body; rather, whenever the Bible describes God as having a body, it is speaking metaphorically. Similarly, the modern existentialist thinker Martin Buber viewed Moses' encounter with God at Mount Sinai as an experience involving a direct Revelation, but not requiring an embodied God.

The other chapters present equally diverse viewpoints. Chapter 4, "Does God Have a Gender?," investigates the question of God's gender, in addition to how masculine images of God might affect how women are viewed in society and whether it is possible to leave a traditional text with male God imagery intact but rethink its meaning. Chapter 5, "What Does It Mean to Declare God Is One?," focuses on God's oneness, along with what it means to bear witness to God's oneness and what it might mean to pray as one (community). Chapter 6, "Does God Intervene in Our Lives?," explores how different strands of Jewish tradition have understood God's involvement in our individual and communal lives, including whether God acts on behalf of the Jewish community, and whether the State of Israel's creation is evidence of divine providence. Chapter 7, "Does God Intervene in History?," discusses how different strands of the tradition have responded to the question of God's intervention when tragedy has befallen the Jewish people, as well as, in the modern era, why God was silent during the Holocaust and whether the experience of great suffering ought to change our relationship to God. Chapter 8, "What Is the Relationship between God and Israel?," considers the relationship between God and the Jewish people, along with what it means to enact a covenant with God and whether this covenant is a metaphor or conveys a literal reality. Chapter 9, "Is It a Binding Covenant?," investigates this concept further, specifically whether the covenant is binding for all time, whether it is necessary to take on a legal commitment to ethical norms for generations to come, and how the doctrine of a special relationship between God and the Jewish people can be maintained in a pluralistic world. Finally, chapter 10, "How Should the Revealed Law Be Understood?," addresses how different strands of Jewish tradition have approached the interpretation of revealed law. It also looks at the rise of a literalist fundamentalist understanding of the revealed law in ultra-Orthodox Judaism and how a foundational document such as the Torah may continue to be reimagined. The latter is a weighty task indeed. For one, while the revealed law involves a choice—one may choose to heed the commandments or choose to ignore them—in the Bible, this choice is also presented as the choice between life and death.

Most chapter sections focus on a single text intended to give you a sense of how the thinker lays out a theological argument. Early on in the section you will find an extended quotation of text. *Do not panic if the quoted text makes no sense to you on the first reading.* I will break down the text into smaller components and walk you through the key points. The most difficult texts are often the most profound.

Finally, this work has an index, enabling you to look up a specific thinker or idea and see how that perspective applies in other contexts.

Choices in This Book

In choosing the thinkers represented here, I sought to strike a balance between various streams of Jewish thought, so that (for example) a mystic and a rationalist could face off in the same chapter. Similarly, I sought out female voices whenever possible. Theology is not just for and by men.

Nor is god-language strictly masculine. For this reason, I have used two different JPS works for Bible translations. For the first five books of the Bible (Genesis, Exodus, Leviticus, Numbers, and Deuteronomy), there is an excellent gender-neutral translation, *The Contemporary Torah: A Gender-Sensitive Adaptation of the JPS Translation*, edited by David Stein. For all other citations, I have made use of the JPS *TANAKH*, which uses male pronouns for God.

You will also notice that certain thinkers appear in multiple chapters, which may be taken as one indication of the individual's greater impact upon Jewish thought. There are exceptions, of course. Maimonides, based on his influence, easily could have been quoted in every chapter, but his work is particularly challenging for beginners, so he appears only sparsely here.

With regard to source texts, whenever possible I have chosen excerpts from full-length works in English or English translation. Some magnificent Jewish thinkers have not yet been translated into English, but since I hope that, like me, you might find a favorite and keep reading, I specifically selected thinkers where an English-speaking reader could easily continue the journey of thought. If a writer particularly intrigues you, I encourage you to review both the notes and the bibliography for ideas on what to read next.

Getting the Most out of This Book

The best way to read theology is to reflect on it. In the case of this book, you will get the most out of it if you read a section and then stop to think about it. I recommend that you only move on to read the subsequent section once you have ruminated on its predecessor. The chapter summary sections are intended to consolidate this understanding, by showing how the various sections relate to one another. If anything in the summary section seems surprising, it is an indication that a closer reading of the opening sections is needed.

In the context of a college course or an adult education program, I would recommend discussing each chapter over two or three class sessions. For the first class session of a lower-division or introductory course, the students could be assigned a chapter's opening sections through the summary. The *Thinking about God Study and Discussion Guide* available at jps.org/books/thinking-about-God will help readers test their understanding of the text and consider their own theological perspectives in context. The second class session could use each chapter's two final questions as the basis of discussion. *Study and Discussion Guide* questions could then help direct a third session on individual responses to key issues in the assigned chapters. For an upper-division course, each subsection might be used as an introduction to reading a longer work by the author. For advanced coursework (or for particularly astute undergraduates) this work could be assigned in the first week of class to fill in any gaps in earlier studies. Seminary students may find it useful in this regard as well.

Also, as a congregational rabbi, I am always thinking about sermons. The three questions opening each chapter might easily be used as sermon prompts, and, conveniently, each of them are buttressed with sufficient textual examples to support rhetorical points. Congregational rabbis can address theological concerns in a nuanced way, using a tightly focused selection of texts.

Alternatively, each chapter could be used as a three- or four-part text-based adult education program. Use of the *Study and Discussion Guide* will help deepen the conversation, by offering a still wider range of texts.

However you choose to read this book, I hope that you enjoy it and engage with it deeply.

Thinking about God

Part 1

Is God the Creator and Source of All Being—Including Evil?

Chapter 1

What Does It Mean to Say That God Created the World?

- How have different strands of Jewish tradition understood God's Creation of the world?
- What is the meaning of the seven-day Creation narrative?
- What is the intended role of humanity?

1.1. A Biblical View: In the Image of God

The opening chapter of the Hebrew Bible features one of the most famous sections of biblical text: "When God began to create the heaven and earth" (Gen. 1:1). God creates the world in six days and then rests on the seventh. Near the end of this narrative, in Genesis 1:26–2:3, God creates humanity.

> And God said, "Let us make humankind in our image, after our likeness. They shall rule the fish of the sea, the birds of the sky, the cattle, the whole earth, and all the creeping things that creep on earth."
> And God created humankind in the divine image, creating it in the image of God—creating them male and female.

God blessed them and God said to them, "Be fertile and increase, fill the earth and master it; and rule the fish of the sea, the birds of the sky and all the living things that creep on earth."

God said, "See I give you every seed-bearing plant that is upon all the earth, and every tree that has seed-bearing fruit; they shall be yours for food. And to all the animals on land, to all the birds of the sky, and to everything that creeps on earth, in which there is the breath of life, (I give) all the green plants for food." And it was so.

And God saw all that had been made, and found it very good. And there was evening and there was morning, the sixth day.

The heaven and the earth were finished and all their array. On the seventh day God finished the work that had been undertaken: (God) ceased on the seventh day from doing any of the work. And God blessed the seventh day and declared it holy—having ceased on it from all the work of creation that God had done. (Gen. 1:26-2:3)[1]

Notably, the name of God in the opening biblical text is not the proper name of the God of the Israelites. The proper four-letter name of God, spelled *yod-hey-vav-hey* (YHVH) in Hebrew and known as the Tetragrammaton (or "four letters," from the Greek *tetra*, meaning "four" and *gram* meaning "letter" or "writing"), was never pronounced, except by the High Priest on Yom Kippur, and only in the era when the ancient Temple stood in Jerusalem. Post-Temple Jews continued to observe this prohibition: if the Temple was not standing, then the name would not be said. As a result, Jews have generally substituted the word *Adonai* (meaning "my Lord") for the four-letter name of God.

Our passage, however, does not refer to God either by the Tetragrammaton or *Adonai*. It uses *Elohim*, a generic word for God—actually a plural noun that is treated like a singular noun because it refers to the singular God. At the time the text was written, the use of the generic word *Elohim* rather than the proper name of God was most likely meant to convey the idea that this text describes an event of universal importance. These events affected all peoples, not just the Israelites. Simultaneously, the narrative suggests that the God of the Israelites was the Creator of all being.

Let's look more closely now at the passage. Returning to the first two lines of the text:

> And God said, "Let us make humankind in our image, after our likeness. They shall rule the fish of the sea, the birds of the sky, the cattle, the whole earth, and all the creeping things that creep on earth."

The question of what it means to be created in God's image—specifically, whether God has a body that we may resemble—will be addressed in chapter 3. For now, a second question arises: what does it mean for humanity to "rule" over the other creatures? Perhaps this text was meant to acknowledge humanity's unusual intellectual capabilities. Perhaps it was intended to stress the need for stewardship of the earth's resources. Perhaps it was envisioned to convey awareness that humans are omnivores capable of eating nearly every other creature as food.

The Hebrew Bible does not let us know by elaborating on these points. Rather, the text continues with the creation of humanity:

> And God created humankind in the divine image, creating it in the image of God–creating them male and female.

In this text, the male and female are created together at the same time. By contrast, in Genesis chapter 2, which features the narrative of Adam and Eve, Eve is created from Adam's rib as God's response to Adam's existential loneliness.

Do the two narratives in chapters 1 and 2 represent two separate traditions that an editor or redactor later joined together? Or is the second narrative an elaboration on the first? Your assumptions about the theological origins of this text will shape your answer. If you believe that the Bible is the product of human hands, then you are more likely to read it as a composite document, comprising multiple traditions over time. If you believe that the text is granted to humanity as direct Revelation from God, you are more likely to assume that the second text is an elaboration on the first.

> God blessed them and God said to them, "Be fertile and increase, fill the earth and master it; and rule the fish of the sea, the birds of the sky and all the living things that creep on earth."

This instruction to "be fertile and increase" is actually the first commandment in the Hebrew Bible. The Mishnah (a discussion of legal questions and pithy sayings redacted in the second to third centuries CE by Rabbi Judah the Prince) suggested, on this basis, that every Jewish male bore the responsibility to have at least one boy and one girl. As the Mishnah text states: "A man must not abstain from *fruitfulness and increase,* unless he already has children: The School of Shammai say, Two sons; but the School of Hillel say, A son and a daughter, because it says, *Male and female He created them.*"[2] Jewish females, however, do not have the same requirement. According to *Yebamoth* 65b, a tractate of the Babylonian Talmud (the body of Jewish law and legend comprising the Mishnah and the Gemara), "A man is commanded concerning the duty of propagation but not a woman. R[abbi] Johanan b[en] Baroka, however, said: concerning both of them it is said, *And God blessed them and God said unto them, 'Be fruitful and multiply.'*"[3] The Gemara that follows this Mishnah includes a debate as to whether the commandment applies to both sexes equally; together the man and the woman produce the child, but only the man has the obligation.

> God said, "See I give you every seed-bearing plant that is upon all the earth, and every tree that has seed-bearing fruit; they shall be yours for food. And to all the animals on land, to all the birds of the sky, and to everything that creeps on earth, in which there is the breath of life, (I give) all the green plants for food." And it was so.
> And God saw all that had been made, and found it very good. And there was evening and there was morning, the sixth day.

Notice that in this very first discussion of food in the Bible, only plants were designated as food. As a result, Jewish vegetarians, among others, have argued that vegetarianism was the originally intended diet for humanity. In the perfection of the early Creation, God had provided a means of sustenance for all these new creatures that did not require spilling blood. Later in the text, however, permission is granted for meat-eating.[4]

Ultimately, God's act of Creation represented an ordering of chaotic impulses to produce a world with structure and purpose. The world was spoken into being. God surveyed this peaceable, orderly garden and declared it "very good."

The last paragraph of our selection describes the origin of Shabbat, the weekly day of rest and reflection Jews observe from sundown on Friday through sundown on Saturday. To this day, this text is recited as part of the sanctification of Shabbat:

> The heaven and the earth were finished and all their array. On the seventh day God finished the work that had been undertaken: (God) ceased on the seventh day from doing any of the work.

And God blessed the seventh day and declared it holy—having
ceased on it from all the work of creation that God had done.

Thus the observance of Shabbat was linked to the narrative of Creation: this cycle of activity punctuated by rest was intended to be
part of the grand structure of the universe.

Perhaps, then, we might conclude: just as God created the world—
ordering chaotic impulses into a structured world—our own creativity in generating order from life's chaos is what marks us as
created in the divine image.

1.2. From the Liturgy:
God Renews Creation Day by Day

After the Romans destroyed the Second Temple in Jerusalem in 70
CE, the theological and liturgical structures of the ancient Israelites
were shattered. The institutions of religion and government were
no longer standing, offering animal sacrifices in the Temple was no
longer possible, and the Jewish people were soon dispersed far from
the Land of Israel.

The Judaism we know today is the product of the ancient Rabbis
who lived from the time of the Second Temple's destruction through
the fifth or sixth centuries. These Rabbis developed a comprehensive
response to the destruction: if it were no longer possible to offer
sacrifices at the Second Temple, then the words of the heart would
be offered in their place.

The Rabbis created a prayer structure that mirrored the sacrificial system in the ancient Temple. Just as sacrifices were brought
three times a day, so too the prayers would be said three times daily:
Shaḥarit ("morning," named for the timing of the service), Mincha
("offering," named for the afternoon meal offering), and Ma'ariv
("setting," named for the sunset). A fourth service, called Musaf ("ad-

ditional," named for the additional offering on Shabbat and festivals), was included to parallel the schedule of the ancient Temple services.

The primary formula used for prayer as well as many of the prayer texts themselves originated in this rabbinic era. Additional prayers were introduced in the subsequent centuries, many of them rewritten or reworked as needs changed.

The following prayer from the *Shaḥarit* service praises God for the work of Creation, which is renewed each day:

> You illumine the world and its creatures with mercy; in Your goodness, day after day You renew Creation. How manifold Your works, O Lord; with wisdom you fashioned them all. The earth abounds with Your creations. Uniquely exalted since earliest time, enthroned on praise and prominence since the world began, eternal God, with your manifold mercies continue to love us, our Pillar of strength, protecting Rock, sheltering Shield, sustaining Stronghold.
>
> Our praiseworthy God with vast understanding fashioned the rays of the sun. The good light He created reflects His splendor; radiant lights surround His throne. His heavenly servants in holiness exalt the Almighty, constantly recounting His sacred glory. Praise shall be Yours, Lord our God, for Your wondrous works, for the lights You have fashioned, the sun and the moon which reflect Your glory.[5]

The kind of prayer in this text is praise. In the context of Jewish prayer, praise texts usually focus on God's redemptive acts, reinforcing the terms of the covenant between God and the Jewish people. Other Jewish prayer forms include thanksgiving, lamentation, and petition.

Let's look closely at the prayer, beginning with the illumination portrayed in the first line:

You illumine the world and its creatures with mercy;

In later mystical thought, the illumination came to be seen as God's unending overflow and was depicted as energy or light. In rabbinic thought, however, it likely referred to the light of the sun and stars.

in Your goodness, day after day You renew Creation.

The philosophy known as Deism suggests that God created the world and then walked away from it. It is also known as the "watchmaker" theory: God was like a watchmaker who created all of the intricate movement within the timepiece, wound it up, and then let it go according to the laws of nature. The ancient Rabbis, however, were *not* Deists. In their view, God was involved in Creation daily, even now.

How manifold Your works, O Lord; with wisdom you fashioned them all. The earth abounds with Your creations.

Note that this affirmation is very different from Proverbs 9:1–6, which teaches that wisdom can be personified, as if it were an angel or heavenly being:

> Wisdom has built her house,
> She has hewn her seven pillars.
> She has prepared the feast,
> Mixed the wine,
> and also set the table.
> She has sent out her maids to announce
> On the heights of the town,
> "Let the simple enter here,"
> To those devoid of sense she says,
> "Come, eat my food

And drink the wine I have mixed;
Give up simpleness and live,
Walk in the ways of understanding."

In Proverbs, wisdom takes action, as a person would: "Wisdom has built her house." By contrast, in our prayer from the morning service, wisdom is described as an attribute of God.

The prayer continues:

Uniquely exalted since earliest time, enthroned on praise and prominence since the world began, eternal God, with your manifold mercies continue to love us, our Pillar of strength, protecting Rock, sheltering Shield, sustaining Stronghold.

Observe that while this prayer book uses the masculine pronoun for God, each of these names for God are actually gender-neutral terms. Thus it is not necessary to think of God as male; the liturgy offers us other images. (For more on this, see chapter 4.)

Our praiseworthy God with vast understanding fashioned the rays of the sun. The good light He created reflects His splendor; radiant lights surround His throne.

In the medieval period, the radiant lights would have been thought of as separate intelligences. Influenced by Greek philosophy, medieval Jewish philosophers such as Maimonides suggested that these heavenly bodies contemplated God as they moved in perfect circles. In the rabbinic era, however, these lights were more likely understood as the sun and stars.

His heavenly servants in holiness exalt the Almighty, constantly recounting His sacred glory. Praise shall be Yours, Lord our God, for Your wondrous works, for the lights You have fashioned, the sun and the moon which reflect Your glory.

The heavenly servants here were the angels. In the rabbinic imagination, the angels spent their time singing praises to God. Isaiah 6:3 records that the angels would cry out, "Holy! Holy! Holy! The Lord of Hosts! [God's] presence fills all the earth!"

In our next text, however, the angels were a bit less adoring.

1.3. A Rabbinic View:
The Trouble with Angels

The Rabbis who created the prayer structures that have become normative in Judaism also authored two types of literature: *halakhah*, the legal materials that form the basis of Jewish law, and *aggadah*, the nonlegal stories and commentaries. Taken together, this collected literature comprises a rich record of rabbinic culture: laws and customs, sermons and stories, jokes and folk-cures.

It is clear that the ancient Rabbis were quite willing to engage in questioning, speculation, and argument. At points, their approach to reading was quite playful. This text from the Talmud provides an account of God's (apparently difficult) relationship with the angels:

R[abbi] Judah said in the name of Rav: when the Holy One was about to create man, He first created a company of ministering angels and asked them: Is it your desire that "we make man in our image" (Gen. 1:26)? They replied: Master of the universe, what will be his deeds? God said: Such-and-such shall be his deeds. Indignantly, they exclaimed: Master of the universe, "what is man that Thou art mindful of him, and the son of man that Thou thinkest of him" (Ps. 8:5)? At once He stretched out His little finger among them and consumed them with fire.

The same thing happened with a second company. The third company said to Him: Master of the universe, what did it avail the former [angels that they spoke to You] as they did? The whole world is Yours, and whatever You wish to do therein, do it.

When God came to the generation of the flood and to the generation of the dispersion of mankind, whose deeds were so corrupt, the angels said: Lord of the universe, did not the first [company of angels] speak justly? He retorted, "Even to old age . . . and even to hoar [grey] hair will I put up [with man]" (Isa. 46: 4).[6]

The opening sentence addresses a difficulty in the biblical text. To whom is God speaking when God says, "Let us make man in our image, after our likeness" in Genesis 1:26? The text explains:

R[abbi] Judah said in the name of Rav: when the Holy One was about to create man, He first created a company of ministering angels and asked them: Is it your desire that "we make man in our image" (Gen. 1:26)?

Here, Gen. 1:26 was read as a question: "So, angels, what do you think—should we make humanity in our image?" (This interpretation is not the only one the ancient Rabbis offered.)

A standard rabbinic practice of the time was to teach in the name of another (e.g., "R[abbi] Judah said in the name of Rav . . ."), in order to give credit where credit was due. You might think of it as the ancient Rabbis' way of producing footnotes.

They replied: Master of the universe, what will be his deeds?

Here and elsewhere in the literature of the ancient Rabbis, the angels often opposed the creation of humanity on account of humanity's ability to choose to sin. Angels, by contrast, were unable to choose to do evil. In this text, the angels clearly considered that fact to be in their favor.

God said: Such-and-such shall be his deeds.

The Rabbis were not interested in specifying what actions humanity might take in the world. To them it was sufficient to clarify that God and the angels had a longer conversation regarding this point. The angelic response was not positive:

Indignantly, they exclaimed: Master of the universe, "what is man that Thou art mindful of him, and the son of man that Thou thinkest of him" (Ps. 8:5)?

The angels might not have been able to choose to sin, but they could be a bit jealous of humanity's high place in God's regard. Note that they were quoting from the Psalms—which were attributed to King David—yet they were doing so before humanity was created. Presumably, then, this conversation was happening well before King David was born. In that case, how did the angels know the text? (We will come back to this question, for it illustrates an important theological point.)

Regardless, God was not interested in the angels' point of view:

At once He stretched out His little finger among them and consumed them with fire. The same thing happened with a second company.

Apparently, God got irritated at the naysayings of two companies of angels, and eliminated them both. Still, God decided to create yet another host of angels:

The third company said to Him: Master of the universe, what did it avail the former [angels that they spoke to You] as they did? The whole world is Yours, and whatever You wish to do therein, do it.

Ultimately, the angels stopped trying to convince God that creating humanity was a bad idea. They pursued a new tack: The whole world is Yours, You get to do what You want — so why are You even asking us, since you seem to already have a predetermined answer in mind? Even with that, it appears that the angels were unable to just let things go:

When God came to the generation of the flood and to the generation of the dispersion of mankind, whose deeds were so corrupt, the angels said: Lord of the universe, did not the first [company of angels] speak justly?

The angels might be unable to choose to sin, but they were not above saying "I told you so" to God.

He retorted, "Even to old age . . . and even to hoar [grey] hair will I put up [with man]" (Isa. 46: 4).

God responded to their "told-you-so" with a biblical quote. In rabbinic literature, quoting the Bible was a common way to settle a question.

But it's not that simple. The idea that the angels quoted the Bible to God or that God quoted the Hebrew Bible to the angels raises the interesting problem of narrative time. The Hebrew Bible can be treated as one long story in which the events in the early parts of the text take place before the events in the later parts. However, if the Hebrew Bible is recounting history, then how do the angels know the text? They quoted from it twice: first, before humanity was created, and second, after the great flood. How could the text exist even before it was supposed to have been written? If the Hebrew Bible coexisted with the angels, describing events that had not yet happened, then the Bible is something other than the sacred history of a specific people.

In this conception of it, the Hebrew Bible serves as the blueprint or building plan for the unfolding of history. Therefore, God and the angels both could and did use (and quote) it as an independent source of truth.[7] Importantly, this approach changes how we, too, might read it. First, it elevates the text: the Hebrew Bible becomes a source of metatruths rather than a recital of history. Second, it removes the biblical text from the flow of history, so that its historical accuracy is no longer the core issue. As a result, interpretation of this passage becomes problematic, but fruitfully so. How are we to understand the biblical text, if it is a blueprint of God's plan, told to us as an extended metaphoric riddle?

1.4. A Medieval View: Ibn Pakuda's Logical Analysis

In eleventh-century Spain, "the encounter between Jewish and Arabic literature was particularly fruitful and intense," says the scholar Dean Phillip Bell. "The Umayyad caliphate dissolved into petty principalities during the Period of the Ta'ifa Kings (1009–91); more rulers and courts meant more opportunities for patronage (as in Renaissance Italy)."[8] The works of the Greek philosophers had been translated into Arabic, and both Muslims and Jews were keenly interested in reconciling the scientific worldview of the Greeks with the piety of the received tradition. The rabbi and Jewish philosopher Bachya Ibn Pakuda, author of the classic work of Jewish devotion *Duties of the Heart*, was particularly adept at negotiating both worlds.[9]

The concern in those days was similar to one we encounter in our own day: how to reconcile biblical narratives with scientific truth. In that era, of course, the scientific understanding of the world centered on Aristotle's theory that the earth was the center of the solar system. The stars were considered to be separate intelligences that moved in a circle, the most perfect shape.

More troubling, however, for those who trusted the truth of the biblical narrative was the suggestion from Greek philosophy that the material out of which the world had been made existed eternally. The Hebrew Bible, on the other hand, made it clear that God had created the world. Even more concerning: the dominant Jewish interpretation asserted that the world was not simply created, but created *ex nihilo*, meaning it was created out of nothing at all.

In 1040, Ibn Pakuda set out to prove in a scientific fashion that God had created the world ex nihilo. His argument was laid out similarly to a geometry proof: he raised each possibility and evaluated it according to logical principles:[10]

Three premises are needed in order to prove that the world has indeed been created from nothingness by a single Creator:

1. Nothing can make itself.
2. Causes are limited in number and there must be a first cause that is unpreceded by any other.
3. Everything that is composite is a thing created.

If these three suppositions are correct, everyone who can apply and combine them will see that the world has indeed been created from nothingness by a single Creator, as will be explained in the following, if God so wishes. . . .

The proof of the validity of these three presuppositions is as follows: Everything that comes into a state of being after having been a nonbeing cannot escape one of the two possibilities—

either it made itself, or something else has brought it into being. And everything we imagine to have made itself cannot escape one of two possibilities—either it made itself before it existed, or after. Both these propositions are impossible. . . .

The proof of the validity of the second is as follows: Everything that has an end also has a beginning, for if it has no beginning, neither can it have an end. One cannot reach the limit of something without a starting point. When we reach the end of something we may conclude that it has also a beginning unpreceded by any other beginning—a first and only cause. . . .

The validity of the third presupposition is shown in the following way: Everything that is composite consists without doubt of more than one component. The components naturally precede the composite thing. And so does the maker who puts together the components. He is before it both naturally and in time. The Eternal One is He, who has no cause. Having no cause, He is unprecedented by any other; being unpreceded, he is also unsucceeded.[11]

Let's break down the commentary, starting with Ibn Pakuda's first point:

The proof of the validity of these three presuppositions is as follows: Everything that comes into a state of being after having been a nonbeing cannot escape one of the two possibilities— either it made itself, or something else has brought it into being. And everything we imagine to have made itself cannot escape one of two possibilities—either it made itself before it existed, or after. Both these propositions are impossible.

First, Ibn Pakuda is saying, if a thing exists, *something* made it. A thing cannot make itself. How else could that thing exist?

The proof of the validity of the second is as follows: Everything that has an end also has a beginning, for if it has no beginning, neither can it have an end. One cannot reach the limit of something without a starting point.

Using similar logic, Ibn Pakuda contends that it is not possible to have an infinite chain of causation. If a series of individual distinct things (such as individuals of a species) exists, then each of these were caused by something. Each cause has one before it, and this process goes back to the cause of all causes.

When we reach the end of something we may conclude that it has also a beginning unpreceded by any other beginning—a first and only cause.

Up until now, Ibn Pakuda is seeking to establish the logical necessity that the world was created by a single cause, which he identifies as God. In his third point, he makes this idea explicit.

The validity of the third presupposition is shown in the following way: Everything that is composite consists without doubt of more than one component. The components naturally precede the composite thing. And so does the maker who puts together the components.

Ibn Pakuda starts out simply with a definition: a composite has component parts. Once he gets to the question of what comes first, however, he introduces atomic theory—not in the sense of our modern, scientific understanding of atoms, but rather, that the world is composed of basic elements that are the building blocks for everything. Composite things are built out of simpler things.

Whatever puts the components together into more complicated things must come before all of those things. Ibn Pakuda identifies this compiler as the "maker." He is working toward identifying God as the first cause of all things:

> He is before it both naturally and in time. The Eternal One is He, who has no cause. Having no cause, He is unprecedented by any other; being unpreceded, he is also unsucceeded.

If things cannot create themselves, Ibn Pakuda concludes, then there must be a Creator. In order to be a first cause of all things, this Creator must be eternal, and uncaused. In short, when reading the Creation narrative of the Hebrew Bible, we should assume that each thing has its cause, all the way back to God, who precedes Creation as its first and only cause.

This particular proof may seem to be fairly straightforward: after all, it only has three points, each of which is made using logic and analysis. However, if you try to chart this proof, it quickly becomes evident that he has made more than three points here. His three premises are actually a cluster of ideas that take some work to unpack.

The same might be said of the biblical account of Creation. It may seem to be a simple seven-day narrative, outlining in grand terms how Creation unfolded, but mapping the way each piece fits together illustrates how many assumptions are hidden in the grand design. In this regard, Ibn Pakuda's attempts to reconcile science and the Creation narrative might remind us of the "intelligent design" arguments posed in our day as a counterpoint to evolution theories. However, what Ibn Pakuda offers is less an apologetic for the biblical text than an explanation of how to use reason to address the problem of belief.

1.5. A Modern View:
Green's Divine Helpmate

Mysticism is a spiritual orientation in which one attempts to achieve union or communion with God by going beyond the boundaries of time or space, either by engaging in specific ritual practices or by studying certain texts that disclose a hidden meaning.

Mysticism may be contrasted with rationalism, which involves analyzing God and faith on the basis of empirical evidence. The dichotomy between mysticism and rationalism was brought to the fore in our time by the American philosopher and psychologist William James, who conceived of these categories as opposing personality traits.

However, in the context of Jewish thought, it is possible to find rational mystics. Bachya Ibn Pakuda, for example, might be identified as a rational mystic. We saw evidence of his rationalism in the proof that God had created the world; much of his writing, however, is inward and contemplative. The scholar of Jewish mysticism and neo-Hasidic theologian Rabbi Arthur Green, the author of our text in this section, might best be defined as a humanistic mystic, for he avoids endorsing the idea of a supernatural God.

Let us now turn to the text, from Green's 2003 volume, *Seek My Face*:

Within being, there is an endless drive for manifestation in ever new varied forms, a drive we see manifest as a life force, but that exists beyond the bounds of what we call "animate" as well. As that force drives ever forward for growth and change, the oneness that it bears within it is stretched ever further. Thus is the One renewed in its singularity, as each new form turns out to be naught but itself once again. The One renews itself by stretching forth into the realm of the many. This drive toward self-extension, ever testing the limits of selfhood, as it were, is the One's search for its "other." The inherent tendency toward variety and diversity, combined with the constant reaching toward more complex forms of life, culminates, according to our ancient tale, in the creation of humanity, the crowning achievement of the "sixth day." Only when a self-conscious human being has emerged, one who can both acknowledge the One and insist on the separateness of individual identity, has the test of self-extension begun to reach its goal. We humans are thus the divine helpmate—the *ezer ke-negdo*, both the partner and the one who stands "over against," or "as opposed to." In the very "otherness" of our self-conscious minds, we serve to confirm the existence of the One.[12]

To best understand the text, we will reread and analyze it in four parts:

Within being, there is an endless drive for manifestation in ever new varied forms, a drive we see manifest as a life force, but that exists beyond the bounds of what we call "animate" as well. As that force drives ever forward for growth and change, the oneness that it bears within it is stretched ever further.

Green's identification of a (divine) life force within all things might be characterized as *pantheism*, the idea that God is present within the world. However, within the gamut of pantheism, there are multiple theological possibilities. And since Green's work is fairly new, there is no scholarly consensus as to which way it should be understood.[13] Some candidates:

- *Animism*: all objects are alive in some way, or inhabited by demigods. Green's work, however, is *not* animistic. For example, Green says that the "life force . . . exists beyond the bounds of what we call 'animate' as well." If his work were animistic, then the life force would exist *within* the world, but could not go *beyond* the world.

‣ *Panentheism*: a singular God is present in all things, but God is greater than the whole of creation. Most of Jewish mysticism falls into this category.

‣ *Acosmism*: the universe is really an illusion and everything is part of God. Some of the Hasidic thinkers take an acosmic view. In my view, a strong case can be made for reading Green's work as acosmic.

Green continues:

Thus is the One renewed in its singularity, as each new form turns out to be naught but itself once again. The One renews itself by stretching forth into the realm of the many. This drive toward self-extension, ever testing the limits of selfhood, as it were, is the One's search for its "other."

In this text, everything that exists is considered to be part of God, which is why Green's work expresses a form of pantheism. However, note closely: at no point is the "other" actually separate from God. For this reason, Green's work appears to qualify as acosmism.

The inherent tendency toward variety and diversity, combined with the constant reaching toward more complex forms of life, culminates, according to our ancient tale, in the creation of humanity, the crowning achievement of the "sixth day." Only when a self-conscious human being has emerged, one who can both acknowledge the One and insist on the separateness of individual identity, has the test of self-extension begun to reach its goal.

Here, Green points to humanity as the consciousness that is able to turn back and face God and stand in opposition as God's other.

At this point, he has also introduced the idea of separation between what is human and what is God. Yet we might ask ourselves: is he saying this separation is real, or is it merely an illusion?

In the last few lines, Green identifies the ultimate goal of Creation:

> We humans are thus the divine helpmate—the *ezer ke-negdo*, both the partner and the one who stands "over against," or "as opposed to." In the very "otherness" of our self-conscious minds, we serve to confirm the existence of the One.

Green's term, *ezer ke-negdo*, "a helper for [or opposite] him," appears in Genesis 2:18, when God becomes aware that Adam, the first man, is in need of a partner: "The Lord God said, 'It is not good for man to be alone; I will make a fitting helper for him.'"

In other words, Green characterizes humanity as the end-point of Creation, the divine helper opposite God.

1.6. A Modern View: Kushner's Sermon

Before we delve into Kushner, it is worthwhile to distinguish between a sermon and an academic lecture on theology. While theological claims can be presented in either setting, a sermon tends to be embedded in its context: one typically preaches *to* someone, with the intent of affecting the nature of his or her faith. An academic lecture, by comparison, attempts to transcend its context: it is usually aimed at making claims that can be verified independently by someone who may or may not be of that faith.

The ability to make this kind of distinction became possible in the wake of the Enlightenment, the period in which the modern world emerged from the medieval worldview. One of the Enlightenment's effects was the creation of a secular space in which it became possible to discuss religion as an academic subject.

This next text is a sermon rather than an academic lecture. In making its argument, it relies on an emotional connection to the text rather than a philosophical proof. Its author, Lawrence Kushner, is a contemporary American rabbi whose writing makes use of the homilies found in rabbinic tradition. Specifically, his text builds upon the aforementioned idea that the Torah serves as the blueprint for Creation.

Some definitions before we dive in. The *sefer Torah* is a parchment scroll containing the handwritten Hebrew text of the Torah (first five books of the Bible). A specially trained scribe called a *sofer* writes out the letters by hand and checks it for errors. *Sefer* ("book") and *sofer* ("scribe") share the Hebrew root letters *samekh-feh-resh*, which mean "to count, number; to recount, tell, narrate."[14] Synagogues use a *sefer Torah* as part of their regular weekly worship services.

B'ray-sheet, which can be translated to mean "in the beginning," is the first Hebrew word in the book of Genesis. (This is often transliterated *bereshit*; here I am following the transliteration in the Kushner excerpt.) It is actually a compound word. Its first letter is *beit* (or *bet*), the second letter of the Hebrew alphabet. When used as a suffix on a Hebrew word, *beit* is a preposition that can mean "in" or "with."

At the beginning of the beginning, God was unable to create the world. No matter how many times and how many different ways God tried to arrange them, the parts wouldn't fit together. The universe kept collapsing because God had no diagram, no design.

God said, "I need an overall plan for My world. I want it to be One, as I am One. . . . I know what I will do, I will use Torah as a blueprint for creation and that way all the parts of the world will fit together, and I and My Torah will be inside everything!"

Long ago, our rabbis understood this. When we read in the Book of Proverbs (8:22) that "God made me as the very first thing," the rabbis understood "me" to mean that the Torah preceded creation. They did not mean the *sefer Torah* we keep in the ark but an idea or a plan that God could use. They discovered this same idea when they realized that there were two ways to translate *b'ray-sheet*, the first Hebrew word in the Book of Genesis.

We usually translate *b'ray-sheet* as "In the beginning." But the rabbis noticed that the Hebrew letter *beit* doesn't always mean "in"; it can also mean "with." If that is so, then *b'ray-sheet* (as in "In the beginning God created the heavens and the earth") also could be saying, "With *ray-sheet* God created the heavens and the earth." And this would mean, suggested the rabbis, that *ray-sheet* must be another name for Torah. In other words, God created the world with Torah. Torah is God's blueprint for the world (*Bereshit Rabba* 1:1).[15]

The image of the universe collapsing over and over before God found the proper structure is drawn from Jewish mystical literature, where it was suggested that the primordial first attempts were the source of evil in the world. The failed worlds left a residue that has gummed up the smooth workings of this present Creation. It is a fascinating thought, because it suggests that God is less than fully omnipotent (limitless in power). Here, the world's workings are depicted as not fully under control; God is not always able to manage them.

The idea that the Torah is "inside everything" draws upon the Jewish philosophical tradition. Some medieval writers suggested that knowing Torah is akin to a science: one must engage in the process of discovering the basis of God's thoughts.

Another interesting feature of this text—and one it shares with many others in the chapter—is Kushner's openness to reading the biblical narrative metaphorically. Here he is following the tradition of the ancient Rabbis. Their willingness to interpret the text as a nonhistorical source of truth has enabled Jews throughout the generations to mine the Bible for theological ideas without having to defend the veracity of its scientific claims.

In this approach, the seven-day Creation text is not taken to be historical—it is not expected to convey in scientific terms precisely how the world came to exist. However, it is taken to be true—in that it addresses the deep structure of reality and God's relation to it.

1.7. Summary of Views

In the *biblical text*, God's act of Creation represented an ordering of chaotic impulses into a world with structure and purpose. The world was spoken into being. God surveyed this peaceable, orderly garden and declared it "very good." The observance of Shabbat is linked to this narrative: a cycle of activity and rest is part of the grand structure of the universe, and our ability to rest on the seventh day is linked to our own creation.

The *liturgical text*, part of the prayer structure the ancient Rabbis created in the wake of the Second Temple's destruction, suggested that God has remained involved in Creation ever since it came into being. In this sense, Creation was not a one-time, concluded event. God continues to renew creation day by day.

The *rabbinic text* proposed that the angels opposed the creation of humanity, and that God's decision to go ahead anyway has been a sore point in their relationship. In the rabbinic imagination, the Torah itself served as the blueprint for the creation of the world. In this conception, the Torah stands outside the flow of historical time.

In the *medieval text*, Bachya Ibn Pakuda's three-point proof, designed to reconcile the biblical narratives with scientific truth, also sought to establish that each thing in the world has its cause, in a chain of causes that goes all the way back to God. In this view, God precedes Creation as its first and only cause.

In the first of two *modern texts*, Arthur Green characterizes humanity as the end point of creation: the divine helper opposite God.

In the second text, Lawrence Kushner suggests that the world could only be created once God had a blueprint. Thus the Torah's creation preceded the Creation of the world. We also saw that the Torah does not have to be literally true (in a historical sense) to be metaphorically true (in a theological sense).

1.8. Meaning of the Seven-Day Creation Narrative

Up until this point, we have looked at various understandings of how God created the world. Now let us address the second of our three questions at the beginning of this chapter: What does it mean to say that the heaven and earth were created in seven days? Jews throughout the ages have advanced many possibilities; we will consider just a few of them here.

Benedict Spinoza (1632–77), one of the most significant figures in Western philosophy, was also an apostate Jew who took a pantheistic view with regard to God: he believed that "God" was synonymous with "the natural world as it engages in its usual natural processes."[16] In Spinoza's conception, the Bible was not making a scientific argument when it spoke of a seven-day Creation; rather, the text's purpose was to motivate the masses to follow its laws.

When reading the Spinoza passage, note that *proximate causes* are those causes closest to the effects they produce. So, for example, if I drop a ball on the floor, the proximate cause of the ball's descent to the floor is my hand releasing it. One could, of course, trace the proximate causes back to less proximate causes such as gravitational forces. Ultimately, one could trace these causes back to Nature or God.

6.1. (64) ... Scripture does not teach matters through proximate causes, but only narrates matters in the order and phrases by which it can move human beings ... to devotion [to] the greatest degree; and because of this, it speaks of God and of the matters quite improperly, no doubt since it is not eager to convince reason, but to affect and occupy human beings' fancy and imagination.[17]

Spinoza is arguing that the biblical text is similar to a sermon: its intention is to move a person to action. It does so by appealing to the emotions rather than to the intellect. Spinoza went on to suggest that the Hebrew Bible purposely appealed to the Israelites' emotions in order to effectuate a successful political structure, led by Moses, to govern them.

Spinoza's thought has been profoundly influential. His argument that the Bible is a composite history of the Jewish people (rather than the revealed word of God) has shaped the field of biblical criticism. In addition, many people today who are deeply skeptical of the Hebrew Bible's claims are—consciously or unconsciously—Spinozist in their views. Spinozists tend to believe that the Bible was attempting to exert political control upon the masses. Further, they agree with Spinoza that God is not a supernatural being who exists independently of Creation, but is synonymous with nature's processes endlessly unfolding. To Spinozists, then, the seven-day Creation narrative was intended to convince the masses of the falsehood that there is indeed a God who controls the world.

Another way of understanding the seven-day Creation story, however, is to read the narrative in its historical context. According to biblical scholarship, the story establishes three key points about the God of the Israelites, as compared to the other gods of the Ancient Near East:

- The narrative suggests that the God of the Israelites was the Creator of all being. God did not need to fight other gods for supremacy and then create the world out of their vanquished carcasses, as is recorded in *Enuma Elish*, the Babylonian creation myth.
- It clarifies that the God of the Israelites had full control over the world in the process of creation. No other forces were capable of thwarting God's power. In contrast, another Ancient Near East creation story has two demigods struggle for power over the material universe.
- It indicates that creation unfolded according to the plan of the God of the Israelites. The repetition of "there was evening and there was morning" reinforces this sense of rhythm and order. Unlike other Ancient Near East myths, in which the ultimate outcome of Creation remains in doubt throughout the narrative, here God has a clear plan that unfolds in a predictable pattern.

A third approach to the Creation text is to read it as a metaphor. The ancient Rabbis suggested that the text existed outside of time and space   which meant that it operated outside of a specific historical context. This approach gave them the freedom to move beyond its most literal interpretation. When addressing Creation, in fact, the Rabbis argued against engaging in speculation as to how the world came to be. For example, they wrote in the Talmud:

Why was the world created with the letter *bet* [which is the first letter of the Torah]: Just as *bet* is closed on three sides and open only in front, so you are not permitted to investigate what is above [the heavens] and what is below [the deep], what is before [the six days of creation] and what is [to happen] after [the world's existence] — you are permitted only from the time the world as created and thereafter [the world we live in].[18]

This reading strategy accepts the narrative as a source of insight into the nature of God and repudiates any attempt to reconcile the seven-day account with scientific discovery.

Finally, it is possible to combine elements of each of these strategies for understanding the meaning of Creation. We might think of the text as poetic, in the sense that it has a multilayered meaning that does not have to be squeezed into a rigid framework. Each of these answers (and more) could be invoked depending on the context in which the text is read.

1.9. Intended Role of Humanity

Turning now to the third question posed at the start of this chapter — What is the intended role of humanity? — again we find multiple understandings.

One possible answer is the centrality of the Jewish people in God's plan for Creation. Adherents to this line of thought have argued that the world was created in order for the Torah to be given to God's people, so that they might observe it in the Land of Israel. Consider, for example, this commentary on Genesis 1:1, by Rashi (Rabbi Solomon ben Isaac, 1040–1105), the great commentator best known for his comprehensive commentaries on the Talmud and the TANAKH:

Said Rabbi Isaac: It was not necessary to begin the Torah except from "This month shall mark for you" (Exod. 12:2), which is the first commandment that the Israelites were commanded. Now for what reason did it begin with "When God began"? Because of [the verse] "He revealed to His people His powerful works, in giving them the heritage of nations" (Ps. 111:6). For if the nations of the world should say to Israel, "You are robbers, for you conquered by force the lands of the seven nations (of Canaan)," they will reply, "the entire earth belongs to the Holy

One, blessed be He; he created it and gave it to whomever He deemed proper. When He wished, He gave it to them, and when He wished, He took it away from them and gave it to us."[19]

Here, Rashi suggests that the Torah could have omitted the entire book of Genesis and the first twelve chapters of Exodus. The entire purpose of the story of the Creation of the world was to establish the Israelites' rights to the land; the past is merely prelude to the future. The difficulty, of course, is that this question merely prompts a larger question: Why, then, did God create all the other peoples of the world? (See the further discussion on this topic in chapter 9.)

A second answer is to think in terms of stewardship. Humanity was created in order to take charge of all the animals and all the earth. Along these lines, the ecologically aware contemporary American rabbi Arthur Waskow argues that the core concerns of our lives—food, money, sex, and rest—define our relationship to our Creator. In this passage, food is the focus:

The archetypical story of Eden talks about cracks and flaws that emerge in the flow of Creation when human beings join in the creative process. Poignantly, hopefully, the Bible and all of Jewish tradition look toward some way of healing the split between the earth and its earthlings. I am no longer so surprised as I once would have been to realize that eating is part of the story of this healing, just as it was part of the story of the flaw.[20]

Waskow suggests that our role is to take care of the earth, to heal it from the after-effects of disobedience. Because Adam and Eve did not heed God's command in the Garden of Eden, as punishment the earth would no longer yield its bounty to humanity without toil. Waskow believes that this disobedience caused "a split between the earth and its earthlings" that needs healing, and that the production and consumption of food is an integral part of the healing process. By observing the commandments regarding food—which include the injunctions to allow the land to lie fallow every seventh year and to let the rest of earth's creatures partake of the land when it is left alone—the earthlings are able to repair the world. In essence, humanity's purpose is to tend to the earth, in order to restore it to its original pristine state.

A third possible answer arises from the Jewish mystical tradition. Perhaps God was seeking a partner in Creation? Perhaps God had such a need of us? For example, consider what the great philosopher and theologian Rabbi Abraham Joshua Heschel (1907–72) wrote in *Man Is Not Alone*:

> Man is not an innocent bystander in the cosmic drama. There is in us more kinship with the divine than we are able to believe. The souls of men are candles of the Lord, lit on the cosmic way, rather than fireworks produced by the combustion of nature's explosive compositions, and every soul is indispensable to Him. Man is needed, he is *a need of God*.[21]

In Heschel's view, God created the world in order to have a partner who would fulfill God's will.

A problem arises, though, with Heschel's idea of an anthropopathic God (a God who has the emotions of a person). What if you believe that God is less like a person and more like an abstract force? Is humanity still commanded in this same manner? Can an impersonal universe have a need for us?

We do not know why God created the earth; we are left to wonder. There appears to be purpose and order to it, and we seem to be here for a reason, yet no clear answers are given. The Jewish tradition argues in favor of interpreting Creation as a gift worthy of praise. In the words of the prayer we read above: "You illumine the world and its creatures with mercy; in Your goodness, day after day You renew Creation. How manifold Your works, O Lord; with wisdom you fashioned them all. The earth abounds with Your creations."

Chapter 2

How Does Evil Exist in a World
with a Good God?

· How have different strands of Jewish tradition addressed the apparent coexistence of evil with a good and all-powerful God?
· Do we have free will to choose good over evil?
· Why does God allow evil to exist?

2.1. A Biblical View:
Romping in the Garden of Eden

In Western civilization, the origins of sin are often traced back to the narrative of Adam and Eve in the second chapter of Genesis. Their disobedience is considered to be the moment in which evil enters the world. In the dominant Christian understanding of this text, everyone born thereafter bears the guilt of Adam and Eve's sin. For this reason, their error is often called the Original Sin.

Jewish tradition takes a different approach. In Hebrew, the word most commonly used to denote "sin," *ḥet* (spelled *ḥet-tet-aleph*), has the connotation of "missing the mark," much in the way an archer might miss a target.[1] In the Jewish understanding, sin is not a state of being—unlike Christians, Jews are not encouraged to think of themselves as "sinners"—but rather refers to a mistake a person has made and will hopefully correct. Ultimately, God makes an accounting of each person's life, evaluating how often the individual has missed the mark and addressed the failings—determining whether the balance is positive or negative.

If the concept of Original Sin is not a fixture of Jewish thought, how might Jews understand the meaning of the Adam and Eve narrative? One possible reading is as a maturation story: Adam and Eve grow from a state of naïve and carefree childhood into sexual and relational maturity. Let us read the text of Genesis 2:25–3:13:

> The two of them were naked, the Human and his wife, yet they felt no shame. Now the serpent was the shrewdest of that God[2] had made. It said to the woman, "Did God really say: You shall not eat of any tree of the garden?" The woman replied to the serpent, "We may eat of the fruit of the other trees of the garden. It is only about fruit of the tree in the middle of the garden that God said: 'You shall not eat of it or touch it, lest you die.'" And the serpent said to the woman, "You are not going to die, but God knows that as soon as you eat of it your eyes will be opened and you will be like divine beings who know good and bad." When the woman saw that the tree was good for eating and a delight to the eyes, and that the tree was desirable as a source of wisdom, she took of its fruit and ate. She also gave some to her husband, and he ate. Then the eyes of both of them were opened and they perceived that they were naked; and they sewed together fig leaves and made themselves loincloths.
>
> They heard the sound of God moving about in the garden at the breezy time of day; and the Human and his wife hid from God among the trees of the garden. God called out to the Human and said to him, "Where are you?" He replied, "I heard

the sound of You in the garden, and I was afraid because I was naked, so I hid."

"Who told you that you were naked? Did you eat of the tree from which I had forbidden you to eat?"

The Human said, "The woman You put at my side — she gave me of the tree, and I ate."

And God said to the woman, "What is this you have done!" The woman replied, "The serpent duped me, and I ate."

At the outset this first man and his new female friend are completely unselfconscious, like children blithely running naked through the sprinklers on a warm summer's day. Sexuality has not yet complicated their relationship.

In this regard, the Garden of Eden is a metaphor for childhood. Adam and Eve have no work to do; their Creator cares for all their needs. They spend their time together without any awareness of shame or otherness. In this sense, Eve quite literally appears to be an extension of Adam, rather than a separate human being with her own conscious identity.

Returning to the top of the text:

The two of them were naked, the Human and his wife, yet they felt no shame. Now the serpent was the shrewdest of that God had made. It said to the woman, "Did God really say: You shall not eat of any tree of the garden?"

These introductory verses also introduce a subtle wordplay. In 2:25, the man and woman are described as being *arumim* (naked), and in 3:1 the serpent is depicted as *arum* (shrewd). The Hebrew root that appears in both words (*ayin-resh-mem*) has three distinct meanings: (1) heap up, pile up, (2) to be shrewd, crafty, (3) to lay bare, uncover, denude.[3] Adam and Eve were unaware of their nakedness. The serpent, on the other hand, was fully aware.

The word *arum* can be used both positively and negatively. In the book of Proverbs, it often conveys the good quality of shrewdness, as in Proverbs 22:3, "The shrewd (*arum*) man saw trouble and took cover; / The simple kept going and paid the penalty." Here, however, the intent is clearly negative. The serpent uses its cleverness to seduce Eve into tasting the forbidden fruit:

> The woman replied to the serpent, "We may eat of the fruit of the other trees of the garden. It is only about fruit of the tree in the middle of the garden that God said: 'You shall not eat of it or touch it, lest you die.'"

Eve's speech has a girlish ring to it. She sounds like a child mimicking the grown-ups as she explains the rules to the snake. Notice that she had only been instructed not to eat the fruit; she is the one who introduces the prohibition against touching the fruit. She seems afraid that any kind of bodily contact might be harmful. Perhaps it could lead to other things?

> And the serpent said to the woman, "You are not going to die, but God knows that as soon as you eat of it your eyes will be opened and you will be like divine beings who know good and bad."

The serpent knows better than Eve; it speaks in the voice of an experienced adult. A new verb is also introduced: *yodea*—know, knowing. To know something is to be acquainted with it, to have gained some wisdom, or to have carnal knowledge of it. A theme running through this story is the link between knowledge (manifested in self-consciousness) and sexuality. That is to say, this narrative is a story of mortality, maturity, *and* morality: in the process of grow-ing up, we learn to take responsibility for our actions, including the responsibility for the consequences of our sexual activity.

> When the woman saw that the tree was good for eating and a delight to the eyes, and that the tree was desirable as a source of wisdom, she took of its fruit and ate. She also gave some to her husband, and he ate. Then the eyes of both of them were opened and they perceived that they were naked; and they sewed together fig leaves and made themselves loincloths.

They now perceive that they are naked. The two key words— *arumim* and *yodea* (here conjugated as *vayedu*)—appear again. Sud-denly aware of the "other," Adam and Eve are able to feel shame (and, presumably, desire). Having tasted the forbidden fruits of adulthood, they are children no more.

> They heard the sound of God moving about in the garden at the breezy time of day; and the Human and his wife hid from God among the trees of the garden. God called out to the Hu-man and said to him, "Where are you?" He replied, "I heard the sound of You in the garden, and I was afraid because I was naked, so I hid."
>
> "Who told you that you were naked? Did you eat of the tree from which I had forbidden you to eat?"

This last quote reflects God's dawning awareness that the unsuper-vised children have been misbehaving. The relationship between Adam and his Creator is much like that of parent and child: just as Adam hid, a child also hides his nakedness (i.e., his emerging sexuality) from his parent. Like every parent, God wants to know:

who told you that you were naked? In the place of his unselfconscious little boy romping naked in the woods, God is suddenly faced with a withdrawn, hiding teenager who has not obeyed the house rules.

In response to their sin, the instantly grown Adam and Eve must now take responsibility for themselves. Adam must work all the days of his life to feed himself and his family. Eve will now bear children, and only with pain. They (and presumably we) have learned that romping naked in the woods can lead to unintended consequences, such as pregnancy. The price of the two humans' encounter with the snake in the garden is parenthood and all of its attendant joys and difficulties.

We might reconsider Adam and Eve in light of this understanding. In order for their disobedience to have been a sin, wouldn't they have needed to receive a more complete set of instructions beyond the admonition, "do not eat of this particular tree"? It could be argued the newly formed humans would have needed to fully understand the consequences of their behavior in order for their actions to qualify as a sin. And if they did not sin, the question arises: was their punishment just? Perhaps, nonetheless, their punishment was intended to teach them the consequences of their behavior.

2.2. From the Liturgy:
The Soul You Have Given Me Is Pure

Let us now return to the question of Original Sin.

Some Jewish interpretations of the Adam and Eve narrative have proposed that Adam and Eve's narrative marked the introduction of evil into the world. Mystical Jewish theologies, for example, have suggested that the heavenly light of God was too great for God's creation to bear. Its containers shattered, creating shards, and the scattering of these broken shards dispersed evil throughout the world. Other mystics have posited that evil arises when competing forces within the divine such as compassion and justice get out of balance. If there is too much compassion, then there is no justice (for then God would have compassion for wrongdoers and never enact any kind of punishment, even for heinous crimes). If there is too much justice, then no one is able to stand before God (for God would know that every person has engaged in wrongdoing at some point, and all would be judged most harshly for their transgressions). Thus, to the mystics, an imbalance in the two attributes allows evil to flourish.

For Christians, the interpretation that humanity is ever after marked by Adam and Eve's Original Sin answers the question as to why a savior is needed to redeem humanity. In Paulist theology, for example, Jesus' sacrifice was intended to atone for this sin.

In contrast to the notion of sin being inherent in every human being upon birth, Judaism offers the *Elohai* ("My God") prayer affirming the purity of the human soul.[4] This prayer appears in the *siddur* (Jewish prayer book), as part of the morning blessings in the daily morning service:

> My God, the soul You have given me is pure.
> You created it, You shaped it, You breathed it into me,
> and You protect it within me.
> For as long as my soul is within me,
> I offer thanks to You,
> Adonai, my God
> and God of my ancestors,
> Source of all Creation, Sovereign of all souls.
> Praised are You, Adonai,
> in whose hand is every living soul and the breath of
> humankind.[5]

Let's look at this prayer in three parts, beginning with its first three lines:

> My God, the soul You have given me is pure.
> You created it, You shaped it, You breathed it into me,
> and You protect it within me.

The Hebrew of the opening line is beautifully rhythmic. For this reason, the text is often set to music.

In the biblical era, the Hebrew word for soul, *neshamah*, referred to the life-breath of the living being. The Hebrew Bible did not distinguish between body and soul, but merely referred to the living being. The word used here for "pure," *tahorah*, referred to the concept of ritual purity, which was defined as an absence: one had not encountered something defiling. Therefore, in the biblical context, a "pure soul" would have been a living, breathing being that had not come into physical contact with a chaotic element, such as life-blood, or a deathly thing, like a corpse. (If, however, one had been defiled, a person could be cleansed through a specified ritual to remove the defilement. This ritual sometimes involved water, for example, immersion in a *mikveh* or ritual bath, or alternatively sprinkling someone with a mixture of water laced with blood or ash.)[6]

In the eras that followed, however, *neshamah* came to mean a soul that might exist separately from the body. The "pure soul" of the Talmudic-era *Elohai* prayer likely referred to a metaphysical state: something beyond the merely physical, in the realm of the intellectual or spiritual. A pure soul, in this context, would have been one that had not been stained by sin. The message of this prayer, therefore, is that there is nothing in the human soul, at least in its natural state, that would prevent an individual from approaching God. In this sense, the prayer could be read as a repudiation of the Christian claim that the Original Sin tainted humanity.

For as long as my soul is within me,
I offer thanks to You,
Adonai, my God
and God of my ancestors,
Source of all Creation, Sovereign of all souls.

During the Roman period, starting about 100 years before the Common Era, at a time when the Israelites came into regular contact with Hellenistic thought, people began to speak of a soul that might somehow transcend and survive the physicality of the body. In response, the Rabbis sometimes rejected Hellenism and at other times incorporated this notion (as well as other Hellenistic ideas).

Praised are You, Adonai,
in whose hand is every living soul and the breath of humankind.

This closing line is known as a *hatimah* in Hebrew, from the root *het-taph-mem*, "to seal, to set a seal upon."[7] The closing follows the standard rabbinic prayer formula, "Praised are You, Adonai." Notice how the ending references humanity's creation: God formed the first human by breathing life into the earthly clay.

If we are born pure, then how is it that we come to be sinners?

2.3. A Rabbinic View:
The Impulse to Good and the Impulse to Evil

The Rabbis argue that we face a choice with regard to sin: we can choose good or we can choose evil.

The next text is an example of *aggadah*, the non-legal stories and commentaries collected by the ancient Rabbis. It is a (surprising) commentary on the following lines from the first chapter of Genesis, intended to better explain their meaning:

> And God saw that this was good. (Gen. 1:10, 12, 18, 25)
> And God saw all that had been made, and found it very good.
>   (Gen. 1:31)

The question at hand is why, at the end of several of the days of Creation, the text says, "And God saw that this was good," but on the last day it says, "And God saw all that had been made, and found it very good." The plain meaning of the biblical text would suggest that God was particularly pleased with the creation of humanity. However, the Rabbis were not always satisfied with the plain meaning, and often suggested a number of alternative possibilities, spurred on by the presence of extra words or unusual locutions in the biblical text. These alternatives opened a window into different understandings of the text—and sometimes even inverted the plain meaning of the text. The Rabbis did not see the need to reconcile all of these alternatives in order to provide the best, most coherent and authoritative rendering; rather, each of these possibilities was allowed to exist side-by-side, as one interpretation among many.

Two terms introduced in the subsequent rabbinic commentary are relevant for our discussion: *yetzer ha-ra*, the impulse to do evil, and *yetzer ha-tov*, the impulse to do good. The Rabbis teach that human nature has both inclinations:

> R[abbi] Samuel bar Naman said: The words "Behold, it was good" refer to the impulse to good and the words "Behold, it was very good" (Gen. 1:31) refer to the impulse to evil. But how can the impulse to evil be termed "very good"? Because Scripture teaches that were it not for the impulse to evil, a man would not build a house, take a wife, beget children, or engage

in commerce. All such activities come, as [King] Solomon noted, "from a man's rivalry with his neighbor."[8]

This is a fascinating, even profound, commentary on human nature. Let us investigate it more closely.

> R[abbi] Samuel bar Naman said: The words "Behold, it was good" refer to the impulse to good.

This phrase "it was good" occurs six times in the first chapter of Genesis. Interestingly, it appears several times after major developments in the creation timeline, but it does not get evenly distributed across the various days of that first week. Here is the complete list:

- On the first day, *when God creates light*: "God saw that the light was good." (1.4)
- On the third day, *when God separates the waters* so that dry land may appear: "And God saw that this was good." (1:10)
- Also on the third day, *when the earth brings forth vegetation*: "And God saw that this was good." (1:12)
- On the fourth day, *when God creates the sun, the moon, and the stars*: "And God saw that this was good." (1:18)
- On the fifth day, *when God creates sea-creatures and birds*: "And God saw that this was good." (1:21)
- On the sixth day, *when God creates the land animals*: "And God saw that this was good." (1:25)

All of these were deemed to be "good." In contrast, God says that the creation was "very good" in verse 31, on the sixth day, when God created humanity. The rabbinic text makes a surprising point in response:

and the words "Behold, it was very good" (Gen. 1:31) refer to the impulse to evil.

How could the impulse to evil be called "very good"? The suggestion seems contrary to good sense.

Note the context for these comments: Each of the verses where "God saw that this was good" refers to events in nature that unfolded *according to laws*. The sun and moon appeared at their appointed times; all of the plants grew according to plan, and each of the creatures followed their instincts to provide food for themselves. None of these things or beings had any choice in the matter.

The only thing that really distinguishes humanity here is the ability to choose between good and evil. We, alone among the creatures, are given the power of choice. Even so, the text asks our question directly:

But how can the impulse to evil be termed "very good"?

After all, we often choose badly. How could our *yetzer ha-ra,* our impulse to do evil, be called "very good"? Here is where we encounter the stunning psychological insight:

Because Scripture teaches that were it not for the impulse to evil, a man would not build a house, take a wife, beget children, or engage in commerce. All such activities come, as [King] Solomon noted, "from a man's rivalry with his neighbor."

Quite often, we are driven to act from a multiplicity of complicated motives. Some of our baser yearnings—such as our desire to be something in the world—motivate our highest achievements. Recognizing this, and rather than spurning the shadow side of our psyche, the Rabbis embraced it. Thus the Rabbis suggested that the *yetzer ha-ra* can also be a motivating force: it can lead us to take risks and move forward with some of the most challenging decisions in our lives. In that sense, our impulse to evil is "very good."

Notice also that the notion of *yetzer ha-ra* appears here, at the very beginning, in the course of Creation. In other words, it is absolutely foundational to our existence. According to the Rabbis, we humans have never existed in some state of unerring bliss, only to have this experience ruined by a tragic mistake. Rather, this passion is part of our very nature. Our goal, as it were, is to make use of it, to apply it toward positive ends.

Returning to the story of Adam and Eve, one might ask: did sin first enter when Eve and Adam ate the forbidden fruit, or when the two hid from God, or when they were expelled? In rabbinic tradition, the answer is "none of the above." Rather, sin entered *when humans were first created*. The capacity to engage in sin was part of their very nature from the start. In fact, one could argue that what marked Adam and Eve as having been created in God's image was *their ability to choose between good and evil*. What they gained from eating from the Tree of Knowledge of Good and Evil, therefore, was the ability to feel shame.

2.4. A Medieval View: Maimonides on Adam's Sin

In the medieval period, Moses Maimonides (1135–1204), a scholar of Jewish law, judge of legal cases, and philosopher of the highest rank, introduced a different understanding of the Adam and Eve story. In his philosophical masterwork, *Guide of the Perplexed* (written as an extended letter to a favorite student), he advanced that the real reason Adam lost his mortality was not his act of eating the fruit of the tree per se, but his act of shifting his attention away from God. Because Adam turned away from contemplation of God to contemplation of lesser subjects — "fine and bad" — he was no longer like the angels, and no longer immortal.

In Maimonides' words:

For the intellect that God made overflow unto man and that is the latter's ultimate perfection, was that which Adam had been provided with before he disobeyed. It was because of this that it was said of him that he was created in the image of God and in His likeness. It was likewise on account of it that he was addressed by God and given commandments, as it says: And the Lord God commanded, and so on. For commandments are not given to beasts and beings devoid of intellect. Through the intellect one distinguishes between truth and falsehood, and that was found in [Adam] in its perfection and integrity. Fine and bad, on the other hand, belong to the things generally accepted as known, not to those cognized by the intellect. . . . [Before Adam's sin,] he had no faculty that was engaged in any way in the consideration of generally accepted things, and he did not apprehend them. So among these generally accepted things even that which is most manifestly bad, namely, uncovering the genitals, was not bad according to him, and he did not apprehend that it was bad. However, when he disobeyed and inclined toward his desires of the imagination and the pleasures of his corporeal senses—inasmuch as it is said: that the tree was good for food and that it was a delight to the eyes—he was punished by being deprived of that intellectual apprehension.[9]

Let's parse this text into six sections, starting at the beginning:

For the intellect that God made overflow unto man and that is the latter's ultimate perfection, was that which Adam had been provided with before he disobeyed. It was because of this that it was said of him that he was created in the image of God and in His likeness.

Note that Maimonides refers solely to Adam rather than to Adam and Eve. The root of the name Adam comes from the red (*adom*) soil (*adamah*) from which he was taken; the name also means "(hu)man" or "(hu)mankind." Arthur Waskow, the contemporary Jewish thinker we met in chapter 1, translates "*adamah*" as "earth" and "adam" as "earthling" in order to highlight the connection between the two Hebrew words. For his part, Maimonides explains, "It is the name of *Adam the first man*, and is a derivative word; for, as the biblical text states, it is derived from the word *adamah*. It is also the term for designating the species."[10] (It is reasonable to assume that Maimonides meant all humans rather than solely men in this context, since the biblical text includes known examples of female prophets and Maimonides does not disambiguate here.)

For Maimonides, it is our intellect that makes us uniquely human and after the image of God. Maimonides argues that prior to Adam's sin, Adam had been contemplating God. In fact, Adam was in contact with an overflow of God's intellect. This overflow is what would make prophecy possible. It is the highest form of intellectual understanding.

> It was likewise on account of it [Adam's intellect] that he [Adam] was addressed by God and given commandments, as it says: And the Lord God commanded, and so on. For commandments are not given to beasts and beings devoid of intellect.

Maimonides suggests that because the first human being was engaged in intellectual apprehension of God at the outset, he was able to receive and understand commandments directly. Furthermore, Adam was fully engaged in discerning the difference between what is true and false, and ignored everything else:

Through the intellect one distinguishes between truth and falsehood, and that was found in [Adam] in its perfection and integrity.

At this point in the discussion, we encounter one of Maimonides' most interesting—and surprising—arguments. He defines the knowledge of what is fine and bad *by its context*. This knowledge, in fact, relates only to the demands of the body and the needs of society:

Fine and bad, on the other hand, belong to the things generally accepted as known, not to those cognized by the intellect.

According to Maimonides, then, true and false are absolutes that exist regardless of the situation in which they are encountered. Fine and bad, however, are determined by their context. Might Maimonides be suggesting that what is considered bad is socially constructed?

In certain cases, the answer is indeed yes. For Maimonides, some things we call "bad" actually relate to social conventions. It is a startling suggestion, as it anticipates, by more than 800 years, the idea of socially constructed conventions. Maimonides was not a modern thinker, but he fundamentally understood that we are shaped by our society.

However, Maimonides also identified three types of evil (as distinct from what is merely "bad") that are not defined by social conventions:

1. The evil associated with beings made of matter, which is subject to decay.[11] Having worked most of his life as a physician, Maimonides often witnessed the suffering attendant on ill health.

2. The evil resulting from some people's "tyrannical domination" over others.[12] Maimonides experienced this kind of

evil directly: as a young man he had to flee his hometown to escape extremist violence.

3. The evil an individual brings on him or herself by behaving in self-defeating ways.[13] These are our bad habits and personal vices, large and small, which Maimonides claimed accounted for much of our misfortune. His *Guide of the Perplexed* was offered as an antidote to such behavior.

For Maimonides, then, the proper definition of evil would be "the kinds of suffering that humans must endure" rather than "a separate force that opposes God's will." In other words, in no sense was evil some sort of independent metaphysical force.

Returning to our text:

[Before Adam's sin,] he had no faculty that was engaged in any way in the consideration of generally accepted things, and he did not apprehend them. So among these generally accepted things even that which is most manifestly bad, namely, uncovering the genitals, was not bad according to him, and he did not apprehend that it was bad.

Here, Maimonides explains one of the most surprising features of the biblical text: how could it be that Adam did not know he was naked, and did not feel shame? Maimonides answers that Adam was not cognizant of his nudity because he was not aware of social conventions regarding nudity. He was solely engaged in discerning what was true and false.

Knowledge of what is true and false is the basis of scientific knowledge. For Maimonides, science is the knowledge of God's effect upon the world.

However, when he [Adam] disobeyed and inclined toward his desires of the imagination and the pleasures of his corporeal senses—inasmuch as it is said: that the tree was good for food and that it was a delight to the eyes—he was punished by being deprived of that intellectual apprehension.

Initially, Adam was so completely absorbed in the realm of the intellect, he thought nothing of his bodily needs. He was like one of the heavenly bodies, which are "endowed with apprehension."[14] In fact, it is possible, based on the text of Genesis 1, that Adam started out in Eden as a disembodied intellect and then took on mortal embodiment by disobeying God. Conversely, it could be that Adam had a body all along (it was, after all, the locus of his sin), but he was initially unaware of it. Given that Moses could subsist without food or drink for forty days, it appears reasonable that one could have a body and not need to care for it when engrossed in the intellectual apprehension of God.

Regardless, Maimonides says, Adam found himself distracted from this pure contemplation by the tree, which he found delightful to view and attractive as a source of food. Turning away from contemplation marked a change in Adam's relation to his body. Adam became aware of his own hunger. Once he acted upon it and ate from the compelling tree, he had newfound awareness of what is good and bad. He was suddenly ashamed of his own nakedness.

In other words, Maimonides is saying that prior to his sin, Adam had been the regular recipient of the overflow of intellect that makes prophecy possible. This overflow is also what accounts for individual providence: prophets experience calamities only in those moments when they break off from perfect contemplation of God.

Ultimately, in the act of shifting his attention away from God, Adam became mortal. Because Adam turned away from the contemplation of God to consider the lesser subjects of good and evil, he was driven out of the Garden of Eden. For Maimonides, the lesson here for us mortals is twofold. First, our highest calling is the contemplation of God. Second, we must regulate our appetites to stay focused on that goal. Neither of these endeavors is easily accomplished. However, if we succeed, then we will not engage in sin. We might become like the perfect and immortal angels.

2.5. A Modern View: Cohen on God's Holiness

Having just read the analysis of a medieval rationalist, let us now look at the thinking of a modern rationalist.

The German Jewish philosopher Hermann Cohen (1842–1918) argued in his masterwork, *Religion of Reason out of the Sources of Judaism* (published posthumously in 1919) that the Adam and Eve story is not meant as proof that humanity is evil from birth. Rather, the text's introduction of sin is indicative of moral development within the Hebrew Bible. After all, Adam and Eve gain moral cognition of good and bad when they realize they have disobeyed God. Cohen explains it this way:

> This idea ... [of] attributing the origin of evil to the predisposition to evil of the human heart, of the human will, cannot be supported by the passages in Genesis. Rather, man has the holy spirit in his heart. To it is issued the call, that is, the calling to holiness. The natural predisposition to evil would be in contradiction to the fundamental commandment of holiness. More fundamentally, it would be in contradiction to God's holiness. "God, the holy One, is sanctified through righteousness" [Isa. 5:16]. The holy God could not have put evil into the human heart.[15]

Let's analyze Cohen's text in three sections.

This idea . . . [of] attributing the origin of evil to the predisposition to evil of the human heart, of the human will, cannot be supported by the passages in Genesis.

Though Cohen was a well-known scholar of Immanuel Kant's philosophy and expressed great admiration for Kant's work, his first point repudiates an aspect of Kant's theology. Kant suggested that evil originated within the human will. He reinterpreted the idea of Original Sin to suggest that we humans are predisposed to this evil, as if we were evil from birth. Cohen argues that the biblical text does not support this reading.

According to Cohen, many biblical narratives are grounded in Ancient Near East creation myths, which were adapted and reinterpreted in a monotheistic context. The Garden of Eden story is one of these; it must be understood as a mythic tale, much like other mythic tales that arise from the same region. It was not devised as proof that humanity is evil from birth.

Furthermore, Cohen holds that the biblical narrative moved from primitive god-concepts (such as the worship of a collection of gods) to higher concepts of monotheism (the worship of a single God). Unlike other Ancient Near East texts, Cohen argues, the Hebrew Bible interrupted its description of the primordial paradise to introduce the effects of sin. Later, it presented an even greater disruption of the idyllic myth, in the form of Cain's murder of his brother.

To Cohen, this rupture is evidence of the text's higher level of moral development. Specifically, he contends, monotheism looks forward towards the future (towards a pristine Messianic Age) rather than backward (back to a pristine primeval age). By introducing disobedience and murder into the myth, and then showing how God interacted with the perpetrators and adjudicated their wrongdoing, the biblical writer moved the ancient text toward a more refined sense of ethics. The important thing in the biblical version is that

Adam and Eve gain awareness of good and bad when they realize they have disobeyed God.

Meanwhile, Cohen maintains, the biblical text mirrors our own internal development: we start out pure (in Eden, as it were) but we make mistakes and must learn what is right. Our mistakes will not taint us forever: though we may suffer a lifelong punishment (as Adam and Eve do, and as Cain does), we are not condemned to endlessly repeat our error. Unlike Kant, who suggests that humanity acts as if it were corrupted from birth, Cohen argues that we always have the ability to choose to do good rather than to commit evil. As Cohen explains:

> Man has the holy spirit in his heart. To it is issued the call, that is, the calling to holiness. The natural predisposition to evil would be in contradiction to the fundamental commandment of holiness.

That is to say, there is a correlation between what God asks of us and our ability to meet God's demand. If we are called to do what is good, it must be within our nature to be able to do what is good. How can we be called to do good if we are undermined by a basic nature that is predisposed to evil? That would mean that God is cruel and the task is impossible. Such a situation is inconceivable:

> More fundamentally, it would be in contradiction to God's holiness. "God, the holy One, is sanctified through righteousness" [Isa. 5:16]. The holy God could not have put evil into the human heart.

Is Cohen arguing here that humans never actually desire to commit evil? At this point, we might ask him: what about the passages in the Hebrew Bible that seem to suggest that evil is inherent? For example, in Genesis 4:7, God says to Cain: "Surely if you do right, / There is uplift. / But if you do not do right / Sin couches at the door; / Its urge is toward you, / Yet you can be its master." Similarly, in Genesis 6:5, just before the story of Noah and the ark, the text states: "The Lord saw how great was man's wickedness on earth, and how every plan devised by his mind was nothing but evil all the time." Is Cohen ignoring the many atrocities committed by humanity?

To the contrary, Cohen was indeed aware of humanity's capacity for evildoing. But he argues that in order to be able to choose between good and evil, a person must first be aware of the consequences of his or her behavior. Adam and Eve, for example, did not have free will when they were in the Garden of Eden because they did not understand the choices that faced them. After their disobedience, they learned about the consequences of their behavior and what it meant to make moral choices. At that point—and only at that point—were they able to become ethical beings.

In other words, in Cohen's view, Kant had the order of precedence wrong. Sin can only be labeled as sin *after* the human awareness of ethics. Without the understanding of sin, no moral choices can be made. By learning the consequences of our actions, we become aware of the possibility to choose.

Nonetheless, doing what is good remains an infinite task. According to Cohen, we are not to accept what *is* as "good enough." On the contrary: We are expected to keep before us the Messianic Age ideal—the ideal of what *ought* to be, which includes caring for the widow, the stranger, and the orphan. This ideal is meant to forever inspire us to higher and greater ethical and moral action.

2.6. A Modern View: Kushner on Bad Things That Happen

In *When Bad Things Happen to Good People*, possibly the best-known work of Jewish theology in American culture, Rabbi Harold Kushner offers a different theological explanation as to why bad things can happen in a world with a good God:

> This is perhaps the philosophical idea which is the key to everything else I am suggesting in this book. Can you accept the idea that some things happen for no reason, that there is randomness in the universe? Some people cannot handle that idea. They look for connections, striving desperately to make sense of all that happens. They convince themselves that God is cruel, or that they are sinners, rather than accept randomness. Sometimes, when they have made sense of ninety percent of everything they know, they let themselves assume that the other ten percent makes sense also, but lies beyond the reach of their understanding. But why do we have to insist on everything being reasonable? Why must everything happen for a specific reason? Why can't we let the universe have a few rough edges?[16]

Written in a sermonic style in the wake of his own son's illness and early death, Kushner explains why it is best to let go of the theological construct that the misfortunes that befall us are sent by God. It may be that some things happen for no particular reason at all. As Kushner writes, "I don't believe in a God who has a weekly quota of malignant tumors to distribute, and consults His computer to find out who deserves one most or who could handle it best."[17] In other words, for Kushner, God is good, and the suffering we encounter in the world is quite real, but God is not *causing* these things to happen, in the sense that there is some transcendent meaning to be found behind the events that unfold. Not everything has to make sense.

According to Kushner, then, God is not all-powerful. For some of us, this is a welcome relief: we are not being punished when bad things happen to us. But it can be disconcerting to think that God is not all-powerful: is omnipotence not part of the definition of what it means to be God?

2.7. Summary of Views

Jewish tradition has approached questions about the reality of evil in the world in divergent ways.

In the Jewish understanding of the *biblical text* recounting Adam and Eve's disobedience, sin is not considered inherent in the individual (as the Christian concept of Original Sin implies), but rather refers to a mistake a person has made and will hopefully correct. The biblical narrative is a story of mortality, maturity, *and* morality: in the process of growing up, we learn to take responsibility for our actions, including the responsibility for the consequences of our sexual activity.

In the *liturgical text*, we saw that in contrast to the Christian notion of the Original Sin which tainted humanity, Judaism affirms the purity of the soul. A prayer in the morning service that affirms the purity of the soul suggests that nothing in the human soul, at least in its natural state, would ever prevent an individual from approaching God. In the biblical context, a "pure soul" would have been a living, breathing being that had not come into physical contact with a chaotic element, such as life-blood, or a deathly thing, like a corpse. If, however, one had been defiled, a person could be cleansed through a specified ritual to remove the defilement.

In the *rabbinic text*, the ancient Rabbis asserted that we face a choice with regard to sin: we can choose good or we can choose evil. The Rabbis also chose to embrace—rather than spurn—the shadow side of our psyche. They acknowledged that some of our baser yearnings—such as our desire to be something in the world—help motivate our highest achievements.

In the first *medieval text*, Maimonides suggested that because Adam turned away from the contemplation of God to consider the lesser subjects of fine and bad, he became mortal and was driven out of the Garden of Eden. For Maimonides, the takeaway is twofold. First, our highest human calling must be the contemplation of God. Second, we must regulate our appetites to stay focused on that goal.

In the first *modern text*, Hermann Cohen argued that the Adam and Eve story was not written as proof that humanity is evil from birth. Rather, the Hebrew Bible's introduction of sin into an ancient myth is indicative of the moral development achieved by the text. After all, Adam and Eve gain moral awareness of good and bad when they realize they have disobeyed God. We, too, can gain moral maturity, by recognizing that what God demands of us (the highest ideal of what is good) is possible. We are to keep before us the Messianic Age ideal—the ideal of what *ought* to be—to inspire us to ever greater ethical action.

In the second *modern text*, Harold Kushner suggested that it is best to let go of the theological construct that the misfortunes that befall us are sent by God. Ultimately, he argued that the best explanation for why a good God allows tragedies to happen might be that we have no neat explanation. In essence, God is not all-powerful, and thus we are not being punished when bad things happen to us.

2.8. The Question of Free Will

Let us return to our second opening question: do we have free will to choose good over evil? In the *aggadic* literature, we find an answer to this question in the form of a conversation between God and Cain that expands upon the biblical narrative. The Bible tells us that Cain, angry that God had accepted his brother Abel's sacrifice but not his own, rose up and killed his brother, at which point God called him to account for Abel's murder.

The following passage from the *aggadic* literature imagines this conversation between Cain and God:

Cain said to God, "Am I [expected to be] my brother's keeper?" (Gen. 4:9). You are the keeper of all creatures, yet You call me to account for him. Cain's question may be understood by the parable of a thief who stole some vessels during the night and was not caught. The following morning, the gatekeeper did catch him and asked, "Why did you steal the vessels?" The thief replied, "I, thief that I am, did not slacken at my trade, but you—your trade is to keep watch at the gate. Why did you slacken in your occupation?" Accordingly, Cain's question is in fact a defiant assertion: I slew Abel—it was You who created in me the impulse to evil. But You are the keeper of all things—yet You let me slay him. It is You who slew him. Had You accepted my offering as You did his, I would not have been jealous of him. Immediately the Holy One countered, "What have *you* done? 'The voice of thy brother's blood crieth'" (Gen. 4:10).[18]

In the text, Cain attempts to blame God for his own sin. God created the inclination to do evil within him; therefore, God was ultimately responsible for his brother's murder. Cain does have a point: God created us with an urge to do evil. But the ancient Rabbis are not satisfied with that answer. Ignoring Cain's accusation, God asks him directly, "What have *you* done?" It is not appropriate to blame God for our sins, the Rabbis are saying. Cain had the power of choice—as we all do—and he could have chosen to do good. Cain could have found a way to make peace with his brother and reconcile with God.

2.9. Why Does God Allow Evil to Exist?

The attempt to answer the question of how God might be good yet still allow evil to exist is known as *theodicy*. Theodicy grows out of our human need to make sense of the world. Those of us who believe in God assume there must be some kind of message from God in the events that happen to us. In effect, we would like to be able to hold together the following three assertions regarding the nature of God and the nature of the world:

1. God is good.
2. God is all-powerful (omnipotent).
3. Evil is real.

Unfortunately, as the German-Jewish philosopher Hans Jonas (1903–93) points out in *Mortality and Morality*, these three assertions, taken together, do not work:

> We can have divine omnipotence together with divine goodness only at the price of complete divine inscrutability. Seeing the existence of evil in the world, we must sacrifice intelligibility in God to the combination of the other two attributes. Only a completely unintelligible God can be said to be absolutely good and absolutely powerful, yet tolerate the world as it is. Put more generally, the three attributes at stake—absolute goodness, absolute power, and intelligibility—stand in such a logical relation to one another that the conjunction of any two of them excludes the third. The question then is: Which are truly integral to our concept of God, and which, being of lesser force, must give way to their superior claim?[19]

To better understand how Jonas reaches this conclusion, let's consider each of the three attributes in turn.

RETHINKING GOD'S GOODNESS

One response to the theodicy question is to reinterpret what the phrase, "God is good." We might construe tragedy as God's will, which is another way of saying that God's will is inscrutable—but still, in the end perhaps all we can fathom is that God is punishing us to teach us a lesson.

Some will say, "God only gives us what we can handle." The ancient Rabbis liked this line of thought: they argued that the many difficulties Abraham faced in his life were God-given tests, to demonstrate his character and faithfulness. Yet one of those tests was the near-sacrifice of his son Isaac. The problem with these kinds of frameworks is they make God out to be quite cruel. We see this as well in the story of Job. After God makes an idle bet with Satan, God lets Satan take away this righteous man's children, livelihood, fortune, house, and health, apparently just to prove a point or win the bet.

This interpretation makes cruelty seem acceptable. If God acts cruelly, then we should be allowed to be cruel as well.

RETHINKING GOD AS OMNIPOTENT

Another line of thought is that perhaps God is not all-powerful. For whatever reason, God cannot prevent tragedies from happening (for more on this, see Kushner's argument in 2.6, as well as the discussion in chapter 7).

Rabbinic literature includes many images of God suffering along-side the Jewish people; for example, God goes into exile with the people after the destruction of the Jerusalem Temple. In our own day, the idea that God is not omnipotent has been repeatedly invoked in the wake of the Holocaust.

RETHINKING THE REALITY OF EVIL

Alternatively, we might affirm that God is good and all-powerful but deny the reality of evil. Much of Hasidic thought takes the position that evil is merely an illusion. The world is a veil that obscures the view of the Divine. The suffering we experience is not actually real—except, of course, that it *feels* real.

My view is that God created a world that specifically allows for chaos. I am influenced by Maimonides' understanding of evil: that is to say, what we call evil is the suffering that is either caused by natural events or is the natural outcome of our free will. Additionally, I believe God has chosen to be self-limited within Creation — hence the presence of chaos. This element of chaos allows for change and growth, for new species and new traits to arise, for artistic expression and new ideas. But that same chaotic space also allows for unwanted mutations, cancerous tumors, destructive events, and natural catastrophes. It is built into the very structure of this world, which is why God does not intervene to change it. It means that we live in a world where eight-year-olds can die of cancer. It also means that we live in a world where there are eight-year-olds.

Evil, therefore, appears to be a necessary by-product of Creation, a Creation that includes free will. If we have the ability to choose to do good, we must also have the ability to choose to do evil. But the reverse must also be true: if we have the ability to choose evil, we must also have the ability to choose good.

Part 2

Does God Have a Personality—or Is God an Impersonal Force?

Chapter 3

Is God Like a Person?

- How have different strands of Jewish tradition viewed the question of God's physical form?
- What is gained when we think of God as a person?
- How is imagining a personal God different from imagining God as an impersonal force?

3.1. A Biblical View: Moses Asks to Behold God's Presence

In much of the biblical narrative, God behaves like an actor in a play: sometimes angry, sometimes gracious, but generally always active and involved. To use the technical terms, the biblical descriptions of God include *anthropomorphic* qualities (having a body that's like a person's) and *anthropopathic* qualities (having the emotions of a person).

The following exchange appears in the book of Exodus after Moses receives two tablets carved with the Ten Commandments on Mount Sinai. When he returns to the people and sees them worshiping a golden calf, he breaks the tablets. In the wake of this turmoil, Moses seeks reassurance regarding his relationship with God.

[Moses] said, "Oh, let me behold Your Presence!" And God answered, "I will make all My goodness pass before you, and I will proclaim before you the name of God and the grace that I grant and the compassion that I show," continuing, "But you cannot see My face, for a human being may not see Me and live." And God said, "See, there is a place near Me. Station yourself on the rock and, as My Presence passes by, I will put you in a cleft of the rock and shield you with My hand until I have passed by. Then I will take My hand away and you will see My back; but My face must not be seen."

God said to Moses: "Carve two tablets of stone like the first, and I will inscribe upon the tablets the words that were on the first tablets, which you shattered. Be ready by morning, and in the morning come up to Mount Sinai and present yourself there to Me, on the top of the mountain. No one else shall come up with you, and no one else shall be seen anywhere on the mountain; neither shall the flocks and the herds graze at the foot of this mountain."

So Moses carved two tablets of stone, like the first, and early in the morning he went up on Mount Sinai, as God had commanded him, taking the two stone tablets with him. God came down in a cloud—and stood with him there, proclaiming the name God. God passed before him and proclaimed: "God! God! a God compassionate and gracious, slow to anger, abounding in kindness and faithfulness, extending kindness to the thousandth generation, forgiving iniquity, transgression, and sin—yet not remitting all punishment, but visiting the iniquity of parents upon children and children's children, upon the third and fourth generations." (Exod. 33:18–34:7)

This text gives the strong impression that God has a body. The inclusion of "hand" and "face" makes it seem like God is distinctly human in form. We also learn that God's presence is able to pass by while Moses is standing on a rock—which would appear to mean that God is not enormous or amorphous. On this basis, it would be possible to conclude that the Bible supports an anthropomorphic understanding of God: God has a body that is more or less human in appearance, and can be seen.

Particularly interesting, however, is that this passage can support precisely the opposite conclusion. From the evidence, one could argue that God does not have a body at all. Moses cannot see God's face because there is no face to be seen.

Which reading makes the most sense? Which reading is the most faithful to the literal meaning of the text? The Bible does not make it clear. It seems, in fact, that for every biblical passage that says God may become visible, another argues that God cannot be seen. An earlier passage in the same book gives a physical description:

Then Moses and Aaron, Nadab and Abihu and seventy elders of Israel ascended; and they saw the God of Israel: under whose feet there was the likeness of a pavement of sapphire, like the very sky for purity. (Exod. 24:9)

Then we have this contravening assertion nearly ten chapters later, included in our main selection:

You cannot see My face, for a human being may not see Me and live.

Since both options are supported by biblical passages, and no one reading is dominant, the question of interpretation falls to us. Do we choose one reading and reject the other? Or do we harmonize the two views?

In the last verses of our selection, the Hebrew Bible seems poised to give us additional insight into the nature of God. God asks Moses to recreate the tablets of the Ten Commandments and then return to

Mount Sinai, where the tablets were originally given. When Moses obeys, God rewards him with new information about God's nature. While passing by Moses, God makes the following declaration:

> "God! God! a God compassionate and gracious, slow to anger, abounding in kindness and faithfulness, extending kindness to the thousandth generation, forgiving iniquity, transgression, and sin—yet not remitting all punishment, but visiting the iniquity of parents upon children and children's children, upon the third and fourth generations."

This statement relates in some way to the question of repentance after the sin of the Golden Calf. This divine message is offered to Moses as if it were some new insight into the nature of God, but it is not explained any further.

The fact that the Bible offers varied and even conflicting depictions of God has led some biblical scholars to suggest that it is a combination of different source-texts. Perhaps the author of Exodus 24 did not know the work of the author of Exodus 33, and vice versa. Alternatively, it could be that the author(s) of the biblical narrative, like the ancient Rabbis, did not see a reason to reconcile these various views of God, but rather presented all of them together.

3.2. From the Liturgy: Forgiveness and God's Body

Among the many insights in the High Holy Day liturgy is the idea that obtaining God's forgiveness is not dependent upon experiencing God's bodily presence.

In the biblical period, the Israelites would achieve atonement by bringing animals and other foodstuffs to the Temple and offering them as sacrifices to God. After the Second Temple's destruction, however, the Rabbis were forced to face their uprootedness and devise a new avenue for obtaining God's forgiveness.

Christianity, too, struggled to respond to the major political and religious upheavals of the time. Early Christian theology debated the meaning of Jesus' crucifixion. Was Jesus the Son of God—that is to say, was he an *embodied* form of the Divine? Did Jesus' death constitute an atonement offering? Did Jesus' sacrifice end the need for the Temple cult?

Rabbinic Judaism came to emphasize a different aspect of the Temple service. The early Rabbis prayed for the day when the Temple would be rebuilt. Their prayers for the resumption of the Temple service expressed a longing to regain Jewish sovereignty in the Land of Israel. In the meantime, they argued, it was not permitted to offer sacrifices elsewhere. In their view, the only sacrifices meaningful to God were those of kosher animals burned on the Temple's altar.

At the same time, the Rabbis concluded that these sacrifices were not the *only* avenue for achieving atonement. Other valid ways to achieve forgiveness included verbal prayer, as this Talmud text attests:

Come and see that the conduct of flesh and blood [human beings] is not at all like the conduct of the Holy One [God]. The conduct of flesh and blood: when a man angers his friend with words, it is questionable whether or not the friend will agree to be pacified by him. And even if you suppose the friend is willing to be pacified, it is questionable whether he will be pacified by mere words or will have to be pacified by compensation. But with the Holy One, there is no question. When a man commits a sin in secret, He is pacified with mere words, as is said, "Take with you words, and return unto the Lord" (Hos. 14:3). (*Yoma* 86b)[1]

In other words, God, unlike human beings, will take a prayer as compensation for having been wronged.

The Rabbis also decreed that prior to Yom Kippur (the Day of Atonement), Jews were to resolve personal disagreements and ask forgiveness of everyone they harmed during the previous year. Having (ideally) put everything in order, worshippers could then approach God on Yom Kippur with the solemn intention of asking God's forgiveness.

Meanwhile, Jewish tradition held that God also decided the individual's fate for the coming year. According to the Babylonian Talmud: "Three books are opened [in heaven] on New Year, one for the thoroughly wicked, one for the thoroughly righteous, and one for the intermediate."[2] The Talmud further explained that the thoroughly righteous were inscribed in the book of life, the thoroughly wicked inscribed in the book of death, and the intermediate judged during the ten days between Rosh Hashanah and Yom Kippur.[3] The ancient Rabbis also concluded that the "intermediate" people (those neither thoroughly wicked nor thoroughly righteous) could in fact repent—if they would repeat the aforementioned passage from Exodus (34:6–7). As the Rabbis explained:

> *And the Lord passed by before him and proclaimed* [etc.] R. Johanan said: Were it not written in the text, it would be impossible for us to say such a thing; this verse teaches us that the Holy One, blessed be He, drew his robe around Him like the reader of a congregation and showed Moses the order of prayer. He said to him: whenever Israel sins, let them carry out this service before Me, and I will forgive them. (*Rosh Hashanah* 17b)[4]

Since that time, Exodus 34:6–7 has become a core component of the Yom Kippur Torah service in the Ashkenazic (northern European) tradition.[5] The following example of how it is cited in the service is drawn from the Reform movement's High Holiday prayer book, *Mishkan Hanefesh*:

Adonai, Adonai—
God, compassionate, gracious, endlessly patient, loving,
and true;
showing mercy to the thousandth generation;
forgiving evil, defiance, and wrongdoing; granting pardon.[6]

Comparing this with the preceding biblical text, however, we might notice something odd: part of the biblical verse is missing. In Exodus, after we are told of God's "extending kindness to the thousandth generation, forgiving iniquity, transgression, and sin" (essentially the same points with slightly different word choices), the text continues: "yet not remitting all punishment, but visiting the iniquity of parents upon children and children's children, upon the third and fourth generations." In the Reform movement's liturgy, the point about extending punishment to the next generations has been left out. The prayer books of other Jewish movements also omit this passage.

Why was the verse truncated? For one, it seems the Rabbis read the Exodus text as attesting to the *potential* scope of God's judgment— God's power to extend judgment into the generations that follow— rather than as a mandatory sentence. In this reading, God can choose not to visit the sins of the ancestors onto the subsequent generations because the individual's sincere repentance eliminates the need for such retribution. Expanding this thinking to the community as a whole, God will accept our heartfelt prayers and suspend the harsh decree.

Also, the Rabbis may have been concerned that worshippers might abandon the hard effort of repentance if they believed that God would not excuse their sins without punishment—and, further-more, would visit their ancestors' sins upon them. The worshipers would already have accepted God's power. When they were already engaged in the process of achieving reconciliation with God, was it really necessary to remind them of God's potential retribution upon them and their children?

Finally, the Rabbis' interpretation could now be clearly distinguished from the Christian interpretation. Theologically, Christianity linked the death of Jesus to the sacrificial worship at the Temple; in the Christian view, the death of Jesus, the embodiment of God, replaced animal sacrifice as the conduit to achieving atonement. For the Rabbis, however, whereas physical sacrifice had indeed once been the method of achieving this atonement, now the words of the heart would be sufficient.

3.3. A Rabbinic View: Where Is God's Place?

In many rabbinic texts, God is described as acting like a human. However, as we've seen, the ancient Rabbis were not literalists when it comes to text. While they may have portrayed God as acting human-like, that does not mean they thought of God as actually being human-like. Their imagery may have been a metaphor.

To illustrate this point, let's evaluate a selection from the midrash (which is a form of *aggadah* or commentary which was written by the ancient rabbis to fill in gaps in the biblical narrative). This text uses the old-fashioned word *caparison*, an ornamental covering for a horse.

> R. Isaac taught: A verse in Deuteronomy speaks of "the skies, the dwelling place of the eternal God" (Deut. 33:27). But we would not have known whether the Holy One, blessed be He, is the dwelling place of the world or whether the world is the dwelling place of the Holy One, blessed be He, unless Moses had come and given us the answer by saying, "Lord, Thou hast been our dwelling place ... from everlasting" (Ps. 90:1).
>
> R. Yose bar Halafta said: We would not have known whether the Holy One, blessed be He, is secondary to His world or wheth-

er His world is secondary to Him unless the Holy One Himself, blessed by He, had made the answer plain by saying, "Behold, there is a place by Me" (Exod. 33:21), meaning: "The place is by Me—secondary to Me—and not I to My place."

R. Abba bar Yudan said: He is like a warrior riding upon a horse, with the caparison hanging down on one side and the other; the horse does the bidding of the rider, but the rider does not do the bidding of the horse.

R. Huna said in the name of R. Ammi: Why is the epithet "Place" used for the Name of the Holy One, blessed be He? Because He is the place of the world, and the world is not His place.[7]

What does this text mean? The first paragraph opens with a verse from Deuteronomy:

R. Isaac taught: A verse in Deuteronomy speaks of "the skies, the dwelling place of the eternal God" (Deut. 33:27).

From this verse, it would seem that God lives in the sky. But the Rabbis ignore the plain meaning. Instead they say:

[W]e would not have known whether the Holy One, blessed be He, is the dwelling place of the world or whether the world is the dwelling place of the Holy One, blessed be He, unless Moses had come and given us the answer by saying, "Lord, Thou hast been our dwelling place . . . from everlasting" (Ps.90:1).

In other words, the Rabbis decide that the verse's true meaning is actually the opposite of its plain meaning. God does *not* live in the sky, because that would mean that God was smaller than the sky.

To reach this conclusion, they consider both options for interpreting the verse: either (a) God is the dwelling place of the world or (b) the world is the dwelling place of God. How might we understand these choices? Imagine drawing a circle to represent God, and then drawing a second circle to represent the world. Which of these two circles is larger? Do they overlap? Does one circle exist inside the other? Which one is more important? The message of option (a) is that God is greater than the world—in effect, greater than the sum of all things. That option might be drawn as a gargantuan God-circle with a much smaller world-circle inside it.

Now imagine option (b): a colossal world-circle with a smaller God-circle inside it. What might this drawing mean? It could mean that God is rather inconsequential to the world; perhaps God set it in motion, or has a small impact upon it. It could also mean that God lives in the world much like the rest of its inhabitants.

Which option is correct, according to the ancient Rabbis? They conclude:

[W]e would not have known . . . unless Moses had come and given us the answer by saying, "Lord, Thou hast been our dwelling place . . . from everlasting" (Ps. 90:1).

The Rabbis quote the Bible to prove that the right understanding is option (a): God is the dwelling place of the world. (They say Moses has "given us the answer" because Psalm 90 is attributed to Moses.) In other words, the Rabbis suggest that God is larger—meaning greater, grander, and more powerful—than the world. The technical term for this position is *panentheism*. God does not live in the world the way other beings do; rather, the world only exists *within* God.

Returning to the original question, Does God live in the sky?, the answer is all the clearer. Since God does *not* live in the world like other residents of the universe do, then when the text speaks of God living in the sky, the image is not meant to be interpreted literally.

Rather, we are meant to view it as an invitation to think deeply about God's relationship to the world.

The second paragraph in our excerpt offers a new question: which is more important in determining the course of things, the ways of God or the ways of the world?

> R. Yose bar Halafta said: We would not have known whether the Holy One, blessed be He, is secondary to His world or whether His world is secondary to Him unless the Holy One Himself, blessed by He, had made the answer plain by saying, "Behold, there is a place by Me" (Exod. 33:21), meaning: "The place is by Me—secondary to Me—and not I to My place."

If the place is defined entirely by its proximity to God, then God must be the most important part of the sentence. Therefore, God's will is primary. Anything else is secondary.

Some readers might find it strange that biblical grammar is used as a proof of God's importance. For the Rabbis, however, the Bible was the ultimate authority, and every one of its details was meaningful. Finding theological messages in grammatical usage was a customary part of their reading strategy.

In the third paragraph, they delve deeper into God's relationship to the world:

> R. Abba bar Yudan said: He is like a warrior riding upon a horse, with the caparison hanging down on one side and the other; the horse does the bidding of the rider, but the rider does not do the bidding of the horse.

We have here an image of God's body in the form of a warrior. But this image is not to be taken literally to mean that God rides about the heavens on horseback. Rather, the Rabbis are teaching that the world is distinct from God, and the world must answer to the will of God, in the same way a horse follows the commands of its rider. Note, also, that the world apparently has a mind of its own!

In the rabbinical literature, one of God's names is "the Place," or *ha-Makom* in Hebrew. Why would God be called "the Place"? Here is the rabbinic answer:

> R. Huna said in the name of R. Ammi: Why is the epithet "Place" used for the Name of the Holy One, blessed be He? Because He is the place of the world, and the world is not His place.

God is called "the Place" here because God is "the Place" where the world is located. According to this text, the whole world exists within God.

3.4. A Medieval View: Maimonides and the Attributes of Action

What if we are wrong to think about God in terms of time or space?

Perhaps everything we might be able to say about God is inadequate—or, worse yet, false. Moses Maimonides, whom we met in chapter 2, argued against making any statements concerning our knowledge of God, out of a deep concern for stating only what is clearly true. Maimonides was not satisfied with approximations or half-truths.

Our text in Exodus 33–34 appears to have been of great interest to Maimonides. He explicitly referred to this passage at least a dozen times in *Guide of the Perplexed*. Not only did he explain each of its key terms and expound on how to read the anthropomorphic passages; he also provided prooftexts to establish the literal meaning of every word and demonstrate its figurative use.

Here Maimonides is commenting on the nature of God. This particular argument is called the *via negativa,* for it constructs an argument through a series of negations.

As for the negative attributes, they are those that must be used in order to conduct the mind toward that which must be believed with regard to Him, may He be exalted, for no notion of multiplicity can attach to Him in any respect on account of them, and moreover, they conduct the mind toward the utmost reach that man may attain in the apprehension of Him, may He be exalted. For instance, it has been demonstrated to us that it is necessary that something exists other than those essences apprehended by means of the senses and whose knowledge is encompassed by means of the intellect. Of this thing we say that it exists, the meaning being that its nonexistence is impossible. We apprehend further that this being is not like the being of the elements, for example, which are dead bodies. We say accordingly that this being is living, the meaning being that He, may He be exalted, is not dead. We apprehend further that this being is not like the being of the heaven, which is a living body. We say accordingly that He is not a body. We apprehend further that this being is not like the being of the intellect, which is neither a body nor dead, but is caused. We say accordingly that He, may He be exalted, is eternal, the meaning being that He has no cause that has brought Him into existence. We apprehend further that the existence of this being, which is its essence, suffices not only for His being existent, but also for many other existents flowing from it, and that this overflow—unlike that of heat from fire and unlike the proceeding of light from the sun—is an overflow that, as we shall make clear, constantly procures for those existents duration and order by means of wisely contrived governance.

Accordingly we say of Him, because of these notions that he is powerful and knowing and willing. The intention in ascribing these attributes to Him is to signify that He is neither powerless nor ignorant nor inattentive nor negligent.[8]

Though the argument is subtle, and often difficult to follow, the description of God's nature offered here is profound. God is unlike anything in the world. In fact, according to Maimonides, God is so completely different than anything in the world, we must depart from our everyday use of language in order to explain what God is.

Some additional definitions will help elucidate the text. By the word *essence*, Maimonides means the defining quality of a given thing. The essence of a child's bouncy ball, for example, is roundness. An *accident*, for Maimonides, describes some aspect of a thing that is not part of its essence. A bouncy ball could be red or blue or another color, so redness is not part of its essence. Redness, therefore, is an accident of the bouncy ball. Both roundness and redness are *attributes* of the bouncy ball. An attribute is either an explanation of a thing's essence (*explanatory attribute*), or an explanation of an aspect of something different than that thing's essence (*accidental attribute*). So, in this case, roundness is an explanatory attribute of the bouncy ball, whereas redness is an accidental attribute of the bouncy ball.

The first category of attributes — explanatory attributes — can be split into two types: those that provide either full or partial explanations of the thing. Roundness is a partial explanation of a bouncy ball, for the ball must also be made of a material that bounces.

According to Maimonides, a full explanation of God is not feasible, because it is impossible to provide a complete definition of God. Any single attribute one might choose would be much too small to encompass the entirety of God.

Furthermore, a partial explanation of God is also not possible, because if it were possible, then God would be some sort of a composite entity composed of attribute A + attribute B + attribute C, etc. Since God is not made up of parts, explanatory attributes cannot be ascribed to God.

Though God exists, this existence is profoundly different from the existence of inert matter or living beings. In our passage, Maimonides writes of God:

> Of this thing we say that it exists, the meaning being that its nonexistence is impossible. We apprehend further that this being is not like the being of the elements, for example, which are dead bodies. We say accordingly that this being is living, the meaning being that He, may He be exalted, is not dead. We apprehend further that this being is not like the being of the heaven, which is a living body. We say accordingly that He is not a body. We apprehend further that this being is not like the being of the intellect, which is neither a body nor dead, but is caused.

An attentive reader will realize that his statement has far-reaching implications. If God is profoundly different than anything in the world, then God does not interact with the world as if with a body (whether dead like the elements or living like the heavens) or with intellect. God does not ever create a hypostasis (a physical manifestation of essence). God is not a person, and never takes the form of a person.

Nonetheless, God is the first cause, that which causes all other things. Maimonides continues:

> We say accordingly that He, may He be exalted, is eternal, the meaning being that He has no cause that has brought Him into existence. We apprehend further that the existence of this being, which is its essence, suffices not only for His being existent, but also for many other existents flowing from it, and that this

overflow—unlike that of heat from fire and unlike the proceeding of light from the sun—is an overflow that, as we shall
make clear, constantly procures for those existents duration and
order by means of wisely contrived governance. Accordingly we
say of Him, because of these notions that he is powerful and
knowing and willing.

Since God is so profoundly different from the world, these positive
statements (that God is "powerful and knowing and willing") do
not adequately explain God's essence. Rather than imperfectly apprehend God's essence, it would be better to admit what we do *not*
know; it would be preferable to use negations to describe God. As
Maimonides continues:

> The intention in ascribing these attributes to Him is to signify
> that He is neither powerless nor ignorant nor inattentive nor
> negligent.

Maimonides is telling us that the only way to speak meaningfully of
God's essence is to use a double negation, to affirm what God is by
denying every deficit or lack. What is more: the more negatives we
employ, the closer we are to the truth.

And since we cannot speak otherwise of God's essence, Maimonides advises us to view any biblical text that refers to God's
physical attributes metaphorically. When, for example, we read
in our passage from Exodus, "I will put you in a cleft of the rock
and shield you with My hand until I have passed by. . . . Then I will
take My hand away and you will see My back" (33:22–23), we are
to accept that the passage is not to be understood literally. There
is no rock, no hand, no back, and no moment when God passes by
Moses. The whole text is a metaphor for Moses' deep understanding
of the nature of God.

3.5. A Modern View: Buber's Dialogic Approach

The existentialist Jewish philosopher Martin Buber (1878–1965) agreed with Maimonides that God does not have an embodied form. A student of the mystical tradition, particularly Hasidic thought, Buber saw the human encounter with God as one of pure presence, in the sense of feeling connected to the Eternal, rather than an experience of coming into contact with a physical being.

In his classic volume *I and Thou*, Buber taught that the world has two basic modes: *I-You* and *I-It*.[9] I-You is a direct encounter:

> The relation to the You is unmediated. Nothing conceptual intervenes between I and You, no prior knowledge and no imagination; and memory itself is changed as it plunges from particularity into wholeness.[10]

Buber is saying that at a moment of true encounter, it is just the I and the You, and nothing else. Words are not necessary, concepts become meaningless, and time slips away.

One might think that an I-You relationship must necessarily involve two persons or a person and God. However, Buber explains that one might enter into it with an animal, a tree, or even a piece of mica. It is possible to encounter the other fully in the moment even when the other side of the relationship is not human, or even animate.

Most of the time, however, Buber says we are engaged in an I-It relationship with the people and things around us. For example, he describes an interaction with a tree:

> I contemplate a tree.
> I can accept it as a picture: a rigid pillar in a flood of light. . . .
> I can feel it as movement: the flowing veins around the sturdy, striving core, the sucking of the roots, the breathing of the

leaves, the infinite commerce with earth and air — and the grow-
ing itself in its darkness.

I can assign it to a species and observe it as an instance, with
an eye to its construction and its way of life.

I can overcome its uniqueness and form so rigorously that
I recognize it only as an expression of the law — those laws according to which the elements mix and separate.

I can dissolve it into a number, into a pure relation between
numbers, and eternalize it.

Throughout all of this the tree remains my object and has its
place and its time span, its kind and condition.

But it can also happen . . . that as I contemplate the tree I am
drawn into a relation and the tree ceases to be an It.[11]

Buber is pointing out various forms of I-It relations in which a tree
is an object and the observer is thinking of it as an object. He can
"accept [the tree] as a picture," "feel its movement," "assign it to a
species," or "dissolve it into a number."

However, Buber explains, it can also happen in rare moments that
"the tree ceases to be an It." Rather than thinking of the tree in generic terms, as an artistic vision or as a representative of its species,
rather than bringing judgment or ideas or concepts to the tree, it is
also possible to experience the tree in its "exclusivity" — and thereby
uplift the moment into an I-You encounter.

Nonetheless, Buber recognizes, this state is not continuous. The
moment will pass and the world will return to the way it was:

Every You in the world is doomed by its nature to become a thing
or at least to enter into thinghood again and again.[12]

Eventually, the observer may try to describe what took place, and
in so doing be pulled back into the I-It realm. In this sense, the I-

You encounter is a kind of peak experience, known only in fleeting moments.

To Buber, I-You relationships mirror the encounter between individuals and God:

> The relation to a human being is the proper metaphor for the relation to God—as genuine address is here accorded a genuine answer. But in God's answer all, the All, reveals itself as language.[13]

When we seek out God, we are indeed met with a presence. But right then and there we encounter a problem: the use of language brings us back to the world of I-It. Nonverbal I-You encounters with God eventually require us to make use of words and concepts. Yet at the same time, Buber says:

> By its very nature the eternal You cannot become an It; because by its very nature it cannot be placed within measure and limit, not even within the measure of the immeasurable and the limit of the unlimited; because by its very nature it cannot be grasped as a sum of qualities, not even as an infinite sum of qualities that have been raised to transcendence; because it is not to be found either in or outside the world; because it cannot be experienced; because it cannot be thought.[14]

If the eternal You cannot be thought, it cannot be written down and taught to others either. To Buber, this basic difficulty is the central problem of religious life.

How, then, did Buber understand Moses' encounter with God back on Mount Sinai? Was this an I-You encounter?

Buber teaches that when Moses asked to see God's face, he received a new understanding of God:

[Moses] now learns two things in one: of the graciousness and mercifulness of YHVH, which are named as His essential attributes, and of His liberty to show those attributes of His to whomsoever He wishes to show them.[15]

In other words, Moses entered into an I-You relationship with God through which God revealed to him the attributes of graciousness and mercifulness.

Did God need to have a body in order for this encounter to take place? Though Moses' encounter with God was real (and it involved a direct Revelation of God's attributes), it did not require an embodied God. Buber's I-You encounter with God is not an experience of coming into contact with a physical being per se, but one of pure presence in feeling connected to the Eternal.

3.6. A Modern View: Green's Non-Dualism

Arthur Green (introduced in 1.5) goes even further than Martin Buber in viewing God and the world (that includes us) as one. To Green, God is not some kind of being "out there" existing independently from us. In his words, "'God' and 'world' are different faces of the same reality, different modes of the only Being there is."[16] Thus he sees Buber's I-You structure as problematic in that it implies a theological dualism: God on one side and the rest of the world on the other.

Instead, Green takes the idea of God's immanence (presence throughout the universe) to heart. God can be known directly when we look inward. As he explains:

Speaking to God is as much of a betrayal as speaking of. Although I continue to use the dualistic language in prayer ("Blessed are You . . ."), I know that I do not mean it in its simplest sense. This language is a way of addressing the One as though it were possible for me to stand outside it in such a moment, as though there really were an "I" who could speak this way to a "Thou." ... On the plane of daily consciousness we continue to see the world as a place of separation between "self" and "Other." As a mystic I understand that all such separation is a betrayal of the ultimate unitive truth, the faith that there is only One.[17]

Green says *all* is one—including God, and including us. To think of God as a person, or even as a "You" (or "Thou") on the other side of a relationship is to abandon this mystical insight. We are all part of God.

3.7. Summary of Views

Does Moses stand on a rock, sheltered by God's hand, and see God's back as God's presence passes by? Does God take a bodily form? It is difficult to say with precision.

The *biblical text* could be read either way: literally—as reporting a series of events taking place in time and space; or metaphorically— perhaps as a series of dream-sequences in which the laws of nature do not apply.

We saw that part of the biblical text is quoted in the *liturgical text* to support a shift in the content of worship: neither an embodied animal sacrifice nor an embodied God is necessary to achieve atonement. Among the many insights in the High Holy Day liturgy is the idea that obtaining forgiveness from God is not dependent upon experiencing God's bodily presence. Rather, God accepts our heartfelt prayers as a valid substitute for the sacrificial system.

While in many rabbinic texts God is described as acting like a human, the ancient Rabbis were not literalists, and such portrayals do not necessarily mean they thought of God as being human-like. Sometimes the Rabbis read texts contrary to their literal meaning if these made for fuller, richer understandings of God's relationship to the world. Our *rabbinic text* cites a verse in Deuteronomy speaking of "the skies, the dwelling place of the eternal God," but the Rabbis decide that God does *not* live in the sky, because that would mean that God was smaller than the sky. In their view, God does not live in the world the same way other beings do; rather, the world exists *within* God.

In the *medieval text*, Maimonides argued that God does not have a body, God does not act like a person, and humans cannot describe God directly. Rather, whenever the Bible describes God as having a body, it is speaking metaphorically. When Moses saw God's back, for example, he learned how God relates to the world.

In the first *modern text*, Martin Buber maintained that the human encounter with God is one of pure presence, in the sense of feeling connected to the Eternal, rather than the experience of coming into contact with a physical being. He explained that humans engage in two kinds of relationships, I-You and I-It. To have an authentic I-You encounter, one needs to be fully present to the moment, and not see the other as an object to identify, describe, analyze, or use. Moses' encounter with God at Mount Sinai was an I-You experience involving a direct Revelation of God's attributes, but not requiring an embodied God.

In the second *modern text*, Arthur Green avers that God is not some kind of being "out there" existing independently from us. The false conception of a separation between "self" and "Other" betrays the ultimate unitive truth: the faith that there is only One. To think of God as a person, or even as a "You" (or "Thou") on the other side of a relationship, is to abandon this mystical insight. We are all part of God.

3.8. Thinking of God as a Person

To return to our second question: What is gained when we think of God as a person?

For many of us, it is much easier to address prayer to a person—or to a person-like Being—than to address prayer to a force or a cause or any other of the multiple abstract ways Jews understand God. Furthermore, particularly during petitionary prayer, it is much easier for many of us to conceive of God as responding to our needs as a human would. For these and other reasons, Jews have tended to create personal God-images: God-as-parent, God-as-king, God-as-warrior, God-as-protector, God-as-nurturer.

Taking this even further, the modern Orthodox thinker Michael Wyschogrod (1928–2015) argued that God must necessarily be like a person, in that God must have a spatial presence with a personality and a proper name if we humans are to be able to engage in a relationship with God:

> If it is man as man who is to have a relation to Hashem [literally "The Name," meaning God], if man is not to cease being man in spite of this relation, then Hashem must be able to enter space and to be near man wherever he is.[18]

If God is unable to be near humans, Wyschogrod asks, how would we know that God is there? We need to somehow perceive God's presence spatially in order to come into dialogue with God.

On the other hand, Maimonides suggested that humanity is able to understand God without having to encounter God as a person with a body and a personality. In his view, persons of extraordinary intellect who have trained their faculties (such as Moses) are particularly able to make this connection. Certain humans can bridge this gap. Alternatively, the American rabbi and theologian Mordecai Kaplan, founder of the Reconstructionist movement, argued that God is not a person who can interact with gifted individuals such as Moses; rather, the Jewish community serves in the role of deciding what God asks of us. In this case it is collective humanity that bridges the gap.

Impersonal God language might also be more accurate intellectually. When we attribute human qualities to God, we simply magnify the best of what humanity is able to create—but our artistic and creative capabilities pale in comparison to the rich variety of the created world. If God is the cause of all things (as Maimonides argues), then this source of Creation is infinitely more subtle and clever than we are. The difference is not simply one of magnitude.

3.9. Imagining a Personal God vs. Imagining God as an Impersonal Force

We conclude with the question: How is imagining a personal God different from imagining God as an impersonal force?

How we think about God is entangled with problems of power and dominion. A personal God is often imagined as an authority, whether it be a ruler or a parent. By contrast, God understood as an impersonal force removes this aspect of power and dominion from the Divine, likening God to the processes of nature or the workings of a computer.

Some social theorists, notably some Jewish feminists, consider any unsymmetrical relationship, including the human-divine one, unacceptable. The stronger partner might use this differential in power to dominate the weaker. The power differential between a personal God and humanity isn't immune from this critique, especially since it might be used to validate other hierarchies in human relationships, such as master/servant or abuser/abused. From this feminist perspective, depersonalizing one's relationship to the Divine might be preferable, not only for a truer understanding of God but also to avoid perpetuating an inequitable and outmoded power structure among human beings. But if God is an impersonal force without relational power over us, are we bereft of an independent being "out there" that can call us to account? Even more, if we avoid these kinds of hierarchical constructs, have we elevated ourselves to the role of God?

Chapter 4

Does God Have a Gender?

- How have different strands of Jewish tradition viewed the question of God's gender?
- Do masculine images of God make it seem that men are more important than women?
- Is it possible to leave a traditional text with male imagery intact but rethink its meaning?

4.1. A Biblical View: What Does Gender Have to Do with It?

We tend to think of biblical imagery for God as being male, but if you look closely, this poem from Isaiah 66:10–16 appears to alternate between masculine (in this case, the avenging male) and feminine (here, the nurturing female) imagery:

> Rejoice with Jerusalem and be glad for her,
> All you who love her!
> Join in her jubilation,
> All you who mourned over her—
> That you may suck from her breast
> Consolation to the full,
> That you may draw from her bosom

Glory to your delight.

For thus said the Lord:
I will extend to her
Prosperity like a stream,
The wealth of nations
Like a wadi in flood;
And you shall drink of it.
You shall be carried on shoulders
And dandled upon knees.
As a mother comforts her son
So I will comfort you;
You shall find comfort in Jerusalem.
You shall see and your heart shall rejoice,
Your limbs shall flourish like grass.
The power of the Lord shall be revealed
In behalf of His Servants;
But He shall rage against His foes.

See, the Lord is coming with fire—
His chariots are like a whirlwind—
To vent His anger in fury,
His rebuke in flaming fire.
For with fire will the Lord contend,
With His sword, against all flesh;
And many shall be the slain of the Lord.

This poetic passage is describing how the vanquished Israelites will return home to Jerusalem. Thus, the first lines express the joy of return:

Rejoice with Jerusalem and be glad for her,
All you who love her!
Join in her jubilation,
All you who mourned over her —

Note the use of "her" in relation to Jerusalem. Jerusalem is commonly characterized as female in the prophetic literature. Similarly, both "Zion," as the personification of a place, as well as "Israel," the community of the Israelites, are often spoken of as female.

Gender is also relevant in Hebrew names for God. All nouns have a gender in Hebrew, a gendered language (as a rule of thumb, nouns that end with the letter *hey* are nearly always feminine; unfortunately, there is no parallel rule for masculine nouns). Some of the nouns related to God in Hebrew are grammatically masculine (e.g., "King," "Redeemer," and "Rock"), but others (e.g., "Indwelling Presence," "Knowledge," and "Water-Well") are feminine.

One might think that the assignment of gender is based on characteristics of the object denoted, for instance that the word for "rock" is masculine because a rock is strong. But that's mistaken. Rather, in Hebrew, as in other gendered languages, words are assigned gender according to their form rather than their specific meaning. For example, in modern Hebrew, disease names often conform to a specific pattern, one that happens to be grammatically feminine: "mumps" is *ḥazeret*, "measles" is *ḥazevet*, and "diabetes" is *sukeret*. This kind of pattern is common in Hebrew, where many of the words in a certain category (such as "diseases") have the same structure.

Sometimes, however, gender is explicitly invoked and its social meaning is used as a metaphor. Consider the next lines of the poem:

That you may suck from her breast
Consolation to the full,
That you may draw from her bosom
Glory to your delight.

The milk of the mother's breast is being compared to life-giving rain. Because the Land of Israel has a dry climate, rain was often employed as a metaphor for abundance and wealth. In effect, the city will be a place of prosperity and ease. Wealth will be as abundant as the rain in the wadis (the dry stream beds that overflow with water after torrential rain).

For thus said the Lord:
I will extend to her
Prosperity like a stream,
The wealth of nations
Like a wadi in flood;
And you shall drink of it.

Upon conveying the joyousness of nurturing overflow in which all will have what they need, the text continues with mother imagery:

You shall be carried on shoulders
And dandled upon knees.
As a mother comforts her son
So I will comfort you;
You shall find comfort in Jerusalem.

In the original Hebrew, the feminine pronoun ("her" before son) does not appear: a more literal translation would be "like a man whose mother comforts him." In this image, the Israelites are akin to the man who is comforted. But who is the mother in this poem? The poem could be read in two ways: either God or Jerusalem could be the mother. Keep this ambiguity in mind when rereading the next lines:

> You shall see and your heart shall rejoice,
> Your limbs shall flourish like grass.
> The power of the Lord shall be revealed
> In behalf of His Servants;
> But He shall rage against His foes.

If Jerusalem is the mother, then God is envisioned as the husband of Jerusalem, and the people of Israel are like children protected by the father (God) and nurtured by the mother (Jerusalem). Alternatively, it could be that God is performing both roles. God may be both the nurturing mother *and* the protecting father.

Now consider these subsequent, explicitly gendered lines.

> See, the Lord is coming with fire —
> His chariots are like a whirlwind —
> To vent His anger in fury,
> His rebuke in flaming fire.
> For with fire will the Lord contend,
> With His sword, against all flesh;
> And many shall be the slain of the Lord.

The biblical author may have used the warrior image to suggest that God should act like an avenging army. As an oft-vanquished people, the Israelites would have found such protection welcome.

At the same time, this portion of the poem clearly depicts the avenging God as male; and its earlier lines described mothers as nurturing. But to say that men are necessarily warlike, or that women are necessarily nurturing, is to take an essentialist position, ascribing behavioral differences between men and women to genetic or inherent factors rather than cultural conditioning alone. Feminist thought tends to reject essentialism and view gender as largely a societal construct.

Essentialism in our God-concept might create a kind of essentialism in our gender roles as well. If God represents our highest ideals, then calling God "He" when we speak of a warrior, or calling God "She" when we speak of a mother reinforces—perhaps even promotes—those understandings of gender identity.

However, this understanding of the text is not the only option when reading this poem. Perhaps we are being told of a thunderstorm in which the thunder-god rains upon the mother-earth? Might the whirlwind of the chariots be the storm clouds and the sword of flaming fire a lightning bolt? Is this a remnant of paganism, a hint of the male storm-god watering the female earth-god? Our interpretation may reflect the image(s) of God we are hoping to embrace.

4.2. From the Liturgy: Our Father, Our King

If a prayer depicts God in multiple roles, such as both nurturing and avenging, does that variety open up space for a wider range of gender identities?

Consider, for example, the text of the *Avinu Malkeinu* ("Our Father, Our King") prayer. Sung in the synagogue on the High Holy Days with great devotion—usually at a point of high drama in the service, when the whole congregation stands and faces the open ark that is home to the Torah scrolls—the prayer poem offers a heartfelt plea to God: for mercy for our sins and retribution against our enemies. Interestingly, the prayer employs two images of God at once: the terrifying and powerful king as well as the nurturing and caring father.

The prayer appears in a variety of ways in Jewish liturgy. The version that follows is from a traditional prayer book, one that does not incorporate Enlightenment ideals into its text. Its use of masculine language throughout this text is consistent with a traditional depiction of God. Many liberal prayer books, on the other hand, contain a rewritten version that either does not use masculine language or leaves the masculine Hebrew text intact but translates it into English in a less-gendered way, such as "Our Parent, Our Sovereign."

> Our Father, our King, remember that we are dust.
> Our Father, our King, please do not turn us away from You empty-handed.
> Our Father, our King, may this moment be a moment of compassion and a time of favor before You.
> Our Father, our King, have pity on us, our children and our infants.
> Our Father, our King, act for the sake of those who were killed for Your holy name.
> Our Father, our King, act for the sake of those who were slaughtered for proclaiming your Unity.
> Our Father, our King, act for the sake of those who went through fire and water to sanctify Your name.
> Our Father, our King, avenge before our eyes the spilt blood of Your servants.
> Our Father, our King, act for Your sake, if not for ours.
> Our Father, our King, act for Your sake, and save us.
> Our Father, our King, act for the sake of Your abundant compassion.
> Our Father, our King, act for the sake of Your great, mighty and awesome name by which we are called.
> Our Father, our King, be gracious and answer us, though we have no worthy deeds; act with us in charity and loving-kindness and save us.[1]

Throughout the many verses of this prayer, the emphasis shifts between God as father and God as king. At the beginning, more weight seems to be given to God the compassionate father:

> Our Father, our King, remember that we are dust.
> Our Father, our King, please do not turn us away from You empty-handed.
> Our Father, our King, may this moment be a moment of compassion and a time of favor before You.
> Our Father, our King, have pity on us, our children and our infants.

Both traditional and liberal prayer books contain many (somewhat differently worded but largely similar) texts petitioning God the compassionate father who seeks our best interests and addresses our basic needs. This section portrays God's immanence, or presence. It also invokes the concept of a personal God who listens to and answers our prayers.

This next section petitions God in a different vein:

> Our Father, our King, act for the sake of those who were killed for Your holy name.
> Our Father, our King, act for the sake of those who were slaughtered for proclaiming your Unity.
> Our Father, our King, act for the sake of those who went through fire and water to sanctify Your name.
> Our Father, our King, avenge before our eyes the spilt blood of Your servants.

Here is the avenging God who demands retribution for sins. This part of the prayer is much less likely to appear in liberal prayer books, because liberal Jews are more at ease with making changes to the prayer book and less comfortable with calls for divine vengeance. This section invokes God's transcendence: God is not close to us, but rather serves as the commanding and awesome power over us.

The next section, a plea for God's gracious care, appears in both liberal and traditional prayer books:

> Our Father, our King, act for Your sake, if not for ours.
> Our Father, our King, act for Your sake, and save us.
> Our Father, our King, act for the sake of Your abundant compassion.
> Our Father, our King, act for the sake of Your great, mighty and awesome name by which we are called.
> Our Father, our King, be gracious and answer us, though we have no worthy deeds; act with us in charity and loving-kindness and save us.

The case could be made that the *Avinu Malkeinu* prayer moves away from essentialism by depicting God in masculine human terms as both a warrior *and* a nurturer. Nonetheless, the expressly masculine language, "Our Father, Our King," in traditional prayer books reinforces the perception that God is exclusively male.

In liberal prayer books such as the Reform *Mishkan Hanefesh*, however, the prayer has been edited to emphasize the merciful and nurturing aspects of God-as-father. Going further, an alternate version of this prayer — offering female imagery translated as "our Soul-Sustainer, Source of Our Life," in place of the masculine Hebrew transliteration "*Avinu Malkeinu*" (meaning "our father, our king" but left untranslated in the prayer text) appears in the Reform closing service (Ne'ilah).[2]

Nonetheless, this kind of revisioning is not offered consistently throughout the Reform High Holiday prayer book. Sometimes, in fact, there is a split between what the Hebrew and the English have to say. In the same closing service, one of the prayers invokes God-as-ruler in the Hebrew (*El Melech Yosheiv al kise rakhamim,* which means "God-as-King is enthroned on the seat of mercy"), yet it presents a genderless God in the English translation ("Majestic God, Your throne is mercy").[3] In this prayer book, God is sometimes genderless, sometimes not, depending upon the text. Similarly, it avoids using the word "Lord" when referring to God; its substitution of "Sovereign" averts rendering the Hebrew text into gendered English terms.

In essence, the issue of gender is more complicated than the pronoun question. There is the question of how gender is expressed, and what assumptions we bring to a given role.

4.3. A Rabbinic View: God's Fire and the Patriarchy

Gender assumptions appear in midrash in less obvious ways as well. This next selection is interesting in its contradictions. While disavowing the use of any kind of imagery for God, it also subtly reinforces a kind of patriarchal power.

Elijah [the Prophet] told the following: One day as I was walking through the greatest city of the world, there was a roundup and I was roughly seized and brought into the king's house. Presently a Parsee priest came to me and asked me, "Are you a scholar?" I replied, "A bit of a one." He said, "If you can answer the particular question I am about to ask, you may go in peace." I replied, "Ask."

So the Parsee priest said, "You people assert that fire is not god. Then why is it written in your Torah, 'Fire burning eternally' [Lev. 6:6]"? I replied, "My son, when our forebears stood at Mount Sinai to receive the Torah for themselves, they saw no form resembling a human being, nor one resembling the form of anything that has breath which the Holy One, blessed be He, created in His world, as is said, 'Take ye therefore good heed unto yourselves—for ye saw no manner of form on the day that the Lord spoke unto you in Horeb' [Deut. 4:15]. For He, the God of gods, the Lord of lords, is the one and only God, whose kingdom endures in heaven and on earth as well as in the highest heaven of heavens. And yet you people saw that fire is god! Fire is no more than a rod to be used upon men on earth. Its use may be understood by the parable of a king who took a lash and hung it up in his house, and then said to his servants, to his children, and to the members of his household, 'With this lash I may strike you, may even kill you'—threatening them, so that in penitence they would turn away from sin. If they do not turn back, then God says, 'I will have to strike them with the lash, will even have to kill them.' Hence, 'Fire burning eternally' is to be read in the light of the verse 'For by fire will the Lord threaten judgement' [Isa. 66:16]. You might suppose that this verse is to be read [literally], 'For by fire will the Lord be judged'. Therefore, elsewhere Scripture declares, 'The Lord thy God is a devouring fire'[Deut. 4:24]."[4]

The Rabbis intended for this text to be read as a literary device rather than accepted as a historical event. We know this is the case because it features Elijah the Prophet. According to rabbinical lore, Elijah the Prophet did not die. Rather, he was taken up to heaven in a fiery chariot—and he has been wandering on earth conversing with Sages, announcing children's births to barren couples, and performing acts of kindness for poor families ever since.

The tale opens with the Parsee priest. "Parsees" are the followers of Zoroastrianism, a religion founded by the philosopher Zoroaster in Persia in the sixth century BCE. As a Zoroastrian, this priest would have held the dualistic belief that two opposing forces—forces of light and of darkness—existed in the world.

Elijah [the Prophet] told the following: One day as I was walking through the greatest city of the world, there was a roundup and I was roughly seized and brought into the king's house. Presently a Parsee priest came to me and asked me, "Are you a scholar?" I replied, "A bit of a one." He said, "If you can answer the particular question I am about to ask, you may go in peace." I replied, "Ask."

So the Parsee priest said, "You people assert that fire is not god. Then why is it written in your Torah, 'Fire burning eternally' [Lev. 6:6]?"

Note that the Parsee priest is taking the biblical text literally, rather than metaphorically. The story continues:

I replied, "My son, when our forebears stood at Mount Sinai to receive the Torah for themselves, they saw no form resembling a human being, nor one resembling the form of anything that has breath which the Holy One, blessed be He, created in His world, as is said, 'Take ye therefore good heed unto yourselves — for ye saw no manner of form on the day that the Lord spoke unto you in Horeb' [Deut. 4:15]. For He, the God of gods, the Lord of lords, is the one and only God, whose kingdom endures in heaven and on earth as well as in the highest heaven of heavens."

Elijah's quotation from Deuteronomy is particularly apt. In the biblical text the final words of that line are "the Lord spoke unto you in Horeb *out of the fire.*" The biblical text has made it clear that God is not synonymous with fire.

From this example we might derive the lesson: whenever one encounters a quotation from the Hebrew Bible in the rabbinic literature (or any literature, for that matter), it is wise to look up the verse to learn what comes before and after the quoted section. No given quote stands alone; it references a much larger universe of meaning.

Since Elijah's answer to the Parsee priest fully addresses the broached issue, the midrashic text could have stopped there. From a feminist perspective, in fact, we might have wished that it did end there, for this next section reinforces a patriarchal system in which the dominant male is in charge of his household and his word is law:

> "And yet you people saw that fire is god! Fire is no more than a rod to be used upon men on earth. Its use may be understood by the parable of a king who took a lash and hung it up in his house, and then said to his servants, to his children, and to the members of his household, 'With this lash I may strike you, may even kill you'—threatening them, so that in penitence they would turn away from sin. If they do not turn back, then God says, 'I will have to strike them with the lash, will even have to kill them.'"

Here God is portrayed as the patriarchal head of household who wields the right and the power to kill its inhabitants if they misbehave. The "fire" of the earlier texts is like a rod that might be used to beat others into obedience. The discussion was intended to be a form of theodicy (an explanation of why, if God is good, evil persists). The presented answer is that God will make use of fire (here representing the trials in our lives) in order to chastise us when we go astray.

Meanwhile, the text also reinforces the foundations of patriarchal power. It upholds the idea that the male head of a household might terrorize its inhabitants with physical violence or the threat of such violence in order to enforce his will. For those who have faced such abusive behavior, this passage is particularly painful: the abuser becomes synonymous with God.

The prophet Elijah now continues his discussion as if there was nothing unusual in this text. He returns to the question as to whether God may be found in the fire. This last passage makes it clear that God is not *in* the fire, but rather that God makes *use* of the fire:

> "Hence, 'Fire burning eternally' is to be read in the light of the verse 'For by fire will the Lord threaten judgement' [Isa. 66:16]. You might suppose that this verse is to be read [literally], 'For by fire will the Lord be judged'. Therefore, elsewhere Scripture declares, 'The Lord thy God is a devouring fire'[Deut. 4:24]. "

Note how a somewhat gender-fluid biblical text (the one we read in section 4.1) was used in support of a patriarchal reading. This shift illustrates how the Greco-Roman world in which the ancient Rabbis lived tended to be all the more explicitly patriarchal in its assumptions. In this case, the passage most strongly reinforcing patriarchal privilege was merely an aside—ancillary to the primary point of the text. In the culture of its time, such ideas regarding gender relations were simply taken for granted.

4.4. A Medieval View:
Scholem Explains the Rise of the *Shekhinah*

From the Greco-Roman to the modern era, the masculine view of God has been dominant in Jewish tradition—but there have been a few exceptions.

One such anomaly appeared during the medieval period with the emergence of the Jewish mystical tradition known as the *Kabbalah*. The word means "that which is received," a reference to the fact that these texts were received as a tradition, conveyed from the mouth of a learned master to a student. In the Kabbalah, the lowest of the divine attributes (both in grandeur and in space) and therefore the closest attribute of God to humanity—the one that represented the indwelling presence of God—was the *Shekhinah*, and it was often envisioned as female.

In the following passage, the scholar of Jewish mysticism Gershom Scholem explains how the idea of the *Shekhinah* captured the imagination of the Kabbalists:[5]

> *'Ein-Sof* [literally "without end," the name given to the original source of all being] is only seldom conceived of as energy or power; It (in the spirit of the Kabbalists, one should use the neuter gender) is purely and simply concealed and transcendent; no statement can be made about It. However, the *Sefiroth* [ten attributes of God], while part of the divine essence (albeit as stages of Himself to us), are primarily bearers of His active and creative force.... The *Sefiroth* are not mere potentialities, but are real, exist[ing] beings. They are hypostases [physical manifestations of God's essence] that have become independent; charged with and emanating energy, they empower and advance the process by which God reveals Himself and makes His great name known....
>
> In this world of *Sefiroth*, each of which can be viewed as a hypostasis of a particular facet of God, the *Shekhinah* receives its new meaning as the tenth and final *Sefirah*. The crucial factor in its new status is unquestionably its feminine character, which, as mentioned above, is not found in any pre-Kabbalistic source, but which now absorbs everything capable of such an interpretation in biblical and rabbinic literature.... The enormous popularity enjoyed by this new mythic understanding of the concept is illustrated precisely by the fact that it filtered down in the form of confused, apologetic distortions in which the *Shekhinah* was identified and compared with the Divine Providence [God's ongoing protection and intervention in human

lives] itself. This fact is undisputable proof that the Kabbalists here touched upon a fundamental and primal need, uncovering one of the perennial religious images latent in Judaism as well.[6]

In the first section of the text, Scholem explains that the highest and oldest attribute of God is genderless:

> 'Ein-Sof is only seldom conceived of as energy or power; It (in the spirit of the Kabbalists, one should use the neuter gender) is purely and simply concealed and transcendent; no statement can be made about It.

Scholem refers to the 'Ein-Sof, the name given to the original, primal source of all being, as "It," based on how the Kabbalists conceived of it. However, Scholem quickly returns to the convention of referring to God as "He."

> The Sefiroth, while part of the divine essence (albeit as stages of Himself to us), are primarily bearers of His active and creative force . . . the Sefiroth are not mere potentialities, but are real, exist[ing] beings. They are hypostases that have become inde-pendent; charged with and emanating energy, they empower and advance the process by which God reveals Himself and makes His great name known.

The ten attributes of God known as the Sefirot were considered to be actual manifestations of God. They were the processes by which God created and still maintains the world. In Scholem's gendered language, they also "empower and advance the process by which God reveals Himself and makes His great name known."

Scholem soon shifts gears to explain the role of the Shekhinah, the feminine face of God:

In this world of *Sefiroth*, each of which can be viewed as a hypostasis of a particular facet of God, the *Shekhinah* receives its new meaning as the tenth and final *Sefirah*. The crucial factor in its new status is unquestionably its feminine character, which, as mentioned above, is not found in any pre-Kabbalistic source, but which now absorbs everything capable of such an interpretation in biblical and rabbinic literature.

As he says, the idea that this tenth attribute is feminine is a late development in Jewish mysticism. However, once it was conceived as such, it immediately became very popular, and a great number of earlier texts were reinterpreted in the context of this idea:

> The enormous popularity enjoyed by this new mythic understanding of the concept is illustrated precisely by the fact that it filtered down in the form of confused, apologetic distortions in which the *Shekhinah* was identified and compared with the Divine Providence itself.

The *Shekhinah*, the feminine face of God, became the force by which God's Providence might be discerned in the world. Scholem elucidates that it took on all kinds of nurturing imagery, in line with the aforementioned motherly qualities offered by the Bible itself (see 4.1). Scholem continues:

> This fact is undisputable proof that the Kabbalists here touched upon a fundamental and primal need, uncovering one of the perennial religious images latent in Judaism as well.

Apparently, there was a latent need among devotees for a feminine dimension to God. The *Shekhinah*, described in feminine terms, became a potent symbol of God's nurturing care.

The following text, written around 1290 by the Spanish kabbalist R. Joseph Gikatilla and translated by Scholem, exemplifies the role of the *Shekhinah* in kabbalistic thinking; Scholem explained that "Gikatilla offers a detailed presentation of each of the ten *Sefiroth*, using numerous quotations and interpretations of biblical passages, each one of the *Sefiroth* appearing under the aegis of one of God's names."[7]

Now take note of a great principle: know that in the beginning of the creation of the world . . . the *Shekhinah* dwelt with the lower ones [i.e., in the earthly world]; and so long as the *Shekhinah* was below, heaven and earth were one. . . . The channels and sources [through which the cosmic effects of the *Sefiroth* flow down] operated harmoniously and emanated from above to below, so that God, may He be blessed, filled everything from above to below. . . . But when Adam came and sinned, the ranks were disrupted, the channels were shattered and the pools [of blessing] were cut off. Thereupon the *Shekhinah* withdrew and the bond [connecting all things] became undone. Then Abraham, Isaac, and Jacob, of blessed memory, came and began to draw the *Shekhinah* back down again, and they prepared for it three thrones and drew it down somewhat, and they made their bodies into thrones for the *Shekhinah*. . . . Thus, in their days the *Shekhinah* was *in suspenso* [literally, "hanging in air"], and found no resting place for its feet on earth, as in the beginning of Creation. But then came Moses, of blessed memory, and all of Israel together with him built the Tabernacle and the vessels, and repaired the broken channels, and put the ranks in order, and repaired the ponds, and drew live water into them from the House of Water Drawing, and then brought the *Shekhinah* back to its dwelling among the lower ones—into the Tent, but not upon the ground as in the beginning of Creation.[8]

The *Shekhinah's* role was to be a conduit between the upper and lower worlds, between God's world of emanation and the human world of the earth. After Adam and Eve disobeyed God, the *Shekhinah* no longer had its feet upon the earth, which meant that God's emanation no longer reached all the way down to humanity. That flow has not been fully restored as yet.

Let's look at the passage more closely:

Now take note of a great principle: know that in the beginning of the creation of the world . . . the *Shekhinah* dwelt with the lower ones [i.e., in the earthly world]; and so long as the *Shekhinah* was below, heaven and earth were one. . . . The channels and sources [through which the cosmic effects of the *Sefiroth* flow down] operated harmoniously and emanated from above to below, so that God, may He be blessed, filled everything from above to below.

The flow of God is explicitly gendered in some Kabbalistic texts as male. Scholem explained, earlier in the book, that for Gikatilla, "The tenth *Sefirah, Shekhinah* . . . is the pool into which life flows, from which it then disperses to all the lower beings according to their natures and needs."[9] The *Shekhinah* receives its flow from above, from the ninth *Sefirah,* known as the *Tsaddik.*[10] This realm of the *Tsaddik* is male, and has explicitly sexual overtones. In Scholem's account:

We now come to the problem of the sexual symbolism which, throughout the Kabbalah, is inseparable from the image of the *Tsaddik* . . . The ninth *Sefirah* not only corresponds to the phallus; it is also, by reason of this allocation, the site of the circumcision, the sign of the Covenant. The vital force concentrated here is externally expressed in the world of creatures as sexual energy; however, the unrestrained power of the procreative drive, as the creative element of the cosmos, is harnessed and restricted within sacred boundaries. The *Tsaddik* is the one who guards and keeps it within these boundaries; he chains this drive, which flows from the river of life, within the limits of the Law, thus maintaining its sacred nature.[11]

As we see, the flow is seminal.

The next portion of our reading contains echoes of the theology of Original Sin (see our discussion in 2.1 and 2.2):

> But when Adam came and sinned, the ranks were disrupted, the channels were shattered and the pools [of blessing] were cut off. Thereupon the *Shekhinah* withdrew and the bond [connecting all things] became undone.

In the Christian interpretation, Adam and Eve's disobedience was the Original Sin that affected all of their descendants; because of it, a sacrifice (in the form of Jesus' death) was needed in order to absolve humanity of that sin. In the Jewish mystical version, the same Fall was understood to have broken the vessels carrying God's light early in the process of creating the world; to this day it remains necessary to repair the world to return it to its original pristine state.

Initially this repair was performed by the Patriarchs. The Patriarchs serve two functions here: they are the individual characters in the biblical narrative and also (allegorically) the names of the attributes of God:

> Then Abraham, Isaac, and Jacob, of blessed memory, came and began to draw the *Shekhinah* back down again, and they prepared for it three thrones and drew it down somewhat, and they made their bodies into thrones for the *Shekhinah*. . . . Thus, in their days the *Shekhinah* was *in suspenso* [literally, "hanging

in air"], and found no resting place for its feet on earth, as in the beginning of Creation.

The Patriarchs' acts improved the situation, but they were unable to fix all the damage on their own. Moses' work—bringing the Revelation of Torah and establishing the forms of worship—had a much greater impact on the status of the *Shekhinah*:

> But then came Moses, of blessed memory, and all of Israel together with him built the Tabernacle and the vessels, and repaired the broken channels, and put the ranks in order, and repaired the ponds, and drew live water into them from the House of Water Drawing, and then brought the *Shekhinah* back to its dwelling among the lower ones—into the Tent, but not upon the ground as in the beginning of Creation.

These descriptions sound like a physical process of building, but they are metaphors for spiritual work.

Note, meanwhile, the passiveness of the *Shekhinah* in this passage. She serves as a conduit of God's blessing, but she does not actively bring it down herself. Each time she is brought into contact with the lower world, it is at the hands of righteous men. This text reinforces a patriarchal view: an active masculine force is brought to bear upon a passive feminine vessel.

4.5. A Modern View: Plaskow's Feminist Critique

In 1975, the Central Conference of American Rabbis (CCAR), the rabbinical arm of Reform Judaism, released a prayer book offering ten different Shabbat evening services, each with a different God concept. *Gates of Prayer* was the work of a movement undergoing tremendous change. A decade earlier, the movement had become aware of a sense of crisis within its ranks. A comprehensive 1965 CCAR survey found that "seventy-one percent [of rabbis] perceived a 'Jewish distance' between themselves and the congregation," the Reform movement historian Michael Meyer reports. "Nearly two-thirds of the respondents [which also included rabbinical students and a sample of the laity] were eager to move closer to Conservative Judaism, but almost the entire remainder, 29 percent, hoped for a thrust in the opposite direction, toward religious humanism.[12] Additional stresses were the movement's debates over whether rabbis should officiate at an intermarriage and the "proper relationship of Diaspora Jews to the State of Israel."[13] Further, women's roles were changing rapidly. At a time when the movement's seminary, Hebrew Union College-Jewish Institute of Religion, had just made the epochal decision to ordain women, the prayer book was an attempt to keep many different factions within the Reform tent.

Various changes were instituted to make the Reform prayer book more inclusive. For example, the editors revised the English titles of the *Avot prayer* ("Patriarchs") from "Our Fathers" to "God of All Generations" and continued the practice of removing the traditional prayer of gratitude for having been born a man.[14] However, not one of the ten services used gender-neutral terms for God, and all of the editors were male.

Judith Plaskow's *Standing Again at Sinai* appeared in 1991, in the midst of the dramatically shifting conversations within the liberal Jewish world. Its feminist critique of Jewish theology was particularly influential in Reform circles. As a Yale-trained professor of Religious Studies, Plaskow argued then that a male-dominated prayer book was not in keeping with feminism's egalitarian ideals. Around this time, many Reform congregations began to add the Matriarchs' names to standard prayers such as the *Avot*, which extols the merits of the Patriarchs Abraham, Isaac, and Jacob.

The practice spread. Nowadays, if one looks at the inside cover of still-extant congregational copies of the 1970s-era *Gates of Prayer*, one usually finds a gender-neutral version of the *Avot* pasted there. In Reform congregations today, this prayer is now known as the "*Avot v'Imahot*" ("Patriarchs and Matriarchs"), for it routinely includes Sarah, Rebecca, Rachel, and Leah.

Eventually, the fact that *Gates of Prayer* had not included the Matriarchs and that it had consistently referred to God as *He* became increasingly problematic, and in 1996, a gender-neutral version was released. It still made use of some masculine language related to God, but this slim, gray-bound volume was widely adopted in place of its much-heavier, blue-bound predecessor. Then, in 2007, a new prayer book series, *Mishkan T'filah*, was developed, this time with a female rabbi, Elyse Goldstein, as its editor and, in another first, input from both female and male lay leaders throughout the movement. The newest prayer book routinely replaced gendered words such as *king* with neutral words like *sovereign* and continued the practice (also found in the 1996 version of *Gates of Prayer*) of not using a third-person pronoun for God, so that it was possible to exclude references to God's gender. *Mishkan T'filah* has since become the most commonly used prayer book in the Reform movement.

It is helpful to read Plaskow's analysis from 1991 in the context of this history:

A feminist critique of Jewish God-language begins with the unyielding maleness of the dominant Jewish picture of God. If the Jewish understanding of God is in many ways a complex and contradictory weave of biblical and philosophical categories, the maleness of God is a consistent theme in all elements of the fabric. God's maleness is so deeply and firmly established as a part of the Jewish conception of God that it is almost difficult to document: it is simply part of the lenses through which God is seen. Maleness is not a distinct tribute, separable from God's anger or mercy or justice. Rather, it is expressed through the total picture of God in Jewish texts and liturgy. God in the Jewish tradition is spoken of in male pronouns, and more importantly, in terms of male characteristics and images. . . . Every blessing evokes God as lord and king of the universe, and throughout the liturgy, he is father God and God of our fathers, lord of hosts, and king of the earth.[15]

These observations remain true for traditional congregations. In prayer books where the original language is retained, God is clearly, overwhelmingly, portrayed as male. Within the context of liberal congregations, where the language has changed, it becomes appropriate to ask: is it sufficient to change God-language, or do we need to change our assumptions about power as well?

According to Plaskow, the problem is not simply one of pronouns. As Plaskow wrote in 1994:

Feminist God-language . . . seeks to give expression not simply to God's presence in ordinary events and situations, but more specifically to the amazing discovery of God's presence moving in and among women. . . .

God was not simply the traditional deity in female form, but a mother birthing the world and protecting it with her womb. The accumulation of female pronouns and images in both their prayers [those of the early innovators Naomi Janowitz and Rabbi Margaret Moers Wenig] and those of later innovators provides a wonderful celebration of women's sexuality and power rare in the culture and still rarer in a religious context.[16]

Images of mothering were intended to counteract the commanding-king imagery suffusing the traditional liturgy. However, the introduction of feminine metaphors was by itself still insufficient for counteracting the dominance of masculine conceptions of God. As Plaskow continued:

> Important as such language was and is as an affirmation of female selfhood in relation to the sacred, there is also a certain naivete in the assumption that the insertion of female pronouns or images into traditional prayers provides a solution to women's invisibility. Rather, insofar as male images of God are part of a larger pattern of hierarchical dualism, female language introduces a contradiction into the pattern that begins to reveal and disrupt it but does not in itself dislodge the larger system of dualisms. God-She can also be the supreme Other in a hierarchical system. Jewish feminist God-language has therefore also tried to address the notion of God as wholly Other, a notion that persists even in female imagery, but more radically challenging traditional metaphors and blessing formulas.[17]

Plaskow is questioning why God must be envisioned as a domineering figure. Remember, for example, the aforementioned God-with-a-whip-of-fire image (in section 3 above). Wouldn't it be better for humanity if we exalted a God-human relationship ideal that provided a better role model for our own relationships? From a feminist point of view, the hierarchy implied in the traditional language about God can be as problematic as its gendered assumptions.

One might argue, however, that Plaskow's analysis of feminist God-language displays aspects of essentialism. The feminist prayers that Plaskow praises substitute masculine images of power—warrior or ruler—with valorizing feminine images of divine creation—mother or caregiver. But why must the male be the warrior and the female be the nurturer? Even in the Bible the assumptions can be more nuanced. Consider the multiple biblical stories of warrior-women: Deborah employs military strategy when fighting a foe with superior weapons (Judges 4–5); Yael single-handedly takes down the opposing army's general with an offer of warm milk and the skillful use of a tent-peg (Judges 4). Can we have a God-concept that embraces both?

For Plaskow, the answer would be yes: we can employ a multiplicity of metaphors when speaking about God. In other words, Plaskow is not advocating essentialism in gender roles. Rather, in place of a hierarchical relationship, Plaskow proposes a different understanding of the nature of God, one in which God is envisioned in more egalitarian terms. As she wrote:

> God is not a being outside us, over against us, who manipulates and controls us and raises some people over others. God is not the dualistic Other who authorizes all other dualism. God is the source and wellspring of life in its infinite diversity. God—as our foremothers seem to have known—is present in all aspects of life, but present not just as father and protector but as one who empowers us to act creatively ourselves.[18]

Over time, Plaskow's view of a feminist God-concept emphasizing the unity behind the multiplicity of being has emerged as the central idea in her work. In 2016, for example, Plaskow wrote the following commentary on her earlier work:

> The part of my chapter on God that expresses most clearly my current perspective is my brief discussion of the nature of monotheism. In the chapter of *Standing Again at Sinai* on the community of Israel, I argued for using a part/whole rather than a hierarchical model to conceptualize Jewish difference. The many subgroups within the larger Jewish community—ethnic, religious, class or gender based, and so on—have their

own distinctive characteristics and identities and, at the same time, are parts of a greater whole, just as Jews are part of larger heterogeneous cultures. . . . Monotheism is not the worship of a single image of God or of a supernatural being projected into the heavens but "the capacity to see the One in and through the changing forms of the many."[19]

In this view of God, the multiplicity of human existence—which includes gendered persons—is all part of a larger picture, in which God is the unity behind this variety.

4.6. A Modern View: Adler and the "Pudding Stone"

Even as congregations become increasingly sensitive to gender imbalances in traditional prayers, it can be difficult for them to adopt revisions to well-known prayers. The core difficulty lies in the performative nature of liturgy. The prayers are more than the sum of their parts: beyond the text itself, there is the lived experience of saying them, with their cadences and choreography. Take, for example, one of the most "performative" of prayers in Jewish liturgy: the *Mourner's Kaddish*. It has a distinctive, recognizable rhythm even to those who do not understand Hebrew. It is said daily for the year following a close relative's death. Its placement in the funeral liturgy is also particularly prominent: the first time a mourner will recite the *Kaddish* for someone is at the moment the casket has come to its final resting place. The *Mourner's Kaddish* marks the moment when the mourning process formally begins.

And so, it is one thing to recognize (for example) that the language in a particular prayer is difficult or theologically problematic; it is another thing entirely to convince a phalanx of mourners that the *Mourner's Kaddish* should be said any differently than it is traditionally done.

As a novice rabbi, I learned this lesson directly, albeit in a different way. A bereaved family desired to have a graveside service on the morning of the burial, which would take place in the afternoon. I explained to them we would not recite the *Mourner's Kaddish* at the graveside service, for we would wait until the burial. We made an announcement to this effect at the start of the service. However, it is one thing to rationally decide and announce such things; it is another thing to enact them. When the time came to end the graveside service, the deceased's Jewish friends simply would not leave. We had not said the *Kaddish*, so the service was not yet complete in their eyes.

In 1988, Rabbi Rachel Adler, one of the first theologians to integrate feminist perspectives into Jewish texts, published *Engendering Judaism*, an erudite study largely of the difficulties faced in revising *halakhah* (Jewish law). She also explained why changing the liturgy is so challenging:

> Jewish liturgy is not like sedimentary rock in which discrete strata are neatly laid down in historical order. It is more like conglomerate or "pudding stone," in which chunks and globules of various earlier rocks are suspended like nuts and raisins in a cake. A new liturgical field does not cover over its predecessor and deposit a completely new layer. . . . The dilemma for feminist Jews is that virtually all the chunks in the conglomerate were created exclusively by and for men. Yet rejecting the conglomeration as a liturgical process and creating totally new liturgies representing the spiritual insights of our own time and gender entail sweeping away the accumulated webs of covenant made possible by conglomerate liturgy without offering an alternative means of fulfilling its covenant-maintaining function. . . . We can find an answer to the feminist dilemma in the nature of the ritual process. The most effective innovations in liturgical ritual transmute familiar and deeply embedded meanings, metaphors,

and forms through processes that unify the communities to which they belong.[20]

Adler begins by pointing out that

Jewish liturgy is not like sedimentary rock in which discrete strata are neatly laid down in historical order.

In fact, Jewish prayer makes use of texts from a wide variety of eras. The Saturday morning *Shaḥarit* service, for example, follows the structure created by the ancient Rabbis, yet is also interspersed with medieval prayers and modern reflections.

Adler continues:

[The liturgy] is more like conglomerate or "pudding stone," in which chunks and globules of various earlier rocks are suspended like nuts and raisins in a cake. A new liturgical field does not cover over its predecessor and deposit a completely new layer.

As a matter of fact, Jewish liturgy, like Jewish theology, is profoundly *intertextual*: each text comments upon the texts that came before it, so that the interplay of the multi-generational texts is akin to a conversation. Adler recognizes that aspects of this discussion are worth keeping—these are, in fact, the foundations of the tradition. Herein lies the difficulty:

The dilemma for feminist Jews is that virtually all the chunks in the conglomerate were created exclusively by and for men.

Elsewhere in the book, Adler cites a story told by Rabbi Laura Geller. Listening to her rabbinical school professor talk about how the prayer book text addresses all aspects of human experience, Geller suddenly realized that key points of her experience as a woman were *not* included, such as the start of her first menses. Women's experiences and concerns have largely not been part of this amalgamation of texts. Adler resumes:

> Yet rejecting the conglomeration as a liturgical process and creating totally new liturgies representing the spiritual insights of our own time and gender entail sweeping away the accumulated webs of covenant made possible by conglomerate liturgy without offering an alternative means of fulfilling its covenant-maintaining function.

The question arises: is it really possible to start fresh? As my *Mourner's Kaddish* example illustrates, Jews' expectations regarding a prayer's performance have been built up over ages of use.

Then there is the even more fundamental question: how is a prayer still Jewish, if it no longer holds all of the layers of textual meaning? Again, Adler:

> We can find an answer to the feminist dilemma in the nature of the ritual process. The most effective innovations in liturgical ritual transmute familiar and deeply embedded meanings, metaphors, and forms through processes that unify the communities to which they belong.

In other words, we need to reinterpret what we have received. It is possible to rethink existing structures to make sense of a new reality. We'll look at examples of this kind of rewriting in the next section.

Historical precedents in Judaism support this approach. For example, the Rabbis reconsidered and eventually replaced the Temple sacrificial system in the wake of the Second Temple's destruction. Nonetheless, creating an egalitarian textual experience takes time and patience: it involves transforming ancient texts in the context of community.

4.7. A Modern View: Falk's Poetic Rewrite

In traditional practice, Jewish parents bless their children at the start of Shabbat. Boys are blessed in relationship to male forebears: "May God grant you the blessings of Ephraim and Menasseh." Girls are similarly blessed in relation to female forebears: "May God grant you the blessings of Sarah, Rebecca, Rachel, and Leah."[21]

In *The Days In Between* (2014), the poet, translator, and liturgist Marcia Falk offered a gender-neutral alternative to blessing children according to their gender:

> The squares of the city will be filled
> with boys and girls playing
> —Zechariah 8:5
> Be who you are,
> and may you be blessed
> in all that you are.[22]

Here, Falk opens up a liturgical space for genuinely appreciating and encouraging each child's unique potential. Falk also allows each individual to decide how to relate to the traditional ("boy" and "girl") categories. Because Hebrew is a gendered language, however, the Hebrew version of Falk's blessing is offered twice, once as grammatically male and once as grammatically female. Furthermore, Falk maintains traditional gender distinctions when she references both "boys" and "girls." What happens, then, when a person does not identify with being categorized as either male or female?

Let's look at this gender question through the lens of the *aliyah*, one of the honors given during a Torah service. The honoree is called up to the *bimah* (meaning "high place," which is the dais where Torah is read) and recites a set of blessings before and after the Torah reading. Originally, only men were called by name up to the *bimah* to recite the blessing before and after the Torah reading. The traditional formula for calling up a Jewish man to recite this blessing (translated into English) is "Rise, [man's Hebrew name], son of [father's Hebrew name]." When boys turn thirteen, they are called up in this manner on the occasion of their bar mitzvah.

When girls started to have a bat mitzvah as a parallel ceremony, the *aliyah* formula was adapted: "Rise, [girl's Hebrew name], daughter of [father's Hebrew name] . . ." In Reform congregations, as women's contributions to the synagogue increased, it became common to add the mother's name as well. For men, the formula became: "Rise, [man's Hebrew name], son of [father's Hebrew name] and [mother's Hebrew name]. . . ." For women, it became: "Rise, [woman's Hebrew name], daughter of [father's Hebrew name] and [mother's Hebrew name] . . ."

What is to be done if a person has no gender? Note that this is not a particularly new question. For example, there have always been intersex people, born with both sexual organs. Broadly speaking, the Talmud has at least six gender designations—*zachar, nekevah, saris, ailonit, androgynos,* and *tumtum*—that is to say: male, female, intersex male, intersex female, both equally at once, and none. In traditional Judaism, the question received detailed legal analysis. Ultimately (generalizing a complex topic), it was decided to ascertain a person's gender largely on the basis of secondary sexual characteristics. Those who are clearly men (in secondary sexual characteristics and gender presentation) receive *aliyah* honors in the Torah service; everyone else is (usually) not eligible.

By contrast, in recent years, Reform Judaism and certain other liberal groups have embraced alternative formulas that sidestep the requirements of gendered language. Here is one such example: "For the honor of the Torah, [person's Hebrew name], from the house of [one parent's Hebrew name] and [the other parent's Hebrew name]." Note that this version does not reference either "son of" or "daughter of." It also does not require conjugating the verb "to rise" with its inherent reference as to whether the person rising is male or female. The call to *aliyah* follows the traditional structure closely enough to *feel like* the usual blessing; only someone listening intently would catch the difference.

A similar issue arises with regard to God's gender. When a person is called up to the Torah, the traditional blessing opens as follows:

LEADER: Let us bless Adonai the blessed One.
CONGREGATION: Blessed is Adonai the blessed One forever and ever.

This traditional blessing requires conjugation of the verb "bless" according to the gender ascribed to God. Also, *Adonai* literally means "Lord," which in turn invokes the (male) sense of mastery and dominance.

Falk offers an alternative to this blessing that can be chanted to the traditional tune:

LEADER: Let us bless the source of life.
CONGREGATION: As we bless the source of life so we are blessed.[23]

This alternative blessing sidesteps the necessity to identify the gender of God by changing the subject of the sentence. Instead of a passive verb conjugated according to the masculine third person (*blessed is God*), we have an active verb conjugated according to the first person plural (*let us bless*). In addition, Falk has replaced the hierarchical *Adonai* with the egalitarian "source of life"—and has done so by emphasizing our own need to bless. Further, this blessing also celebrates a feminine aspect of God: childbirth. The "source of life" is what births or creates us all.

4.8. Summary of Views

How might we conceive of God's gender, or of God's roles as framed through the traditional lens of gender?

Notably, the *biblical text* contains both masculine and feminine God imagery. Saying that "men are necessarily warlike because they are men" or that "women are necessarily nurturing because they are women" is to take an essentialist position with regard to gender. Feminism has tended to reject essentialism.

In the *liturgical text*, the *Avinu Malkeinu* prayer has allowed Jews to move away from essentialism by depicting God in masculine human terms as both a warrior *and* a nurturer. Nonetheless, its traditional language — "our Father, our King" — reinforces the perception that God is exclusively male.

The *rabbinic text* disavowed using any kind of imagery for God, yet also subtly continues to reinforce a kind of patriarchal power. God is portrayed as the patriarchal head of household who wields the right and the power to kill its inhabitants if they misbehave.

The *medieval text* expounded upon the idea of the tenth *Sefirah* (attribute of God) being the *Shekhinah*. A late development in Jewish mysticism had led to this conception of a divine feminine aspect of God. Immediately the idea became very popular, and a great number of earlier texts were reinterpreted in its light. The *Shekhinah* became the passive female waiting to be redeemed.

The first *modern text*, Judith Plaskow's *Standing Again at Sinai* (1991), played an influential role in the creation of prayer books more in keeping with feminism's egalitarian ideals.

In the second *modern text*, Rachel Adler pinpointed the difficulty inherent in updating Jewish liturgy. Because the liturgy, like Jewish theology, is so profoundly intertextual—each text commenting upon the texts that came before it over the generations—these foundations of the tradition must be maintained. Yet women's experiences and concerns have largely not been part of this conglomeration of texts. Adler counsels building a more inclusive prayer book over time, upon the strata of the received texts.

In the third *modern text*, Marcia Falk updates the traditional and explicitly gendered Shabbat blessing for one's children with a new blessing that ostensibly casts aside gender alignment. However, because Hebrew is a gendered language, the Hebrew version of her blessing appears twice, once as grammatically male and once as grammatically female. She also offers a nongendered blessing for God; her rewrite of the *Barhu* ("Bless") prayer celebrates the creative aspects of God and emphasizes humanity's need to bless.

4.9. Implications of Masculine Images of God

We have been taking it for granted, up until now, that masculine God-images promote a patriarchal understanding of the relationship between men and women. At this point in the discussion, it might be helpful to question that assumption. Is it really the case that masculine images of God make it seem like men are more important than women?

The work of the biblical scholar Tikva Frymer-Kensky might shed some light on this question. Frymer-Kensky approaches the issue through the lens of monotheism. She asks in the preface to *In the Wake of the Goddesses*, "If the world of the gods and goddesses exemplifies gender relations and gender ideology, does the concept of gender change when there is only one god?"[24] Her answer is that some aspects change:

> In pagan religion, the stories about gods and goddesses exemplify and model the relationships between humans in society. Tales of goddesses illustrate and articulate societal ideals about women, and stories about gods and goddesses provided sacred example and divine warrant for the gendered structure of society. In the Bible, ideas about women and gender are conveyed in stories about human women.[25]

Frymer-Kensky acknowledges that women occupy a subordinate position to men within the social structures of the biblical world. Nonetheless, she writes:

> When we survey the biblical record of the goals and strategies of women, a startling fact emerges. There is nothing distinctively "female" about the way that women are portrayed in the Bible, nothing particularly feminine about either their goals or their strategies. The goals of women are the same goals held by the biblical male characters and the authors of the stories. Conversely, those goals which might be considered female-specific, such as female solidarity and rage, are completely absent from the biblical record. Women pursue their goals as actively as men, and use the same techniques and strategies that men in their situation could be expected to use.[26]

This is a rather surprising observation. We are accustomed to thinking of the Bible as patriarchal in its approach to gender.

Why would the Bible portray men and women as acting similarly? Frymer-Kensky argues that Hellenism transformed Jews' understanding of the text:

Israel's ideas about sex and gender changed after the conquest of Judea by Alexander the Great in 333 B.C.E. Jewish thinking about these matters was inherently unstable and was already undergoing modification, but the direction was firmly established by the confrontation with Greek civilization, which considered itself greatly superior to the East and actively promoted the spread of Greek culture. Jewish tradition has long held that there were two factions of Jews, the "Hellenizers," who adopted Greek modes of dress and behavior, and the pious, who did not. However, even the most loyal and pious were influenced by Greek ideas, and Hellenistic Judaism develops in dialogue with Greco-Roman civilization. . . . Greek philosophy portrayed females as inherently and essentially different from men, and fundamentally less valued. The male-female distinction was one of the great polarities of the Greek dualistic system. . . . In all such divisions in Greece, women were considered "natural" and untamed, even animal-like; the males represented civilized humanity.[27]

It is an interesting thought: What if patriarchal ideas about gender originate from ancient Greece rather than the Bible? Perhaps we might reclaim that lost Eden?

However, lest we think that a mere return to the Bible would resolve the difficulties, Frymer-Kensky points out that the rabbinical texts picked up this Hellenistic understanding of gender and applied it to the vast structure of Jewish law:

The rabbinic system represents a dramatic change from the Bible in the conceptualization of women and of sex. In place of the Bible's portrayal of women and men as fundamentally similar, the rabbis express a gender-polarized view of humanity. In place of the Bible's silence about sexual attraction, the rabbis portray sexual attraction as a mighty, at times dangerous and irresistible, force.[28]

In other words, there is still much inequality to address in the rabbinic system.

Nonetheless, we have a new insight here: the narrative of a singular God that appears in the Bible need not reinforce patriarchal ideas. Specifically, Frymer-Kensky argues, women and men in these texts are clearly equals in their intelligence, skill, and devotion, if not equal in their roles and expectations.

While she is not alone in her judgments, not all scholars agree with her conclusions. The feminist scholar Phyllis Trible notes three possible feminist approaches to the text:

> One approach documents the case against women. It cites and evaluates long neglected data that show the inferiority, subordination, and abuse of the female in ancient Israel and the early church. By contrast, a second approach discerns within the Bible critiques of the patriarchy. It upholds forgotten texts and reinterprets familiar ones to shape a remnant theology that challenges the sexism of scripture. Yet a third approach incorporates the other two. It recounts tales of terror *in memoriam* to offer sympathetic readings of abused women. . . . At the same time, it continues to search for the remnant in unlikely places.[29]

For her part, Frymer-Kensky argues that the masculine imagery in the Bible (such as God-as-king or God-as-soldier) need not be taken as a model for human gender relations. She lays blame, rather, on the misogyny of the surrounding culture for shaping biblical interpretations retroactively.

4.10. Rethinking the Meaning of Traditional Texts with Male Imagery

Changing the prayer book is a daunting task, for it is a composite document, created over centuries, representing the accumulated worship practices of a sprawling religious civilization. Further, attempts to edit the text may be met with resistance. Is it possible to leave a traditional text with male God imagery intact but rethink its meaning?

In some cases, it may be possible. In 2016, for example, I reflected on how we might reapproach the traditional text of the *Avinu Malkeinu*:

> What is interesting about this prayer is that the congregation is not identifying with the powerful one in this dynamic; rather, the congregation is identifying with the powerless subjects and dependents of this God-father-king. The worshipers are expected to feel—especially after fasting all day [on Yom Kippur]—as if they were at the mercy of this awesome power and begging for their very lives.
>
> In other words, this prayer is asking that all of the members of the congregation—including the leadership—understand in a most visceral way what it means to be utterly powerless.
>
> Is this not a most radical inversion of power?[30]

As Frymer-Kensky's work indicates, our readings of many of the texts as patriarchal may be superficial; the biblical narrative offers images of men and women that transcend our current and possibly conventional conceptions of gender. Creative, nonsexist reinterpretation of the Bible and the prayer book may be possible.

On the other hand, change is profoundly difficult and particularly slow when religion is involved. Plaskow's point from 1991 is still relevant: "God's maleness is so deeply and firmly established as a part of the Jewish conception of God that it is almost difficult to document: it is simply part of the lenses through which God is seen."[31]

There are those who would argue, on this basis, that the project cannot be accomplished without a break from the past. One such option, for some feminists, is to engage in Goddess worship. As Melissa Raphael writes in *Introducing Thealogy*:

> A Goddess feminist is one who identifies and opposes patriarchal structures of religious and social power and whose religious practice is not only centred on the Goddess but also supports all women's right of access to the sacred and to autonomous religious self-expression and organization.[32]

Goddess feminists reject the masculine God language entirely. Frymer-Kensky's position, on the other hand, is explicitly in opposition to this understanding. Frymer-Kensky explains that she wrote her book *In the Wake of the Goddesses* specifically to respond to the emergence of this movement:

> This modern literature on the Goddess was alien to my understanding of the worship of these ancient deities. There was not one Goddess, there were many goddesses; they were not enshrined in a religion of women, but in the official religion of male-dominated societies; they were not evidence of ancient mother-worship, but served as an integral part of a religious system that mirrored and provided the sacred underpinnings of patriarchy.[33]

Fymer-Kensky insists that the societal organization, not the pantheon, determines whether the worship is patriarchal or not.

What is likely to happen in the future? Each of the layers of the "pudding stone" reflects the concerns of the era. Hopefully ours will contribute a more nuanced understanding of gender.

Chapter 5

What Does It Mean to Declare
God Is One?

· How have different strands of Jewish tradition viewed the
  practice of reciting the *Shema*?
· What does it mean to bear witness to God's oneness?
· What might it mean to pray as one (community)?

5.1. A Biblical View: Hear, O Israel

Drawn from Deuteronomy 6:4, the declaration known as the *Shema*—
"Hear, O Israel! The Lord is our God, the Lord alone"—provides a
succinct profession of faith, affirming the singularity and uniqueness
of God. The ancient Rabbis considered the *Shema* to be so important,
they prescribed its recitation twice daily, based on the exhortation
in Deuteronomy 6:7 to repeat these words "when you lie down and
when you get up." To further its twice-daily recitation, they included
the *Shema* in the morning and evening liturgy.

In its original context, however, the verse does not stand out as
theologically distinctive, in the sense that one must be committed
to the regular recitation of this statement affirming the oneness of

God. Consider, for example, this selection, which includes the verses that appear before and after the *Shema*:

> And this is the Instruction—the laws and the rules—that your God has commanded [me] to impart to you, to be observed in the land that you are about to cross into and occupy, so that you, your children, and your children's children may revere your God and follow, as long as you live, all the divine laws and commandments that I enjoin upon you, to the end that you may long endure. Obey, O Israel, willingly and faithfully, that it may go well with you and that you may increase greatly [in] a land flowing with milk and honey, as God, the God of your ancestors, spoke to you.
>
> Hear, O Israel! God is our God, God alone. You shall love your God with all your heart, with all your soul, and with all your might. Take to heart these instructions with which I charge you this day. Impress them upon your children. Recite them when you stay at home and when you are away, when you lie down and when you get up. Bind them as a sign on your hand and let them serve as a symbol on your forehead; inscribe them on the doorposts of your house and on your gates. (Deut. 6:1–9)

As this text unfolds, Moses is delivering speeches to the people just before his death. He tells the Israelites that God has been kind and merciful to them in giving them a good land and a set of commandments by which to live.

In Hebrew, a commandment from God is known as a *mitzvah* (plural: *mitzvot*). This idea that the mitzvot are a gift from God is a core concept in Jewish thought. To understand it better, let us look at this text piece by piece.

And this is the Instruction—the laws and the rules—that your God has commanded [me] to impart to you, to be observed in the land that you are about to cross into and occupy, so that you, your children, and your children's children may revere your God and follow, as long as you live, all the divine laws and commandments that I enjoin upon you, to the end that you may long endure.

The performance of the commandments is closely tied to possession of the Land of Israel. The land is offered as a reward for loyalty.

This text may have offered a coveted sense of security to a nomadic people concerned about finding grazing land sufficiently abundant in food for their flocks. If so, the theology would have been attractive because it suggested that the chaos of the natural world might be tamed through good behavior. The core idea was that God's protection was available. The world was not as dangerous as it might seem. But this security came at a price: obedience.

It is also possible, however, that this text originated from an era later than its setting. Biblical scholars posit that it likely reflected the interests and anxieties of a much later age, projected backward into the past. If that is the case, then the text would have had resonance for Israelite farmers and city-dwellers as well. As an often-subjugated people living at the crossroads of major empires, the Israelites were deeply concerned about remaining in the land of their ancestors.

Regardless of the era in which this passage was written, in all likelihood it reflected the anxieties of a people beset with challenges who did not feel fully secure in the world. The *Shema* passage would have reminded them that only the Lord could guarantee them the land.

Consider this context, then, when rereading the passage containing the *Shema*:

Obey, O Israel, willingly and faithfully, that it may go well with you and that you may increase greatly [in] a land flowing with milk and honey, as God, the God of your ancestors, spoke to you.

Hear, O Israel! God is our God, God alone. You shall love your God with all your heart, with all your soul, and with all your might.

The emphasis here is on hearing and heeding this instruction. Genuine security is in the people's grasp—but only if they will listen!

Notice the underlying assumptions. Should one fail to receive divine care, it is not because of a weakness or lack on God's part, but rather the result of some kind of weakness or lack of obedience on the part of the petitioner.

Note also the comment that "God is our God, God alone." Many translators have a different take on this text: it is often translated as "God, our God, is one." Hebrew allows for this ambiguity, as it does not make use of the verb "to be" (grammatically, the "copula") in the present tense. This translation of the Hebrew phrase as "God alone" addresses the concern that the Israelites might engage in monolatry (the worship of one god above all other gods), urging them to adopt monotheism (the worship of a single God to the exclusion of all others). As we will see in the next sections, the verse later becomes a commentary on the singular and unique nature of God.

The next part of the text explains how the Israelites would go about remembering to obey:

Take to heart these instructions with which I charge you this day. Impress them upon your children. Recite them when you stay at home and when you are away, when you lie down and when you get up. Bind them as a sign on your hand and let them serve as a symbol on your forehead; inscribe them on the doorposts of your house and on your gates.

The Israelites were expected to repeat this instruction and set up reminders everywhere they might look in order to remember it. The commandments would need to be taught to the next generation, so that their observance would not lapse after the Israelites left the wilderness. Without these precautions, the mitzvot might be forgotten. Note the fear of loss here. Israel must guard against the loss of memory to prevent a consequent loss of land.

In later eras, the *Shema* received different interpretations. For the generations that followed, it was taken to be a declaration regarding the singular nature of God. It also became a form of prayer.

5.2. From the Liturgy: The *Shema* and Its Blessings

How did the Rabbis who included the *Shema* in the morning and evening liturgy understand the meaning of "God is one"? At minimum, the word "one" might have specified that the addressee of the prayer service is singular rather than plural—a declaration of monotheistic faith. However, the Rabbis probably also meant to declare that God is wholly singular in *type*: absolutely unique. The Rabbis may have elevated this verse as a polemic against the nonmonotheistic faiths around them. In 4.3 we discussed a fictional disputation between the prophet Elijah and a Parsee (Zoroastrian) priest: there, the Rabbis argued that God was singular and not dualistic.

The *Shema*'s inclusion in the liturgy prompts the question: is the *Shema* a prayer? Or, to be more precise: should every focused recitation of this statement—regardless of its setting—be considered a prayer?

The liturgical text that follows includes the *Shema* and part of the *V'ahavta*, ("And you shall love"). The words appearing in italics are instructions to the worshiper; the words in regular type are the words of the prayer. The instructions are meant to be enacted in a fairly literal manner. When the text mentions the head-*tefillin* (leather boxes containing specific biblical texts tied with leather straps to the worshiper's forehead), for example, the worshiper is to touch the head-tefillin, confirming that this commandment has been observed.

> *The Shema must be said with intense concentration. In the first paragraph one should accept, with love, the sovereignty of God; in the second, the mitzvot as the will of God. . . .*
>
> *The following verse should be said aloud, while covering the eyes with the right hand:*
>
> Listen, Israel: the Lord is our God, the Lord is one.
>
> *Quietly:* Blessed be the name of His glorious kingdom for ever and all time.
>
> *Touch the hand-tefillin at * and the head-tefillin at **.*
>
> Love the Lord your God with all your heart, with all your soul, and with all your might. These words which I command you today shall be on your heart. Teach them repeatedly to your children, speaking of them when you sit at home and when you travel on the way, when you lie down and when you rise. *Bind them as a sign on your hand, and **they shall be an emblem between your eyes. Write them on the doorposts of your house and gates. . . .
>
> If you indeed heed My commandments with which I charge you today, to love the Lord your God and worship Him with all your heart and with all your soul, I will give rain in your land in its season, the early and late rain; and you shall gather in your grain, wine and oil. I will give grass in your field for your cattle, and you shall eat and be satisfied. Be careful lest your heart be tempted and you go astray and worship other gods, bowing down to them. Then the Lord's anger will flare against you and He will close the heavens so that there will be no rain.

The land will not yield its crops, and you will perish swiftly from the good land that the Lord is giving you.[1]

The initial instruction sounds fairly straightforward, but as we will see, the true meaning of the phrase "intense concentration" is not obvious. Beginning at the top of our selection:

The Shema must be said with intense concentration. In the first paragraph one should accept, with love, the sovereignty of God; in the second, the mitzvot as the will of God.

The focus of this concentration is two aspects of our relationship with God. Accepting the sovereignty of God involves recognizing that there is no other power in the universe equal to God. In this context, "accept[ing] the mitzvot as the will of God" means accepting that the recitation of the *Shema* is just one of many obligations under Jewish law. One is also to accept the *Shema* "with love," because God gave these commandments—the needed instructions in how to live a moral life—as an expression of God's love.

The liturgy continues:

The following verse should be said aloud, while covering the eyes with the right hand:
　　Listen, Israel: the Lord is our God, the Lord is one.
　　Quietly: Blessed be the name of His glorious kingdom for ever and all time.

Covering the eyes while saying the *Shema* allows the worshiper to focus on the recitation without distraction. This practice likely has medieval roots; it is often attributed to the mystics of Safed in Israel.

Notably, the one-line communal response known as *Baruch Shem Kavod* ("Blessed is the Honored Name") that typically follows the

Shema's recitation (here rendered as "Blessed be the name of His glorious kingdom for ever and all time") is not found in the biblical text. The Jewish scholar and Conservative rabbi Isaac Klein argues that "this insertion dates from the period of Roman rule, when emperor worship was practiced. The insertion was intended to emphasize that only God, who is eternal, is to be praised. As a matter of prudence, it was said quietly."[2]

After the interpolation, the prayer book gives directions to worshipers and then quotes from the original Deuteronomy text:

> *Touch the hand-tefillin at * and the head-tefillin at ***
> Love the Lord your God with all your heart, with all your soul, and with all your might. These words which I command you today shall be on your heart. Teach them repeatedly to your children, speaking of them when you sit at home and when you travel on the way, when you lie down and when you rise. *Bind them as a sign on your hand, and **they shall be an emblem between your eyes. Write them on the doorposts of your house and gates.

This section is taken literally. These words are taught to children, recited twice a day (based on "when you lie down and when you rise"), bound on the hand and between the eyes (using the hand-tefillin and head-tefillin), and posted on the doorposts of the house (by means of a *mezuzah*, a little box or tube containing a small scroll of part of the *Shema* text affixed to the door).

The next paragraph is yet another interpolation. In reading it, one might ask: why was it necessary to interrupt the flow of the original biblical text?

> If you indeed heed My commandments with which I charge you today, to love the Lord your God and worship Him with all

your heart and with all your soul, I will give rain in your land in its season, the early and late rain; and you shall gather in your grain, wine and oil. I will give grass in your field for your cattle, and you shall eat and be satisfied. Be careful lest your heart be tempted and you go astray and worship other gods, bowing down to them. Then the Lord's anger will flare against you and He will close the heavens so that there will be no rain. The land will not yield its crops and you will perish swiftly from the good land that the Lord is giving you.

As previously noted, the biblical text is insistent about the need to heed these commandments. This interjection may have been added to reinforce this point: Obedience is necessary for good things such as abundant crops to manifest. Conversely, one's failure to obey the commandments will incite God's retaliation and cause the transgressor to perish.

Not all Jewish movements are comfortable with this theological position, however. Specifically, liberal Jews often object to the idea that God rewards or punishes behavior in a direct way through control of the seasons. For this reason, it has become fairly commonplace for liberal prayer books to provide alternatives to the paragraph. Various liberal movements have approached the substituted texts differently, but both the American Reconstructionist movement's *Kol Haneshamah* (1989) and the Israeli Reform movement's *Ha-Avodah sheba-Lev* (1982) prayer books offer Deuteronomy 30:15–20 as an alternative.[3] Similar to the traditional text, the alternate text suggests that the Israelites' choice between observance and nonobservance of the commandments has lasting consequences: "See, I set before you this day life and prosperity, death and adversity." The difference is that God is not using "the early and late rain" in order to reward or to chastise the Israelites.

On the other hand, it is also possible to read the last interpolated paragraph metaphorically. Human action (or inaction) affects the environment in a multiplicity of unseen ways. Some of God's commandments concern the need to be a caretaker of the earth. For example, Deuteronomy 20:19 states: "When in your war against a city you have to besiege it a long time in order to capture it, you must not destroy its trees, wielding the ax against them. You may eat of them, but you must not cut them down. Are trees of the field human to withdraw before you into the besieged city?" In other words, the trees must be protected to prevent starvation in future years. In that case, we might view the injunction to "heed My commandments with which I charge you today" as a needed warning: we humans might create unintended consequences if we are not observant of God's laws.

5.3. A Rabbinic View: A Deathbed *Shema*

As we saw, Rabbi Isaac Klein postulated that the community's *Baruch Shem Kavod* insertion was introduced during the period of Roman rule in order to acknowledge that God is preeminent over all other rulers—though the insertion was (and continues to be) said in an undertone as a matter of prudence. However, the ancient Rabbis—who actually lived during the Roman era—suggest that the text is actually older, and offer a different reason for its recitation:

And what is the reason that we do recite it [that is, why is "Blessed be the name of His glorious kingdom (etc.) recited in response to the *Shema*]⁴?—Even as R. Simeon b. Lakish expounded. For R. Simeon b. Lakish said: *And Jacob called unto his sons, and said: Gather yourselves together, that I may tell you* [*that which shall befall you in the end of days*]. Jacob wished to reveal to his sons the "*end of days*." Whereupon the *Shechinah* [indwelling presence of God that allows for prophecy][5] departed from him. Said he, "Perhaps, Heaven forfend! there is one unfit among my children, like Abraham, from whom there issued Ishmael, or like my father Isaac, from whom there issued Esau." [But] his sons answered him, "Hear O Israel, the Lord our God the Lord is One: just as there is only One in thy heart, so is there in our heart only One." In that moment our father Jacob opened [his mouth] and exclaimed, "Blessed be the name of His glorious kingdom for ever and ever." Said the Rabbis, How shall we act? Shall we recite it, — but our Teacher Moses did not say it. Shall we not say it — but Jacob said it! [Hence] they enacted that it should be recited quietly.[6]

The ancient Rabbis link the *Baruch Shem Kavod* text to the patriarch Jacob. In so doing, they play on a textual ambiguity: when the *Shema* says "Hear, O Israel," the text may be referring to Jacob, who is also called Israel.

The Rabbis continue:

And what is the reason that we do recite it? — Even as R. Simeon b. Lakish expounded. For R. Simeon b. Lakish said: *And Jacob called unto his sons, and said: Gather yourselves together, that I may tell you [that which shall befall you in the end of days]. Jacob wished to reveal to his sons the "end of days." Whereupon the Shechinah departed from him.*

The text in italics is from Genesis 49:1. Towards the end of the book, Jacob/Israel is on his deathbed. Calling his sons to visit him, he announces that he has something he wishes to tell them. In the ancient Rabbis' understanding of the verse, Jacob/Israel wishes to tell his sons about the prophecy he has received concerning the end of days. However, the *Shekhinah* (indwelling presence of God that allows for prophecy) departs from Jacob/Israel just as he opens his mouth. Jacob/Israel then wonders why this prophetic understanding has left him:

> Said he, "Perhaps, Heaven forfend! there is one unfit among my children, like Abraham, from whom there issued Ishmael, or like my father Isaac, from whom there issued Esau."

To the ancient Rabbis, prophecy was a gift bestowed upon the meritorious. Here, Jacob/Israel worries that he has lost his prophetic gift in the presence of his sons because one of them is unworthy of hearing such prophecy. He then recalls that his esteemed grandfather and father each had a child who was perceived as undeserving: Abraham had Ishmael and Isaac had Esau. Now he is concerned that one or more of his sons is somehow deficient in his piety. Apparently, he need not have been troubled, for the sons break into a recitation of the *Shema* in his presence:

> [But] his sons answered him, "Hear O Israel, the Lord our God the Lord is One: just as there is only One in thy heart, so is there in our heart only One." In that moment our father Jacob opened [his mouth] and exclaimed, "Blessed be the name of His glorious kingdom for ever and ever."

It is a beautiful image: Surrounding their father, the sons of the dying patriarch spontaneously break into recitation of the *Shema* and thereby affirm their commitment to keeping his religious values. He, for his part, affirms the sovereignty of God.

The power of this scene, in turn, provides the Rabbis justification for the regular recitation of this phrase in response to the *Shema*:

Said the Rabbis, How shall we act? Shall we recite it,—but our Teacher Moses did not say it. Shall we not say it—but Jacob said it! [Hence] they enacted that it should be recited quietly.

One probably should not read this text as history. Establishing that Jacob/Israel was a historical figure, in fact, is exceedingly difficult, so attributing ritual practices to his lifetime is even more fraught.

The question that the Rabbis faced, rather, was that of the status of the "Blessed is God's glorious kingdom" response. On the one hand, it was not biblical in origin, but on the other, it clearly was a very old custom. They enact a compromise: imbuing the practice with (assumed) biblical origins, and thus determining the recitation must be said; but since its origins cannot be proven, deciding to recite the phrase in a quiet voice. Also interesting here is the apparent need to ground liturgical practice in some kind of lived experience. As a matter of authority, it should have been sufficient to state that the phrase comes from Jacob/Israel. However, the Rabbis did not exactly give us a directive—you shall do this because Jacob/Israel did so— but rather appeal to the pathos of a deathbed scene.

Perhaps we are getting closer to an answer as to how a statement of faith (such as that found in the *Shema*) might become a prayer. It is offered as an invocation in the hope that it might be adopted as the foundation of all belief.

5.4. A Medieval View: Maimonides' Meditation

In the twelfth century, Moses Maimonides (introduced in 2.4) explained how to make use of the *Shema* as a focus for contemplation. The following excerpt is drawn from his *Guide of the Perplexed*, perhaps the most important work of medieval Jewish philosophy. Written as a book-length letter to a promising student, it lays out how Maimonides believed a person should think about God.

The first thing that you should cause your soul to hold fast onto is that while *reciting* the *Shema'* prayer, you should empty your mind of everything and pray thus. You should not content yourself with *being intent* while *reciting the first verse of Shema'* and saying *the first benediction*. When this has been carried out correctly and has been practiced for years, cause your soul, whenever you read or listen to the *Torah*, to be constantly directed—the whole of you and your thought—toward reflection on what you are listening to or reading. When this too has been practiced consistently for a certain time, cause your soul to be in such a way that your thought is always quite free of distraction and gives heed to all that you are reading of the other discourses of the prophets and even when you read all the *benedictions*, so that you aim at meditating on what you are uttering and at considering its meaning. If, however, while performing these acts of worship, you are free from distraction and not engaged in thinking upon any of the things pertaining to this world, cause your soul—after this has been achieved—to occupy your thought with things necessary for you or superfluous in your life, and in general with *worldly things*, while you eat or drink or bathe or talk with your wife and your small children, or while you talk with the common run of people. Thus I have provided you with many and long stretches of time in which you can think all that needs thinking regarding property, the governance of the household, and the welfare of the body. On the other hand, while performing the actions imposed by the Law, you should occupy your thought only with what you are doing, just as we have explained. When, however, you are alone with yourself and no one else is there and while you lie awake upon your bed, you should take great care during these precious times not to set your thought to work on anything other than that intellectual worship consisting in nearness to God and being in His presence in that true reality that I have made known to you and not by way of affectations of the imagination. In my opinion this end can be achieved by those of the men of knowledge who have rendered their souls worthy of it by training of this kind.[7]

To Maimonides, the highest form of prayer was the contemplation of God. In fact, he believed the original practice of sacrificing animals at the Temple once a year to atone for one's sins had been created as a "gracious ruse" to allow humanity to transition away from worshiping idols. God's real intention had always been to promote verbal prayer, leading, ultimately, to contemplation of the one true God. As he explained in *The Guide of the Perplexed*:

For one kind of worship — I mean the offering of sacrifices — even though it was done in His name, may He be exalted, [it] was not prescribed to us in the way it existed at first; I mean to say in such a way that sacrifices could be offered in every place and every time. . . . All this was intended to restrict this kind of worship, so that only the portion of it should subsist whose abolition is not required by His wisdom. On the other hand, invocation and prayers are made in every place and by everyone whoever he may be.[8]

Returning to our original text, Maimonides wrote that one is not able to launch into the contemplation God desires of us without careful preparation. The first step is to employ a technique drawn from the practice of meditation: emptying one's mind of extraneous thoughts.

The first thing that you should cause your soul to hold fast onto is that while reciting the *Shema‘* prayer, you should empty your mind of everything and pray thus.

Students of meditation will be familiar with this technique; those who have attempted meditation for any length of time know it takes practice to master. Most beginning practitioners find this first step exceedingly difficult: stray thoughts keep interrupting the meditation. One must sit many times before this kind of stillness is achieved.

When engaging in this meditation, Maimonides advised that one should go beyond the usual actions prescribed by Jewish law:

You should not content yourself with *being intent* while *reciting the first verse of Shema‘* and saying *the first benediction.*

Maimonides' method demands more of the worshiper than the usual requirement of focus in prayer. Accomplishing this step will require regular repetition of this technique, possibly for years. Only then will it be possible to move to the next stage.

When this has been carried out correctly and has been practiced for years, cause your soul, whenever you read or listen to the *Torah*, to be constantly directed—the whole of you and your thought—toward reflection on what you are listening to or reading.

Torah is normally read in communal services on Mondays, Thursdays, and Saturdays. Maimonides proposes that these occasions offer an opportunity to expand one's contemplative practice. While the *Shema*-focused meditation could be done at home alone, the Torah-focused meditation would take place in the context of congregational worship, where one would necessarily encounter a greater number of distractions.

> When this too has been practiced consistently for a certain time, cause your soul to be in such a way that your thought is always quite free of distraction and gives heed to all that you are reading of the discourses of the prophets and even when you read all the *benedictions*, so that you aim at meditating on what you are uttering and at considering its meaning.

In other words, one should start with this singular affirmation expressed by the *Shema*, and then work methodically towards expanding this capacity for concentration in prayer, including during the regular benedictions of the prayer service.

> If, however, while performing these acts of worship, you are free from distraction and not engaged in thinking upon any of the things pertaining to this world, cause your soul—after this has been achieved—to occupy your thought with things necessary for you or superfluous in your life, and in general with *worldly things*, while you eat or drink or bathe or talk with your wife and your small children, or while you talk with the common run of people. Thus I have provided you with many and long stretches of time in which you can think all that needs thinking regarding property, the governance of the household, and the welfare of the body. On the other hand, while performing the actions imposed by the Law, you should occupy your thought only with what you are doing, just as we have explained.

Eventually, Maimonides says, a practitioner may be able to clearly differentiate between the prayer-state and mundane-state of mind, and to transition between them at will. During the prayer-service, for example, while "performing the actions imposed by the Law," one should not be thinking about other things. But one may take time to think about other things, such as the "governance of the household" or "the welfare of the body," during the congregational announcements.

The quiet time at the end of the day is ideal for reflection:

> When, however, you are alone with yourself and no one else is there and while you lie awake upon your bed, you should take great care during these precious times not to set your thought to work on anything other than that intellectual worship consisting in nearness to God and being in His presence in that true reality that I have made known to you and not by way of affectations of the imagination.

In your precious moments alone, when it is possible to think without interruption, Maimonides counsels, do not waste time thinking about business or household concerns. This quiet time is designated for contemplation at the highest level. One should spend this time thinking carefully about the nature of God, reviewing one's study in the mind's eye, and making connections and inferences on the basis of what one knows.

You can recite the *Shema* as your text for contemplation.

5.5. A Modern View: Schneerson's Explicit Mysticism

Sholom Dovber Schneerson (1860–1920), the Fifth Rebbe of the Lubavitch Hasidim (also known as the Chabad movement), wrote extensively on the mystical themes of the *Shema*. He also instructed his followers on how best to focus their attention during worship, in keeping with the Hasidic custom of Rebbes serving as spiritual advisors to their followers.

Schneerson's use of G-d instead of "God" reflects the traditional Jewish community's reticence to spell out the name of the Divine. Maimonides wrote in his legal work, *Yesodei HaTorah* ("The Foundations of the Torah") 6:2 that one must not erase the divine name. Even a single letter of the divine name, and even a letter that is a prefix or a suffix unrelated to the name of God, must not be erased. Referring to G-d rather than spelling out the name avoids the use of any form of the divine name, which in turn releases the author from responsibility for ensuring that the text is never defaced or damaged. While the traditional reticence applies to Hebrew texts, it extends to English based on the notion of creating a protective fence around the Torah (*sayag*).

Here is Schneerson's text, from 1899, explaining how the recitation of the *Shema* can be a mystical experience:

> During *Krias Shema* [the general meditative theme during the recitation of] the verse *Shema Yisrael* . . . is that of G-d's Unity— from the perspective of the worlds: how He is One in the seven firmaments, on earth, and throughout the four corners of the globe—utterly Singular, as explained at length elsewhere. During the recitation of *Baruch Shem Kavod,* [the general meditative theme is] how the creation of the worlds and their vivification derives solely from the name of His glorious Kingdom, which is merely an intensely refracted glimmer [of His light].
>
> A person should reflect on all the foregoing themes, at length, and in detail, so that he understands each topic well, can bind himself to it, and can concentrate deeply on it. In this way, the subject becomes absorbed and well settled in his mind and [consequently] the person's heart becomes excited over the goodness and wondrousness of the *Ein Sof*-light. He is aroused

with a love, a yearning, a desire, and a longing to cleave to G-d—not desiring anything alien, G-d forbid. Rather, he has but one aspiration, one that is focused on G-d alone. Through this love, his observance of Torah and its mitzvos [or *mitzvot*] will be infused with an inward and essential vitality. The person will be close to G-dliness in all of his affairs.[9]

Schneerson begins by explaining what one is to do during recitation of the *Krias Shema*, the "Hear O Israel" verse in Deuteronomy 6:4:

During *Krias Shema*, [the general meditative theme during the recitation of] the verse *Shema Yisrael* . . . is that of G-d's Unity—from the perspective of the worlds.

Krias Shema is normally done with great concentration: one should cover the eyes so as to focus on its recitation alone. Schneerson takes this a step further: a worshiper should not only be intent on its recitation, but also be thinking about the nature of God in the context of Jewish mysticism.

Hasidic mysticism speaks of two worlds: the upper (heavenly realm) and the lower (earthly realm). Human action in the earthly realm can affect the heavenly realm, healing rifts and repairing the upper world. Thus, the worshiper should focus on God's unity above and below.

How He is One in the seven firmaments, on earth, and throughout the four corners of the globe—utterly Singular, as explained at length elsewhere.

According to Kabbalistic thought, divine energy continually flows through the *sefirot* (ten attributes of God) in order to endlessly create and renew the world. The seven firmaments Schneerson references here are the seven lower *sefirot*, through which the light-energy of God flows into the lower world or earthly realm. These also correspond to the realm of emotion; the top three *sefirot* are the realm of the intellect.

Schneerson asserts that God's overflowing light-energy is what enables the world to continue to exist:

> During the recitation of *Baruch Shem Kavod*, [the general meditative theme is] how the creation of the worlds and their vivification derives solely from the name of His glorious Kingdom, which is merely an intensely refracted glimmer [of His light].

The divine energy is indeed visualized as a kind of light, but it is to be understood metaphorically. It is not light in the sense of what can be seen with the eyes. Humanity sees the divine light as if it were a reflection in a darkened mirror, for humans are not capable of gazing upon it directly.

> A person should reflect on all the foregoing themes, at length, and in detail, so that he understands each topic well, can bind himself to it, and can concentrate deeply on it.

Meditating on the meaning of prayers is a common Hasidic technique for deepening one's devotion. Hasidic prayer services often include Kabbalistic focusing-meditations, which start with a standard formula: "Here I am, ready to perform the mitzvah of. . . ."

> In this way, the subject becomes absorbed and well settled in his mind and [consequently] the person's heart becomes excited over the goodness and wondrousness of the *Ein Sof*-light.

Ein-Sof is understood as "the transcendent aspect of God that is entirely unknowable to humans."[10] When the meditation is performed correctly, with full intentionality, it can elicit a feeling of elation. In fact, it can be the source of a feeling of profound connection:

> He is aroused with a love, a yearning, a desire, and a longing to cleave to G-d—not desiring anything alien, G-d forbid. Rather, he has but one aspiration, one that is focused on G-d alone.

A larger concern within Hasidic theology is the presence of "alien" desires. The "alien" source, also called the "other side," is said to pull the worshiper away from full concentration on the divine. Thus the emphasis in this meditation is upon fixing one's concentration on God and God alone.

> Through this love, his observance of Torah and its mitzvos [or *mitzvot,*] will be infused with an inward and essential vitality. The person will be close to G-dliness in all of his affairs.

In this context, the prayer-act is a way station in the process of cleaving to God.

Both Maimonides and Schneerson use the *Shema* as the focus of concentration, but they differ with regard to the end point. For Maimonides, contemplation to the point of immersion is the end goal. For Schneerson, and Hasidic worship on the whole, the person's own sense of being separate from God dissolves into the greater unity. The prayerful recitation of the *Shema* is the first step in a mystical experience through which the worshiper will be filled with God's light—to the point that his deeds reflect God's will rather than his own.

5.6. A Modern View:
Soloveitchik Is Ever the Rationalist

This next text strikes a distinctively different note. Joseph Solove-itchik (1903–93), the talmudist, modern Jewish philosopher, and father of modern Orthodoxy in America, took a decidedly rational and intellectual approach to reading the *Shema*. Interestingly, his comments seem to be a direct response to the Schneerson passage—and may have been. He knew Schneerson personally, first in Berlin and later in New York.[11]

Though both men were the product of rabbinic dynastic families, the two were far apart philosophically.[12] How different becomes readily apparent as one reads this excerpt from Soloveitchik's volume of lectures from the 1950s titled *Worship of the Heart*:

> Reading the *Shema* does not entail the state of consciousness required for prayer. "Accepting the yoke of Heaven" is not tan-tamount to entering the Divine presence. The state of reading *Shema* is not identical with that single mood in which man is driven into the company of God. For the performance of *Shema* is not the movement of going and coming to God. It is rather a sedate, placid experience. No encounter takes place. The ele-ment of the dialogue is lacking in this ritual. It expresses itself more in the form of declaration, confession, profession of faith. Whether this solemn profession takes the form of soliloquy, in which man declares and challenges himself, or a colloquy—in which he addresses himself to a thou—is irrelevant. What is important is the fact that if there is a thou in *Shema*, the thou is not God but a finite being like myself.
>
> Of course, God is also experienced when one reads *Shema*, but not in a sense of fellowship or communion via the grammati-

cal thou. God, in the experience of reading *Shema*, is "He," the third person, the remote transcendent Being Whose yoke we do accept, Whose will we must abide, Whose might we respect and fear, Whose authority we acknowledge, yet into Whose presence we must not venture, Whose Being is hidden from us. The emphasis in *Shema* is found in the phrase *malkhut Shamayim* (the kingdom of Heaven), the majesty of God, *majestas Dei*, whose main attribute is inaccessibility and remoteness on the one hand, and absolute might and power on the other.[13]

Soloveitchik begins by arguing that any mystical attentiveness to the recitation of the *Shema* is misguided. Reading the *Shema* does not entail the state of consciousness required for prayer.

"Accepting the yoke of Heaven" is not tantamount to entering the Divine presence. The state of reading *Shema* is not identical with that single mood in which man is driven into the company of God. For the performance of *Shema* is not the movement of going and coming to God. It is rather a sedate, placid experience.

Soloveitchik contends that any mystical attention to the *Shema* is on the wrong track, because the performance of the *Shema* is not intended to effect any kind of interaction with God. Furthermore, during recitation of the *Shema* there is no experience of mystical union with an aspect of the Divine:

No encounter takes place. The element of the dialogue is lacking in this ritual. It expresses itself more in the form of declaration, confession, profession of faith. Whether this solemn profession takes the form of soliloquy, in which man declares and challenges himself, or a colloquy—in which he addresses himself to a thou—is irrelevant. What is important is the fact that if there is a thou in *Shema*, the thou is not God but a finite being like myself.

He notes that Jews recite the *Shema* not for *God's* sake but for the *worshiper's* sake. The intended audience is the one who is making the statement, which is why the *Shema* opens with "Hear, O Israel"—it is not addressing God but Israel, each member of the whole collective. That is also why the verb form appears in the singular: it is addressed individually to each person who recites the verse.

The use of the word "thou" here appears to be a commentary on Martin Buber's *I and Thou*. Buber (see chapter 3) spoke of having I-Thou moments of encounter with God. Soloveitchik opposed thinking about the *Shema* in such terms: "If there is a thou in the *Shema*, the thou is not God but a finite being like myself." In reciting the *Shema*, Soloveitchik maintains, we are not entering into an encounter with God; rather, we are *reminding ourselves* of this relationship to God.

> Of course, God is also experienced when one reads *Shema*, but not in a sense of fellowship or communion via the grammatical thou.

This recitation is not an encounter but a lesson, left for us by a distant God. That great transcendent distance is not made smaller by making this declaration.

> God, in the experience of reading *Shema*, is "He," the third person, the remote transcendent Being Whose yoke we do accept, Whose will we must abide, Whose might we respect and fear, Whose authority we acknowledge, yet into Whose presence we must not venture, Whose Being is hidden from us.

Note here the theme of obedience. In this sense, Soloveitchik's reading of the *Shema* text hews fairly close to its meaning in its original setting.

There are some differences, however. The theological structure presented in the biblical text is that of a commanding God who asks for obedience in exchange for security. In this interpretation, the motivation to perform the commandments is less direct and less punitive. The commandments are all that humanity may know of God, and our access to them attests to God's great love for us.

> The emphasis in *Shema* is found in the phrase *malkhut Shamay-im* (the kingdom of Heaven), the majesty of God, *majestas Dei*, whose main attribute is inaccessibility and remoteness on the one hand, and absolute might and power on the other.

We may desire God, and wish to be close to the Divine, but—and here Soloveitchik reiterates the point—the *Shema*, in its regular recitation, is actually a reminder of the great distance between humanity and the Creator.

Perhaps at least to Soloveitchik, then, the recitation of the *Shema* in the midst of a worship service is intended to remind us that no matter how much our hearts may desire to transcend that great distance between God and humanity, God remains God and humanity remains humanity.

5.7. A Modern View: Schachter-Shalomi's Embodied Prayer

Zalman Schachter-Shalomi (1924–2014) offered yet another interpretation of how the *Shema* might be experienced: as an embodied prayer.

Schachter-Shalomi was one of the founding lights of the Jewish Renewal Movement, a loose confederation of individuals and prayer groups seeking to encourage active engagement in meditative and mystical prayer. His early training with the Lubavitcher (Chabad) movement (in 1938 Belgium and 1940s America) influenced his later thought: "We did meditation in Lubavitch before the word was bandied about in this country [America]," he said. "Experiencing and staying in touch with the inner life was what Lubavitch gave me."[14] In the sixties he forged a new path, adopting liberal ideas such as feminism, egalitarianism, and environmentalism.

Here, he shows just how the *Shema* might be experienced as embodied prayer. His suggested role-playing exercises are aimed at helping the reader move past the mere recitation of the text on a page.

Sh'ma'—"hear," understand, and in the hearing, make your *ayin*, the final letter of the word, big! *Yisra'el* [Israel]—'God-wrestler,' you, the person, one of 600,000 letters of God's Torah. *Y-H-V-H*—*Adonai*—all the levels of reality in which God Gods forever and always. *Eloheinu*, "our God," our nature and our being in God's being. This *Y-H-V-H* is, was, and will be *Ehad*, one, unique, altogether, infinitely loving "One."

Now, omit the word '*Yisra'el*' and substitute your own name for it. Say it again with all the significance and meaning it has when you address it to your own situation, with your own concerns.

Now, say the *Sh'ma'* again, and this time, instead of *Yisra'el*, put the name of a person to whom your heart wishes to send this message, and say it addressing that person most lovingly, speaking from your own truth.

Now, visualize yourself on your own deathbed, wanting to leave the world with one last statement before you pour your whole life-experience into God's ocean of consciousness. Or, even more intensely, you might imagine yourself with a group of Jews in a gas chamber. You cannot escape the fact that this is the end, so you join them in one last shout . . . "*Sh'ma'*!"

Now imagine the expansion of the universe is done. God is reabsorbing it, taking it back into the Eternal Being, and this galaxy is plunging into a black hole. As you say the *Sh'ma'* now, imagine your voice and awareness merging with that of a universe dipping into the infinite *mikveh* [body of water used for ritual purification] of God.

Then, after you have gone with your heart and mind to all of these places, say the *Sh'ma'* a fifth time bringing all the four situations together. When you have done this, you will have the sense of what the kabbalists used to call a *yihud*—a "unification."[15]

This first sentence encourages the reader to dwell deeply on the meaning of the word *Shema*.

Sh'ma'—"hear," understand, and in the hearing, make your *ayin*, the final letter of the word, big!

The instruction to make the Hebrew letter *ayin* big is paradoxical: The *ayin* (the last letter in the word *Shema*) is a letter with no sound—or perhaps, at most, a guttural noise. How does one make a big sound out of a letter with no sound? We might say that pause at the end of the word *Shema* (which might be translated as "Hear!" or "Heed!") offers a moment of silence, to consider the implications of hearing and understanding.

Schachter-Shalomi continues to work his way through the *Shema* word-by-word, so it can be understood viscerally:

Yisra'el [Israel]—"God-wrestler," you, the person, one of 600,000 letters of God's Torah. *Y-H-V-H*—*Adonai*—all the levels of reality in which God Gods forever and always.

The word "Israel" means "one who wrestles with God." Here "Israel" is both a singular and plural noun: singular, in the sense that those who say the *Shema* in this manner are a "God-wrestler" like their forebear Jacob/Israel; and plural, in the sense that these various individuals are like the 600,000 Hebrew letters that come together to make the Torah text.

He avows that Y-H-V-H (the unpronounceable name of God) can be understood as a verb: God is an ever-unfolding process that occurs in the physical and metaphysical worlds. His juxtaposition of God (as a noun) Gods (as a verb) recalls a concept articulated by Benedict Spinoza (see chapter 1). Spinoza believed that God exists within and animates all things (pantheism). Thus God can be likened to "nature in the process of naturing"—nature doing what nature does.

In the next line, however, Schachter-Shalomi differentiates his thinking from that of Spinoza's: God is present in all things, but *greater* than the whole of Creation (panentheism). Thus, we are a small subpart of God's being:

Eloheinu, "our God," our nature and our being in God's being. This *Y-H-V-H* is, was, and will be *Ehad,* one, unique, altogether, infinitely loving "One."

Next, Schachter-Shalomi suggests a series of visualizations. Note the progression from the personal sphere to the larger world:

Now, omit the word *"Yisra'el"* and substitute your own name for it. Say it again with all the significance and meaning it has when you address it to your own situation, with your own concerns.

Now, say the *Sh'ma'* again, and this time, instead of *Yisra'el,* put the name of a person to whom your heart wishes to send this message, and say it addressing that person most lovingly, speaking from your own truth.

At this point, Schachter-Shalomi asks worshipers to imagine their own deaths. As the scholar Rabbi Norman Lamm explains, the *Shema* "was recited as the dying words of Jewish martyrs, in keeping with the example of R. Akiva who (according to the Talmud, *Berakhot* 61b) uttered the Shema as he was executed by the Romans in the aftermath of the revolt against Rome in the second century C.E."[16] This idea, that the *Shema* is connected to martyrdom and the deathbed, is woven deeply into Jewish practice (see chapter 7). Pious Jews have traditionally recited the *Shema* as their final words.

> Now, visualize yourself on your own deathbed, wanting to leave the world with one last statement before you pour your whole life-experience into God's ocean of consciousness. Or, even more intensely, you might imagine yourself with a group of Jews in a gas chamber. You cannot escape the fact that this is the end, so you join them in one last shout . . . "*Sh'ma'!*"
>
> Now imagine the expansion of the universe is done. God is reabsorbing it, taking it back into the Eternal Being, and this galaxy is plunging into a black hole. As you say the *Sh'ma'* now, imagine your voice and awareness merging with that of a universe dipping into the infinite *mikveh* of God.

The idea of pouring "your whole life-experience into God's ocean of consciousness" recalls an image from Hasidic thought: each of us is like "a drop in the ocean"—when we die, we dissolve into the whole. The image of "a universe dipping into the infinite *mikveh* of God" invokes a similar metaphor. The *mikveh*, or ritual pool used for purification, is always of "living waters," either a natural body of water (ocean, lake, or river) or filled with water from a natural source (such as rain).

At this juncture, Schachter-Shalomi appears to be returning to his roots:

Then, after you have gone with your heart and mind to all of these places, say the *Sh'ma'* a fifth time bringing all the four situations together. When you have done this, you will have the sense of what the kabbalists used to call a *yihud*—a "unification."

This kind of contemplation of the *Shema* has long been a core feature of Chabad (Lubavitch) thought. As the scholar Louis Jacobs explains, "The more zealous of the [C]habad devotees have been known to spend a whole hour and more lost in contemplation while reciting the first verse of the Shema."[17]

Chabad thought is often characterized as *acosmic*: suggesting that the cosmos—specifically, the whole world of death, destruction, and evil—is not real. Only God is real; everything else is an illusion. To imagine one's own death is to lift the veil that separates illusion from reality. In this view, then, the *Shema* is more than a prayer. It becomes the point at which it is possible to recognize the fundamental unity of God behind the illusion.

5.8. Summary of Views

Drawn from Deuteronomy 6:4, the declaration known as the *Shema*— "Hear, O Israel! The Lord is our God, the Lord alone"—provides a succinct profession of faith, affirming the singularity and uniqueness of God. The ancient Rabbis considered the *Shema* to be so important, they prescribed its recitation twice daily, based on the exhortation in Deuteronomy 6:7 to repeat these words "when you lie down and when you get up." To further its twice-daily recitation, they included the *Shema* in the morning and evening liturgy.

In the *biblical text*, however, the *Shema* does not seem to stand out as bearing this theologically distinctive meaning. The emphasis does not appear to have been on God's oneness. Apparently, it served to remind the Israelites that only God could guarantee them land. The Israelites were expected to repeat this instruction—and to set up reminders everywhere they looked in order to remember to do so. The commandments would need to be taught to the next generation, so their observance would not lapse after the Israelites left the wilderness.

The Rabbis who included the *Shema* in the morning and evening liturgy, applying the wording of the biblical text to the *liturgical text*, may have elevated this verse as a polemic against the nonmonotheistic faiths around them. They also interpolated material into the biblical text, so that its recitation did not merely repeat the text found in the Bible. The additional text reinforced the need to obey God's commandments.

The *rabbinic text* extols an image of the patriarch Jacob's sons breaking into recitation of the *Shema* as they surround him on his deathbed. This story served to imbue an old liturgical practice—the "Blessed is God's glorious kingdom" response portion of the *Shema*—with (assumed) biblical origins, and simultaneously to ground the practice in lived experience. This offers insight into how a statement of faith, such as this one attesting to God's oneness, might become a prayer. It is offered as an invocation in the hope that it might be adopted as the foundation of all belief.

The *medieval text* introduced another use for the *Shema*: a text for contemplation when one is engaged in a meditative state. To Maimonides, the highest form of prayer was the contemplation of God. In fact, he believed the original practice of sacrificing animals at the Temple once a year to atone for one's sins had been created as a "gracious ruse" to allow humanity to transition away from worshiping idols. God's real intention had always been to promote verbal prayer, leading, ultimately, to contemplation of the one true God. Maimonides suggests that quiet time at the end of day should be designated for contemplation at the highest level. One should spend this time thinking carefully about the nature of God, reviewing one's study in the mind's eye and making connections and inferences on the basis of what one knows.

In the first of our *modern texts*, Schneerson avers that when a Jew directs his attention to the recitation of the *Shema*, he should also be thinking about the nature of God in the context of Jewish mysticism. In Hasidic mysticism there are two worlds: the upper (heavenly realm) and lower (earthly realm). Human action in the earthly realm can affect the heavenly realm, healing rifts and repairing the upper world. Hence, the worshiper should focus on God's unity above and below.

In the second *modern text*, however, Soloveitchik suggests that any mystical attentiveness to the *Shema* is misguided, because its recitation is not intended to invoke interaction with God. Jews recite the *Shema* not for God's sake, but for the worshiper's sake. The intended audience is the one who is making the statement, which is why the *Shema* opens with "Hear, O Israel "—it is not addressing God but Israel, each member of the whole collective. This recitation is not an encounter but a lesson left for us by a distant God "whose authority we acknowledge, yet into Whose presence we must not venture."

In the third *modern text*, Schachter-Shalomi presents a series of role-playing exercises to help the worshiper experience the *Shema* as embodied prayer. Influenced by the Chabad/Lubavitch thought that only God is real—everything else is an illusion—he viewed the *Shema* as more than a prayer. It becomes the point at which it is possible to recognize the fundamental unity of God behind the illusion.

5.9. The Meaning of Bearing Witness to God's Oneness

Early in this chapter, we discussed why Jews say God is *one*: the idea that God is singular, unique, extraordinarily unlike anyone or anything else. Transcending time and space, God is beyond our definitions, more than our imaginations allow.

This is actually a crucial point. When we try to define God—to tame our God-concepts so they might be comprehensible—we tend to imagine things that are not God. Affirming the singularity and uniqueness of God helps us to recognize that God is so much bigger, and grander, than our comprehensions.

A recent trend in Jewish practice is to incorporate contemplation (along the lines of what Maimonides suggests) into a regular practice of meditation.

Here is one way to use the *Shema* to focus the breath and bear witness to God's oneness. The following meditation integrates Arthur Green's teaching: "Y-H-W-H as *Sh'ma Yisra'el* is stasis, the great transcendent Oneness; Y-H-W-H as *Baruckh Shem* is process, the One within the everchanging many."[18] In the combination of the *Shema* coupled with the *Baruch ha-Shem*, the response said after the *Shema*, God's oneness is envisioned as a tension between stasis (the aspect of God that is eternal and unchanging) and process (the endlessly creative aspect of God).

> *As you breathe in, say "Shema."*
> *As you breathe out, say "Baruckh Shem Kavod."*

Each breath becomes an affirmation of the theological concept that God is both transcendent—beyond us yet also immanent—within us. One's own breath becomes one with that of the creator-God who spoke the world into being and sustains it with every breath.

5.10. Praying as One (Community)

I find that when leading prayer-services I have a kind of uncanny ability to discern whether or not the congregation is praying, almost to a person. In my experience, the process of prayer generates a kind of energy that can somehow be sensed. It feels like an electrical current: one can tell, in a sense, who is "plugged in" and who is "turned off" to the current—and if too many people fall into that latter category, the prayer current gets blocked in an almost physical way. That's why both the seating arrangement and the composition of the congregation seem to matter so much.

It could be that I am aware, in some subtle way, of a change in breathing or focus. It is true that a congregation deep in prayer together, well-connected to one another, will start to breathe as one. A kind of energy animates the prayer-experience. It is similar to the energy that rouses fans and players at a sports event or makes people feel like they want to cry at weddings: a shared emotion fills the room.

One could identify this sense of energy with a Jewish mystical concept. *Shefa*, the endless outpouring of God, might be visualized as a light or energy that cannot be measured or directly observed. I myself tend to think in these terms in moments when this energy seems truly palpable. To me, when we invoke God's presence and become one in the recitation of the *Shema*, *shefa* brings our community into contact with the Divine.

Part 3

Does God Redeem—or Might God Not Redeem?

Chapter 6

Does God Intervene in Our Lives?

- How have different strands of Jewish tradition viewed the question of God's involvement in our individual and communal lives?
- Does God act on behalf of the Jewish community?
- Is the creation of the State of Israel evidence of divine providence?

6.1. A Biblical View: Hannah Prays for a Son

Nowadays most people view infertility as a physical problem to be addressed by targeted medical interventions. Most of us also believe that a child's biological sex is determined by genetics (or the interplay of genetics and development). The biblical view, however, was that God chose when to open or close a woman's womb, and God decided upon the sex of her child. Furthermore, God might be persuaded to change those decrees. Thus the plight of a barren woman who pleads with God appears as a trope (recurring literary theme) in the Hebrew Bible. The story of Hannah is one such example.

A man named Elkanah has two wives: Peninnah, who has given birth to many children, and Hannah, who is barren and longs for a child. Each year the family makes a pilgrimage to Shiloh to offer sacrifices.

One such day, Elkanah offered a sacrifice. He used to give portions to his wife Peninnah and to all her sons and daughters; (but to Hannah he would give one portion only—though Hannah was his favorite—for the Lord had closed her womb. Moreover, her rival, to make her miserable, would taunt her that the Lord had closed her womb. This happened year after year: Every time she went up to the House of the Lord, the other would taunt her, so that she wept and would not eat. Her husband Elkanah said to her, "Hannah, why are you crying and why aren't you eating? Why are you so sad? Am I not more devoted to you than ten sons?"

After they had eaten and drunk at Shiloh, Hannah rose— The priest Eli was sitting on the seat near the doorpost of the temple of the Lord—In her wretchedness, she prayed to the Lord, weeping all the while. And she made this vow: "O Lord of Hosts, if You will look upon the suffering of Your maidservant and will remember me and not forget Your maidservant, and if You will grant Your maidservant a male child, I will dedicate him to the Lord for all the days of his life; and no razor shall ever touch his head."

As she kept on praying before the Lord, Eli watched her mouth. Now Hannah was praying in her heart; only her lips moved, but her voice could not be heard. So Eli thought she was drunk. Eli said to her, "How long will you make a drunken spectacle of yourself? Sober up!" And Hannah replied, "Oh no, my lord! I am a very unhappy woman. I have drunk no wine or other strong drink, but I have been pouring out my heart to the Lord. Do not take your maidservant for a worthless woman; I have only been speaking all this time out of my great anguish and distress." "Then go in peace," said Eli, "and may the God of Israel grant you what you have asked of Him." She answered, "You are most kind to your handmaid." So the woman left, and she ate, and was no longer downcast. Early next morning they bowed down low before the Lord, and they went back home to Ramah.

Elkanah knew his wife Hannah and the Lord remembered her. Hannah conceived, and at the turn of the year bore a son. She named him Samuel, meaning, "I asked the Lord for him." (1 Samuel 1:4–20)

Notably, all of the main characters in this story have meaningful names that shed light on the text. Elkanah is a compound name. *El* is a name for God, and the root of *kanah* is "to acquire"; however, whenever this root is used in relation to God (and God alone), it also means "to create." Elkanah thus belongs to God because he was created by God.[1] Eli, on the other hand, means "my God" (or "God belongs to me"). And so, both men have possessive names relating to God, but one is "owned by" God and the other "owns" God. This point is sharpened when one considers that Eli is a priest and Elkanah fathers a child who will be dedicated to the priesthood prior to his birth.

Samuel is that child. Hannah had prayed for his delivery, so she gives him a name that (she believes) means "I asked the Lord for him." Modern etymologists say that Samuel's name means "God heard" (or God "heeded"). In effect, the child is what Hannah asked of God.

As for Hannah's own name, it means "to be gracious." Her name is likely derived from the two-letter Hebrew word *ḥen*, spelled *ḥet-nun*, which means "favor, grace, charm." There is some scholarly debate on this issue, however. If the root of her name is the verb-stem *ḥet-nun-nun*, then it means "to show favor, be gracious," but it also may be derived from the three-letter root *ḥet-nun-heh*, which has the primary meaning of "to encamp" and the secondary meaning of "to be gracious."[2] More likely, all of these were intended at once, as a kind of multilayered pun. Hannah's willingness to station herself at the Temple for a long period of time (to encamp) and to pour out her heart there is pleasing to God and inclines God to show favor and be gracious to her. Her prayer is pleasing, which is why God opens her womb.

The name of Elkanah's other wife is also laden with meaning. Peninnah means "coral" or "pearl"–perhaps an allusion to pregnancy, for pearls are formed inside oysters.[3]

This use of meaningful names is fairly common in biblical literature. Ancient Hebrew audiences would have picked up on these cues right away, recognizing each person in the drama as being destined to play a specific role in its unfolding. This kind of deep structure might have been intended to convey the idea that God is guiding the action toward the realization of larger goals. In theological discussions, this concept is known as providence, God's ongoing protection of human beings.

Providence undoubtedly plays a key role in this drama. Hannah is clearly convinced that if she argues her case with enough passion and skill, she just might change the divine decree. Along these lines, the feminist biblical scholar Nehama Aschkenasy suggests that Hannah's prayer is an attempt to renegotiate the boundaries of her life with God. As Aschkenasy writes, "God is viewed as a protagonist who, though invisible and uncommunicative, is made to enter into some kind of discourse with the woman and become a party to the negotiations."[4] Hannah's God, therefore, is a personal God, one who listens and intervenes.

Apparently, God is indeed swayed by her presentation. Thus, Aschkenasy maintains:

> Hannah's faith in the power of her prayer is so strong that it seems that God has no choice but to follow suit and comply with her request. She has made a one-sided bargain with God, but she has made [God] an active partner in bringing her wish to fruition.[5]

Hannah is clearly successful. In the rabbinic imagination, in fact, Hannah becomes the example to follow when praying, because God clearly favors her intense focus and passion.

This story might also be read as an implicit criticism of the office of the priesthood. Eli's name conveys a sense of possessiveness — "God is mine, and mine alone." Eli is sitting idle at the doorway of the shrine, passing judgment on a woman who comes with a genuine need. This woman who pours out her heart is the one whom God heeds.

Taking this idea further, Hannah's story might be considered subversive of the power wielded by the exclusively male priesthood. If God might heed the prayer of a woman and not just the prayer of the male authorities, then women have their own avenues for accessing God's care. God's response empowers Hannah. Not only does she seek to change her lot; she discovers that she has the power to change it.

This text opens up many layers of questions. It suggests that when it comes to providence, gender is not destiny; Hannah is able to transcend her predicament by appealing directly to God. On the other hand, is it not also true that Hannah remains relegated to fulfilling a woman's traditional role? Taking a broader view, we might also ask: to what degree do each of our current circumstances reflect God's providence?

6.2. From the Liturgy: A *Tkhines* for a Pregnancy

As the example of Hannah demonstrates, one might pray to God for a successful pregnancy and a healthy child.

Tkhines prayers emerged in the Ashkenazic Jewish world in the middle of the seventeenth century. Written in Yiddish specifically for women and printed as prayer books, they "offered a liturgy of daily prayer for women to say once a day as an alternative to, but based upon, the Hebrew liturgy."[6]

These prayer books met a new need. The Ashkenazic community in Eastern Europe experienced a series of deadly pogroms that destroyed communities and created a flow of immigrants westward. "From 1648, large numbers of Jews fled from the atrocities of the Cossack massacres, led by Bogdan Chmielnicki," the Yiddish scholar Devra Kay explains, "and it is estimated that at least 100,000 Jews were murdered in Poland and the Ukraine over a two-year period. Entire Jewish communities were wiped out, and many of the Jews who managed to escape migrated westward and settled in towns such as Amsterdam and Prague."[7]

These unsettled and dangerous times created a cross-fertilization of religious ideas, as well as a new market for publishers. "The influx of new immigrants necessitated the printing of liturgical and other religious books to replace those left behind," Kaye writes. "Those who survived the massacres, but remained in the East, also needed to replenish the books that had been destroyed in the turmoil."[8] Meanwhile, Kaye acknowledges, Yiddish printers may have recognized the business opportunity this presented and helped build demand, motivated both by the potential spiritual and profit rewards. "Women were the predominant readership of Yiddish books."[9]

The prayers in the *Tkhines* spoke to women's specific concerns, such as pregnancy and childbirth. In the *Tkhines* that follows, a pregnant woman entreats God "to protect me and my child." Childbirth in the medieval period could be perilous for both woman and baby. Absent modern medical techniques, a difficult delivery could go horribly wrong. And so was a woman's heartfelt plea: *please, God, do not make this pregnancy a death sentence for me or for my child.*

> God of Hosts
> I call out to You
> To protect me and my child,
> And when it comes to the time

When my child shall be brought into the world,
May You protect me, mighty God
And powerful God,
And awesome God . . .

Lord of the whole world, God on high.
Great and awesome God,
Who can praise You enough?
Who can know how to speak
Of the Great strength that You give to me?
I beg You, God on high,
Let my prayer be accepted by You,
As You accepted the holy sacrifices
That were brought every day
To the Altar.

And may my prayer be accepted
As You accepted the prayer of Hannah the prophetess,
When she was blessed with her fruit.
You heard her prayer
And she gave birth to the prophet Samuel.
So may my prayer
Which I send to You
From the bottom of my heart,
Come before You,
And may You answer my call
With great mercy and compassion.

And I beg You, God on High,
And the God of my forefathers,
Accept my prayer.
Amen. Seloh.[10]

This prayer is unusual in depicting the woman as having "Great strength." In most of the *Tkhines* prayers, the petitioner describes herself as weak or foolish. For example, one of the other *Tkhines* for pregnant women includes the following lines:

How can the Blessed Name show me mercy
When He has chosen me to rule over cows
And over all animals,
And all things on the earth,
And yet I, foolish woman that I am,
Cannot rule over my own body,
But have sinned and transgressed many times
And have been worse than a cow or an ox
Or a donkey.[11]

The fact that in the act of bearing children a woman is characterized differently could be understood in varying ways. Perhaps, the prayer book's printer may have been attempting to appeal to a wide range of moods and temperaments: in order to be profitable, the prayer book would need to find a wide readership. Some women would find the "strong" prayer resonant, whereas others would be drawn to the less-confident characterization. Alternatively, in this context, it could be that woman's strength was acknowledged only when she was fulfilling her God-given role as a mother. In that case, the prayer book served to reinforce her society's expectations for the trajectory of her life story.

It is not a surprise that Hannah is mentioned in the third stanza, as she is the ideal biblical example to follow. Not only was Hannah successful when she engaged in the very same kind of petition; the Rabbis also cite her as the model for praying with sincere intention. She was profoundly focused, pouring out her heart intently.

Interestingly, this efflorescence of female prayer did not last: Kay cites a seventy-year span, from 1648 to 1718, when this kind of prayer book was readily bought and used. It is not clear as to why these prayer books for women were abandoned as a genre, or why they ceased to attract a readership.

6.3. A Rabbinic View: Hannah Persuades God to Act

The ancient Rabbis responded to the story of Hannah by filling in details regarding her words to God:

> "O Lord of *Tzevaot* ["hosts"], if Thou wilt but look on the affliction of Thy handmaid!" (1 Sam. 1:11). R. Eleazar said: From the day the Holy One created His world, there was no one who called the Holy One [Lord of] *Tzevaot* ("hosts") until Hannah came and called Him [Lord of] *Tzevaot*—for she spoke up to the Holy One: Master of the universe, out of all the hosts of hosts that You created in Your world, is it so difficult for You to give me just one son?
>
> By what parable may Hannah's petition be illustrated? By the one of a king of flesh and blood who made a feast for his servants. A poor man came and, standing by the doorway, begged them, "Give me a morsel of bread," but no one heeded him. So he forced his way into the presence of the king and said, "My lord king, out of the entire feast you have made, is it so difficult in your sight to give me one morsel of bread?"
>
> Another comment: Hannah used to go up to the Sanctuary on festal pilgrimages, and when she observed all Israel gathered there, she would say to the Holy One: Master of the universe, You have all these hosts, but among them not even one is mine.[12]

The first paragraph of our text comments on the "Lord of Hosts," the unusual name for God that Hannah invokes when she prays for a son. According to Ernest Klein's *Etymological Dictionary*, the Hebrew noun *tzeva* (spelled *tzaddi-vet-aleph*; the plural is *tzevaot*) means: (1) army, host, (2) military service, war, warfare, (3) service, (4) fixed time.[13]

The Rabbis are careful readers of Hebrew, sensitive to nuances in the language. And so R. Eleazar's understanding of the text is based upon an elaborate pun built upon a *homophone* (two words with different spellings that sound the same). The two words of the homophone are the verb *tzavah* (spelled *tzaddi-vet-hey*), which means "to be willing, to wish," and the adjective *tzaveh* (also spelled *tzaddi-vet-hey*), which means "swollen." Taken together, Hannah's prayer about *tzevaot* means that Hannah *wishes* to have a *swollen* belly. Hannah thus calls out to the Lord of *Tzevaot* to acknowledge that God will determine whether or not her wish to become pregnant will be granted.

In the next part of the passage, the focus shifts to the efficacy of her prayer. She is successful because she enters the Temple in order to make her plea:

By what parable may Hannah's petition be illustrated? By the one of a king of flesh and blood who made a feast for his servants. A poor man came and, standing by the doorway, begged them, "Give me a morsel of bread," but no one heeded him. So he forced his way into the presence of the king and said, "My lord king, out of the entire feast you have made, is it so difficult in your sight to give me one morsel of bread?"

Praying at her home was like standing in the doorway and asking for bread, but praying at the Temple at Shiloh was like entering into the presence of a king. Apparently, God pays more attention when the prayer comes from a holy place. And in Jewish law, the poor have a right to make a claim on the rich to be fed. By framing the encounter in these terms, the Rabbis communicate that Hannah's cause is just.

The last part of the talmudic discussion focuses on Hannah's response upon seeing the multitudes make the pilgrimage to Shiloh:

> Hannah used to go up to the Sanctuary on festal pilgrimages, and when she observed all Israel gathered there, she would say to the Holy One: Master of the universe, You have all these hosts, but among them not even one is mine.

This comment is the closest to the literal meaning of *tzevaot* (hosts).[14] Here, Hannah is saying, a whole host of people is present for the pilgrimage festival, yet none of the children are hers.

Throughout this text, Hannah is objecting to her situation. In the first paragraph, the rabbis have her recognizing that God is responsible for her predicament and makes a wish that it might be fixed. In the second paragraph, they imagine her making her childlessness known, with the understanding that she is merely asking for what is rightfully hers. In the third paragraph, the rabbis suggest that she would be seeking equity in the distribution of wealth: why should she be left out of this bounty?

The Rabbis' analysis of Hannah's narrative indicates that they considered it appropriate for women to pray, based on the biblical story's demonstration that God heeds the prayers of women. They characterized the request for a child as a demand for equity, analogous to a beggar asking for food. In their view, God has a responsibility to deliver on the promise to Abraham that his descendants will be as numerous as the stars in the sky. God is both approachable and subject to persuasion.

6.4. A Medieval View:
Ibn Pakuda Argues for Predetermination

What if Hannah's petition is granted because God has previously decided her fate—that is to say, her prayer changes nothing? Bachya Ibn Pakuda, introduced in chapter 1, contended that everything in the world has already been determined; the outcome is already known to God.

In his eleventh-century masterwork, *Duties of the Heart*, Ibn Pakuda affirmed God's continued decree in the world after God's initial creation of it:

[O]ne should be certain of the fact that everything that happens anew in this world, after creation, is made perfect by two things. The first is the Creator's decree and His will to bring them into being out of nothingness; the second, causes and means, some near and some far, some explicit and some implicit, all working to complete what He has determined to be, all working to bring them into existence with His help.

An example of a near cause is the drawing of water from the depths of the earth by the water wheel, or by the troughs which draw the water up from the well with the wheel. An example of a far cause is the man who ties the beast to the wheel, so that it may turn it and thus draw up the water from the depths of the well to the face of the earth. Those causes which are between the man and the troughs are the media between the two, namely the beast, the wheels which turn each other, and the rope. When some misfortune befalls one of the above-mentioned causes, the purpose which they were to serve is not achieved. The same is true of all other actions brought into existence. They are performed by man and others only with God's predetermination, as it is said (1 Sam. 2:3): Multiply not exceeding proud talk; Let not arrogancy come out of your mouth; for the Lord is a God of knowledge and by Him actions are weighed.[15]

Ibn Pakuda is insisting that God is omnipotent: God decides all outcomes. The world unfolds the way it does because God decrees it.

Notice the idea of perfection here: in Ibn Pakuda's estimation, we are living in the best of all possible worlds. However, Ibn Pakuda suggests, sometimes there is a gap between God's decree — God's decision that something be so — and its execution. Ibn Pakuda provides two examples of what might cause such a gap. In the first case, a man (the primary cause of the action) is drawing water up from a well by turning the wheel (a process Ibn Pakuda calls the intermediate cause). In the second case, when the man has an animal turn the wheel to draw the water, man again is the primary cause. One could claim that the animal causes the water's movement, but in the final analysis the man is responsible.

These two simple scenarios can be used to explain God's relationship to the earth. God is ultimately the cause of all things, but for many of these outcomes God makes use of intermediate causes to create the desired outcome. Just as a man might tie an animal to the wheel to draw water, so too might God enact decrees through natural processes. While this process can be disrupted, these disruptions, too, are part of God's plan: "They are performed by man and others only with God's predetermination."

Interestingly, the prooftext Ibn Pakuda brings to demonstrate this point is a line from the narrative of Hannah: "As it is said: Multiply not exceeding proud talk; Let not arrogancy come out of your mouth; for the Lord is a God of knowledge and by Him actions are weighed" (1 Samuel 2:3). After Hannah bears her child, she dedicates the child to Temple service and authors a psalm for the occasion. The psalm's theme is that God knows all who are truly righteous and will eventually give them their reward. The text goes on to feature a series of images of reversals:

> The bows of the mighty are broken,
> And the faltering are girded with strength.
> Men once sated must hire out for bread;
> Men once hungry hunger no more.
> While the barren woman bears seven,
> The mother of many is forlorn.
> The Lord deals death and gives life,
> Casts down into Sheol and raises up.
> The Lord makes poor and makes rich;
> He casts down, He also lifts high.
> He raises the poor from the dust,
> Lifts up the needy from the dunghill,
> Setting them with nobles,
> Granting them seats of honor. (1 Samuel 2:4–8)

The psalm contributes to Ibn Pakuda's conclusion that God intervenes in the world in order to reward the faithful. When he says, "One should be certain of the fact that everything that happens anew in this world, after creation, is made perfect," he is assuring the faithful that any disadvantage they experience in the present time will be righted in the end.

6.5. A Modern View: Heschel's Partnership with God

In the view of Abraham Joshua Heschel (1907–72), God is intimately involved in the affairs of humanity, as a partner in redeeming the world.

Heschel's legacy includes a prolific and profound body of theological work, scholarly activity in philosophy and rabbinics, teaching and mentorship of a generation of rabbis, and direct activism in the realm of civil rights. "For him, politics and theology were always intertwined," his daughter Susannah Heschel recalls in an introduction. "After the civil-rights march in Selma, he said, 'I felt my legs were praying.' Even as social protest was for him a religious experience, religion without indignation at political evils was also impossible: 'To speak about God and remain silent on Vietnam is blasphemous', he wrote."[16]

A descendant of multiple interconnected Hasidic dynasties, Heschel was expected to become a rebbe like his forefathers, but as a young man he left that cloistered world to earn a PhD in philosophy. While in the course of his lifetime he articulated a great many original Jewish ideas, his theological thinking was nonetheless grounded in the Hasidism of his childhood. Hasidism encouraged its followers to empty out their own individual egos in order to do God's will. It also emphasized that the trials and tribulations we encounter in this world are merely illusions: God is the one true reality. Heschel took this Hasidic view and applied it to the modern world.

In the following passage, taken from *God in Search of Man*, Heschel begins by questioning: "By whose grace, by what right, do we exploit, consume and enjoy the fruits of the trees, the blessings of the earth?" By the close, it is evident: by God's grace, by God's right.

We are endowed with the ability to conquer and to control the forces of nature. In exercising power, we submit to our will a world that we did not create, invading realms that do not belong to us. Are we the kings of the universe or mere pirates? By whose grace, by what right, do we exploit, consume and enjoy the fruits of the trees, the blessings of the earth? Who is responsible for the power to exploit, for the privilege to consume?

It is not an academic problem but an issue we face at every moment. By the will alone man becomes the most destructive of all beings. This is our predicament: our power may become our undoing. We stand on a razor's edge. It is so easy to hurt, to destroy, to insult, to kill. Giving birth to one child is a mystery; bringing death to millions is but a skill. It is not quite within the power of human will to generate life; it is quite within the power of the will to destroy life.

In the midst of such anxiety we are confronted with the claim of the Bible. The world is not all danger, and man is not alone. God endowed man with freedom, and He will share in our use of freedom. The earth is the Lord's and God is in search of man.[17]

Heschel knows that his urgent question has a specific answer in Jewish tradition. An observant Jew recites, "Blessed are You, Our God, Sovereign of the world, creator of the fruit of the tree" before eating any such fruit. God is the one who creates this bounty, and the Jew is obligated to sanctify God before consuming it.

Here, Heschel is drawing attention to a core biblical concept: God, the Creator of heaven and earth, gave human beings dominion over the earth. Early in the book of Genesis, God grants humans the privilege to exploit and consume. First, God gives Adam the fruit of the trees of the garden. Later, God expands human beings' privileges: Noah can also eat certain animals, so long as he pours their blood onto the ground (see 1.1 above). At the same time, Heschel is all too aware of the dangers inherent in such privileges: "This is our predicament: our power may become our undoing." As a refugee from the Holocaust, Heschel narrowly missed suffering the same fate as his mother and sisters, who were murdered by the Nazis. He knows human brutality all too well—that "it is so easy to hurt, to destroy, to insult, to kill."

Since God's involvement in the world does not mean that God will save us from our most destructive impulses, Heschel argues that we are called to be partners with God in transforming the world. God is not solely responsible for the consequences of human behavior, but neither are we left alone in the universe. God is in search of humanity. God is in search of humans who will make the world what God conceived it to be.

Heschel teaches that we have the power to choose to do good or to do evil—but we have to live with the knowledge that each choice we make can unleash a cascade of unintended results. That is why God gave us the commandments: to help us structure our lives so as to do what is right.

In Hasidic thought, God's interaction with the world is envisioned as *shefa*, a kind of overflow, like an endless outpouring of golden light, that fills us up in prayer and enables us to enact God's will on earth. *Shefa* is also a source of creative, healing energy. In some Hasidic circles, the leader is asked to create amulets, to help heal someone or help a woman bear a healthy child. This is the practice of *theurgy*, employing rituals and sacred objects in the attempt to effect some change in God's relationship to the world.

One the one hand, Heschel echoes the Hasidic viewpoint that validates such practices, in that he affirms humanity's partnership with God in drawing down God's goodness. His writing is also imbued with a mystical element, in the sense of seeking contact with the divine. On the other hand, Heschel's observations are devoid of magical thinking, in the sense that he was not advocating creating amulets or charms. He was writing his theological works in mid-twentieth-century America, a decidedly nonmystical environment. He chooses to proclaim—to a much wider audience than the Hasidic world—the urgent need for an ethics grounded in the Bible's prophetic message: "God endowed man with freedom, and He will share in our use of freedom. The earth is the Lord's and God is in search of man."

If, as Heschel says, we are expected to work in partnership with God to enact God's will on earth, then in that sense, too, Hannah's quest to bear a child of her own was the best kind of prayer. She sought to partner with God to increase holiness in the world. And, understanding the true nature of God's blessing, she subsequently dedicated her son to the priestly service.

6.6. A Modern View: Kaplan's Rejection of Supernaturalism

Mordecai Kaplan (1881–1983), "one of the most radical Jewish thinkers of the twentieth century" according to his biographer, Mel Scult,[18] believed that supernatural conceptions of God—even Heschel's nonmagical conception of a supernatural God who searches out humanity to help effect God's goodness—were no longer tenable in the modern age.

Instead, Kaplan proposed a fundamentally new approach to God. Instead of a "being" acting independently in the world, Kaplan's student Rabbi Steven Carr Reuben explains that Kaplan understood God as "the transcendent power that we experience in the everyday miracles of our lives, in the best and highest ideals of the human mind and heart. . . . The way to find God wherever we are, Kaplan taught, is to wittingly demonstrate the qualities we identify as Godly. . . . We may find God in the support we extend to someone who is hungry. We may find God when we stand up for those who need it most."[19] In Kaplan's own words: "The best argument for the existence of God is a godlike human life."[20]

Kaplan's reimagining of Judaism as an evolving civilization of the Jewish people was another radical contribution, and sparked the creation of Reconstructionist Judaism. The movement seeks to connect the individual to the community through religious and social events and to leave space for nonmagical, nonsupernatural God-language. In addition, Kaplan originated the bat mitzvah coming-of-age service for girls to parallel the longstanding bar mitzvah tradition for boys; his daughter Judith was the first to have a bat mitzvah ceremony.

In the following passage, taken from *Judaism without Supernaturalism* (1958), Kaplan argues that since God does not intervene in our lives in any supernatural fashion, we must accordingly revise our understanding of what we mean when we say "God":

The only alternative to the traditional and supernaturalist conception of God's self-manifestation that can make a difference in people's lives is not the metaphysical approach but the social-behavioral one. . . . *It is the business of religion not to give a metaphysical conception of God, but to make clear what we mean by the belief in God, from the standpoint of the difference that belief makes in human conduct and striving. . . .*

The freedom and responsibility of which human nature is capable are the natural manifestations, on a self-conscious level, of the cosmic principle of polarity. Freedom expresses the pole of selfhood, and responsibility the pole of otherhood, or cooperation. Is the human polarity of freedom and responsibility, with its promise of human metamorphosis into a higher type of being, futile dreaming and self-delusion, or is it as existentially real as the world of sense and sound we inhabit? If the latter is the case, then the self-conscious will to salvation is the immanent aspect of that cosmic reality for which no term can be more appropriate than "God." Whatever else human beings may have sought to express by the term "God," it has always had the connotation of man's responsibility for what he does and his freedom to choose between right and wrong, good and evil.[21]

At the outset of the passage, we encounter Kaplan's pragmatism, here meaning the philosophical approach of evaluating ideas according to their results:

> The only alternative to the traditional and supernaturalist conception of God's self-manifestation that can make a difference in people's lives is not the metaphysical approach but the social-behavioral one. . . . *It is the business of religion not to give a metaphysical conception of God, but to make clear what we mean by the belief in God, from the standpoint of the difference that belief makes in human conduct and striving.*

Scult explains that "For the most part, Kaplan may be described as a pragmatic believer. His first question in understanding a ritual or any kind of historical phenomenon was to ask how it had traditionally functioned. Did it continue to function as it had in the past?" In this case, Kaplan has concluded that traditional conceptions of God were not currently functioning. Therefore, he suggests how the God-concept might be reconstructed, based on his understanding of the human condition:

> The freedom and responsibility of which human nature is capable are the natural manifestations, on a self-conscious level, of the cosmic principle of polarity. Freedom expresses the pole of selfhood, and responsibility the pole of otherhood, or cooperation.

Think of two poles: on one side is the individual's need for freedom and self-determination, on the other side the group's need for cooperation on a common goal. Kaplan says that these two poles, operating separately but in tandem, have cosmic significance. These poles manifest themselves within the individual (who must struggle with the tension between participating in a group and listening to an inner voice) and in the community (which must address the individual's needs but also pursue the group's concerns).

Kaplan goes on to ask whether this tension between freedom and cooperation is existentially real, in the sense that it is part of the fundament of the universe, reflecting an aspect of God.

> Is the human polarity of freedom and responsibility, with its promise of human metamorphosis into a higher type of being, futile dreaming and self-delusion, or is it as existentially real as the world of sense and sound we inhabit?

He argues that it does:

> If the latter is the case, then the self-conscious will to salvation is the immanent aspect of that cosmic reality for which no term can be more appropriate than "God." Whatever else human beings may have sought to express by the term "God," it has always had the connotation of man's responsibility for what he does and his freedom to choose between right and wrong, good and evil.

That is to say, our desire to improve ourselves ("the self-conscious will to salvation") is what is godly in us. In Kaplan's view, there is no external God who intervenes in our lives in any way. God, rather, is reflected in our will to enact our own personal salvation. We do so by making choices in our lives, specifically choosing good over evil. When we enact goodness in our lives, we become living embodiments of God.

In Kaplan's view, Hannah's prayer would not have changed her situation. Her infertility was a physical, not a metaphysical, problem. There is no supernatural God who could have intervened to respond to her prayer. God, however, would have been present when she willed to do good—to enlist her newborn son into priestly service.

6.7. Summary of Views

The *biblical text* tells us that Hannah, a barren woman, was tormented by her desire to bear a child. She prayed intently for a child at the temple at Shiloh, and God granted her wish. Ultimately, she was held up as an example of effective prayer. Hannah's story might be considered subversive in relation to the power wielded by the exclusively male priesthood. The narrative reinforces the idea that God might heed the prayer of a woman and not just the prayer of the male authorities, intimating that women have their own avenues for accessing God's care. Moreover, God's response empowers Hannah. Not only does she seek to change her lot; she discovers that she has the power to change it.

The *liturgical text*, a *Tkhines* (a Yiddish prayer articulating women's specific concerns) for a pregnant woman, cited the story of Hannah. Childbirth in the medieval period could be perilous for both woman and baby. And so a woman's heartfelt plea in the *Tkhines* was: *please, God, do not make this pregnancy a death sentence for me or for my child.* The text reinforced the possibility that God might heed a woman's prayer.

The *rabbinic text*, drawn from the Talmud, upheld Hannah as the example to follow when praying, because God clearly favored her intense focus and passion. This story might also be read as an implicit criticism of the office of the priesthood. Eli's name conveys a sense of possessiveness—"God is mine, and mine alone." Eli is sitting idle at the doorway of the shrine, passing judgment on a woman who comes with a genuine need. This woman who pours out her heart is the one whom God heeds.

In the *medieval text*, Ibn Pakuda argued that everything that occurs in the world does so because God so wills it. He quoted as his prooftext the psalm attributed to Hannah, which suggested that God eventually rewards the faithful. Any disadvantages they experience in the present world will be righted in the end.

In the *first modern text*, Abraham Joshua Heschel asserted that God's involvement in the world does not mean that God will save us from our most destructive impulses. Rather, we are expected to work in partnership with God in order to enact God's will on earth.

In the *second modern text*, Kaplan maintained that a supernatural God does not intervene in our lives in any way. He redefined God as our human will to improve ourselves and thereby enact our own personal salvation. We do so by making life choices, specifically choosing good over evil. When we enact goodness in our lives, we are living embodiments of God. Hannah's prayer would not have changed her situation. God, however, would have been present when she willed to do good—to enlist her newborn son into priestly service.

6.8. Does God Act on Behalf of the Jewish Community?

Up until now, this chapter has addressed the providence question solely on the plane of individual experience. But this concept also has broader application. Many events in Jewish history have been framed in terms of God's providence.

This concept is particularly apparent in the Passover narrative. Traditionally, the seder (festival meal recounting the story of the Exodus from Egypt) is organized around the principle that the Exodus is the truest, best example of God's providential intervention in history. During the *maggid* ("storytelling") section of the seder, Jews read about the four children and their questions. When the simple child asks, "What is this?," Jews are instructed to give that child a theological answer drawn from Exodus 13:14: "And when, in time to come, your son asks you, saying, 'What does this mean?' you shall say to him, 'It was with a mighty hand that the Lord brought us out from Egypt, the house of bondage.'" Thus the first answer, the very first thing that Jews teach children, is this theological narrative, the story that forms the bedrock of Jewish tradition. Only as the child matures into wisdom is one to explain Jewish laws and customs.

God's hand in the Exodus narrative is made explicit in the seder in other ways as well. Also in the recounting of events during the *maggid* portion of the seder, Jews are expected to declare that we "did not overpraise Moses," to ensure we have given God proper credit. (By contrast, Mordecai Kaplan created a Haggadah that exalted Moses' role.)

However, God's apparent willingness to respond to suffering on the national scale, as retold each year at Passover, raises even more questions. Does God's providence extend to every generation, or only certain ones? And if this narrative unfolds according to God's will, why does the Israelites' liberation require the Egyptians' suffering? In other words, does God's providence extend to the good *and* the bad? The seder demonstrates awareness of the cost of this redemption—ten drops of wine symbolizing each of the ten plagues are spilled—but this memorial does not quiet the theological concern.

6.9. Is the Creation of the State of Israel Evidence of Divine Providence?

For nearly two thousand years, ever since the destruction of the Second Temple in Jerusalem by Titus and the dispersal of the Jews at the hands of the Roman armies, Jews have looked longingly toward *Eretz Yisra'el* (the Land of Israel) with the thought of return. From a theological point of view, this idea of return has a specific historical precedent: after the destruction of the First Temple in 587 BCE, the elites were brought in chains to Babylonia, where they dreamt of returning to rebuild the Temple anew. This experience of exile and return, attested by many biblical passages that celebrate the ideal of return, created a powerful framework for viewing the second destruction and consequent Diaspora. For example, Psalm 126, "A song of ascents," confidently asserts in its opening lines: "When the lord restores the fortunes of Zion / —we see it as in a dream— / Our mouths shall be filled with laughter, / Our tongues, with songs of joy." As a result, to many Jews the establishment in 1948 of *Medinat Yisra'el* (the State of Israel) in *Eretz Yisra'el* (the Land of Israel) by *am Yisra'el* (the Jewish people) seemed nothing short of miraculous.

How are Jews to understand the establishment of the state that fulfilled the Bible's teaching in their own generation?

One could say that the creation of Medinat Yisra'el came down to a series of worldly events for which men and women were solely responsible, e.g., the political Zionists who immigrated to then-Palestine and labored to make a harsh desert bloom, the soldiers in the armed conflict, the participants in the international diplomacy.

Other thinkers, however, such as Rabbi Abraham Isaac Kook ("Rav Kook"), a spiritual leader who served as a chief rabbi during the British Mandate, considered the efforts toward creation of Medinat Yisra'el as evidence of the "first flowering" of the messianic redemption—the event that would ingather all the exiles and bring *am Yisra'el* back to *Eretz Yisra'el*.[22] When he voiced this idea in the 1920s, his position was a minority opinion, but since his death, a national-religious movement has grown up around his thought. His followers now view the State of Israel in eschatological terms, a progressive step toward the end of days, when the Messiah comes.

To Kook and his followers, the whole world is filled with evidence of divine providence. Viewing the creation of the state as proof of providence leads believers to cast worldly events—even small mundane events in the state—as having transcendent meaning.

Chapter 7

Does God Intervene in History?

- How have different strands of Jewish tradition viewed the
  question of God's intervention when tragedy has befallen the
  Jewish people?
- Why was God silent during the Holocaust?
- Should the experience of great suffering cause us to change
  our relationship to God?

7.1. A Biblical View: What Was Meant
for Evil, God Meant for Good

The biblical story of Joseph conveys the message that God sometimes
intends ostensibly evil actions for good—as Joseph says, "so as to
bring about the present result—the survival of many people."

Joseph, one of the youngest of twelve brothers, is his father Isaac's
favorite child. This favoritism is a familial pattern: Isaac preferred
Joseph's mother Rachel over his other wife (Rachel's sister Leah).
Exacerbating the tension over favoritism is Joseph's irritating habit
of telling his brothers about his nightly dreams—each dream illus-
trating that Joseph will one day rule over them all. In their anger and
jealousy, the brothers throw him into a pit to die, but later decide
it would be better to sell him into slavery. They take his distinctive

multicolored coat (a gift and emblem of Isaac's favoritism), dip it in animal's blood, and concoct a story to tell their father.

In time, by correctly predicting a famine, Joseph goes on to become the Pharaoh's second in command. As vizier he institutes steps that stave off famine in Egypt. Eventually, Joseph's family seeks refuge in Egypt, and in due course they discover, much to their surprise, that Joseph is not only alive; he now holds a high position in the Egyptian government. In an emotional scene, a weeping Joseph reconciles with his brothers, and then seeks to be reunited with his father. All is well for a while.

When their father dies, however, the brothers fear that Joseph has been waiting for this moment to exact his revenge. We pick up the text at Genesis 50:15-21.

> When Joseph's brothers saw that their father was dead, they said, "What if Joseph still bears a grudge against us and pays us back for all the wrong that we did him!" So they sent this message to Joseph, "Before his death your father left this instruction: So shall you say to Joseph, 'Forgive, I urge you, the offense and guilt of your brothers who treated you so harshly'. Therefore, please forgive the offense of the servants of the God of your father's [house]." And Joseph was in tears as they spoke to him.
>
> His brothers went to him themselves, flung themselves before him, and said, "We are prepared to be your slaves." But Joseph said to them, "Have no fear! Am I a substitute for God? Besides, although you intended me harm, God intended it for good, so as to bring about the present result—the survival of many people. And so, fear not. I will sustain you and your dependents." Thus he reassured them, speaking kindly to them.

We see in the text that the brothers asked three times for Joseph's forgiveness, first through a messenger and then twice when speaking before Joseph himself.

Joseph's response to his brothers, however, makes it clear that he has already forgiven them. He interprets the misfortunes in his life in theological terms: everything was part of God's plan for him ("although you intended me harm, God intended it for good, so as to bring about the present result—the survival of many people"). His theology acknowledges the brothers' evil actions ("you intended me harm"), and his commitment to rise above it ("I will sustain you and your dependents"). Joseph is indeed righteous. He extends forgiveness readily and recognizes the value of his own suffering; good has been brought into the world.

Even so, this interpretation has unfortunate consequences. When suffering is given theological meaning, it suggests that things had to turn out this way; God, in effect, is the author of the suffering, purposely bringing it about in service of a greater good. We may decide to turn evil into good; that is praiseworthy. However, if it is *God* who turned evil into good, it appears like a kind of abuse. Why is it necessary for the evil to exist in the first place? Could we not skip straight to the good?

On the other hand, notice that the author does not attribute the evil to God's will. Notice also that the passage does not make the argument that things had to happen this way. Rather, in these words of Joseph, the biblical author articulates a theology that allows for healing and forgiveness, in asserting that God has transformed the negatives into something positive.

7.2. From the Liturgy:
The Martyrdom of Jewish Sages

The medieval liturgical poem "Eileh Ezkarah" ("These I Remember") memorializes the martyrdom of ten scholars in Roman times. Rabbi Lord Jonathan Sacks notes that when the story of this martyrdom is told through the reading of this poem each Yom Kippur, "the emphasis is on the way [the martyrs] gave their lives for faith—as if to say that though the destruction of the Temple brought sacrifices to an end, Jews did not cease to make sacrifices for the sake of God. Often they gave their lives."[1]

The narrative arc of the poem suggests that an evil Roman ruler punished the Jews of his day for the crime of kidnapping Joseph, on the theory that justice had not yet been served. The question of why God allowed this martyrdom is not answered, though the refrain casts blame on the Jewish community as a whole for having sinned—which may indicate an assumption that God had intervened in history. As much as the Romans were blamed for the persecutions, the Jews of the time also had to bear collective guilt for an event that took place in the biblical era.

> These I remember, and I pour out my soul within me, for evil
> ones have swallowed us, like a cake not yet turned—when
> during the Caesar's rule there was no deliverance for the
> ten martyrs of that empire.
>
> > Whilst the ruler studied our holy book from [sages]
> > likened to heaps of grain,
> > considering and discerning our written tradition,
> > he happened to open at "These are the statutes,"
> > and devised an evil plan
> > as he read, "One who steals a man and
> > sells him, and is found out
> > shall surely be put to death."
>
> > > We have sinned, our Rock; forgive us our Creator.
>
> The heart of this wicked idol worshiper grew haughty;
> he ordered that his palace be filled with shoes,
> and summoned ten great sages
> with profound understanding of the law and its reasoning.

He declared: "Judge this case with precision—
do not pervert it by making false statements,
but bring true justice to light:
what is the verdict if a man is found kidnapping
one of his brothers from the children of Israel,
treating him as a slave and selling him?

> We have sinned, our Rock; forgive us, our Creator.

When they answered: "That kidnapper shall be put to
death,"
He said: "Then what of your ancestors, who sold their
brother,
Trading him with a traveling company of Ishmaelites,
Handing him over for the mere price of shoes?" . . .

O Gracious One, look down from Your heights,
See the spilled blood of the righteous,
   their vital essence,
From Your concealed place behold this
And remove the stains of sin,
God, King, who sits upon a throne of compassion.

> We have sinned, our Rock; forgive us, our Creator.[2]

The first part of this liturgical text speaks to the history of Jewish persecution during the Roman era:

These I remember, and I pour out my soul within me, for evil ones have swallowed us, like a cake not yet turned—when during the Caesar's rule there was no deliverance for the ten martyrs of that empire.

The sages of the rabbinic era (after the destruction of the Second Temple in 70 CE) experienced a series of persecutions at the hands of the Romans. The tradition particularly remembered the martyrdom of these ten.

The phrase, "like a cake not yet turned" is unclear, as its import has been lost. The following explanation is an educated guess. When making pita bread (or, similarly, flat cakes), a large rounded clay oven is used, with a chimney at the top, a fire at the bottom, and an opening on one side. A skillful baker will lean toward the fire, reach into the oven's dome with a baker's board, and slap a ball of dough against the inside wall. This flattened dough ball will cling to the wall like a spongey starfish while it bakes. Once the circle of dough has finished baking on one side, the dough will begin to peel away from that side of the oven, and start to fall toward the fire. The baker will use the baker's board to catch the half-baked dough. Then the baker will slap the uncooked side of the dough back against the oven wall so as to bake it on the other side. Again, it will fall off when it is done. A "cake not yet turned," therefore, might be one that falls straight into the fire without being caught by the baker. The image suggests that God did not prevent this martyrdom from happening, the way a baker might prevent a cake from falling. God is apparently not paying attention to the needs at hand. Rather, the lives of these sages have been cut short well before their time.

> Whilst the ruler studied our holy book from [sages]
> likened to heaps of grain,

"Heaps of grain" is a measurement of wealth. In this setting and others, the sages were accounted Judaism's greatest treasure.

> considering and discerning our written tradition,
> he happened to open at "These are the statutes,"
> and devised an evil plan

as he read, "One who steals a man and sells him, and is
found out
shall surely be put to death."

The rabbinic literature contains multiple examples of theological discussions with Romans in which the Romans dispute aspects of rabbinic thought and then receive correction from the Rabbis. However, this poem more accurately reflects the patterns of interaction present in the medieval Christian era, such as we will see in 7.4 below, than the early Roman era. In the medieval period, Jews would be summoned for disputations with representatives of the church, and Jewish texts would be used as evidence of the wrongness of their ways.

We have sinned, our Rock; forgive us our Creator.

Note that the refrain indicates that the Jewish community as a whole has sinned. This kind of theology—the idea that such trials are chastisements or punishment for sin—has been fairly common in all eras, but it has also been rightfully criticized since the Holocaust as a form of "blaming the victim" for an inflicted abuse.

The heart of this wicked idol worshiper grew haughty;
he ordered that his palace be filled with shoes,
and summoned ten great sages
with profound understanding of the law and its reasoning.

The wicked ruler has created a trap: no record of retribution or punishment for the sins of the brothers appears in the biblical text. This poem reflects a situation in which the foe is a knowledgeable reader of the Hebrew Bible.

He declared: "Judge this case with precision—
do not pervert it by making false statements,
but bring true justice to light:
what is the verdict if a man is found kidnapping
one of his brothers from the children of Israel,
treating him as a slave and selling him?

We have sinned, our Rock; forgive us, our Creator.

Here we encounter the idea that the Jews should bear collective guilt for an event that took place in the biblical era—an idea similar to the Christian concept of Jewish guilt for the death of Jesus.

The text makes it clear that visiting collective punishment upon the community is evil. It is wickedly unfair to use a people's texts against them, to visit retribution upon them for events recorded in the sacred texts written well before their birth. This text, in fact, may be intended as an indirect reprimand of Christian persecution of Jews for being "Christ killers." How can the present-day community be held responsible for what happened in biblical times?

When they answered: "That kidnapper shall be put to
    death,"
He said: "Then what of your ancestors, who sold their
    brother,
Trading him with a traveling company of Ishmaelites,
Handing him over for the mere price of shoes?"

The remainder of the poem describes the Jews' terror in response. The sages asked for three days to deliberate, during which the martyrs purified themselves. The sages did not respond further to the questioning; they knew it was a trap and there was no way to survive it. The death of each of the martyrs is described with great emotion.

At the very end, the poem asks God to bear witness to this martyrdom and to forgive the Jewish community's sins:

> O Gracious One, look down from Your heights,
> See the spilled blood of the righteous, their vital essence,
> From Your concealed place behold this
> And remove the stains of sin,
> God, King, who sits upon a throne of compassion.
>
> We have sinned, our Rock; forgive us, our Creator.

The poem's refrain, "We have sinned, our Rock; forgive us, our Creator," certainly fits with the task of atonement during the High Holiday season, but it has been rightfully criticized, particularly after the Holocaust, as an example of excusing the victimizer. In its defense, it may accept the martyrdom not at the hands of the Romans but as God's intervening punishment of the community. Alternatively, this refrain might subtly be lodging a protest: if we have sinned, forgive us—but also, tell us how we have sinned!

7.3. A Rabbinic View:
Why Does Suffering Happen?

As the last text illustrates, some of the sages in the rabbinic period met a painful and prolonged death at Roman hands. There are other stories of sages being burned alive, wrapped in a Torah scroll with wet wool placed over their hearts to prolong the agony.

Consider their situation for a moment from a theological point of view. The kingdom had been soundly defeated, the Temple was a charred ruin, and the Romans were ruling over the people with harrowing brutality—yet God was agonizingly silent. When the ancient Rabbis asked, "Why does God allow the righteous to suffer?," their question had genuine urgency.

In response, the Rabbis suggested multiple possibilities (including alternatives we will explore in the next chapter). The text in this section offers a particularly difficult answer, for it argues that these kinds of suffering are chastisements of God's love. It represents one of the mainstream Jewish views. In our era, however, it seems particularly difficult to accept.

> Rabba (some say, R[abbi] Hisda) says: if a man sees that painful sufferings visit him, let him examine his conduct. For it is said: *Let us search and try our ways, and return unto the Lord* (Lam. 3:40). If he examines and finds nothing [objectionable], let him attribute it to the neglect of the study of the Torah. For it is said: *Happy is the man whom Thou chastenest, O Lord, and teachest out of Thy law* (Ps. 94:12). If he did attribute it [thus], and still did not find [this to be the cause], let him be sure that these are chastenings of love. For it is said: *For whom the Lord loveth He correcteth* (Prov. 3:12).
>
> Raba, in the name of R[abbi] Sahorah, in the name of R[abbi] Huna, says: If the Holy One, blessed be He, is pleased with a man, he crushes him with painful sufferings. For it is said: *And the Lord was pleased with [him, hence] he crushed him by disease* (Isa. 53:10). Now, you might think that this is so even if he did not accept them with love. Therefore it is said: *To see if his soul would offer itself in restitution.* Even as the trespass-offering must be brought by consent, so also the sufferings must be endured with consent. And if he did accept them, what is his reward? *He will see his seed, prolong his days.* And more than that, his knowledge [of the Torah] will endure with him. For it is said: *The purpose of the Lord will prosper in his hand* (Ps. 94:12).[3]

Parsing out each of these comments, let's investigate the biblical quotations and their context.

Rabba (some say, R[abbi] Hisda) says: if a man sees that painful sufferings visit him, let him examine his conduct. For it is said: *Let us search and try our ways, and return unto the Lord* (Lam. 3:40).

After the Romans' destruction of the Second Temple in 70 CE, the Rabbis looked to the book of Lamentations—which mourned the Babylonians' destruction of the First Temple in 587 BCE—for a useful theological structure by which to respond to catastrophe. They took the lesson that when faced with tragedy, one should search one's deeds and find where one has sinned, for such events were assuredly examples of God's retribution.

For the Rabbis of the era, attributing theological significance to their plight was imperative. If they assumed that the destruction was wrought by God on account of the people's own sins, then at least they could take comfort in the thought that they had some control over their future. In Deuteronomy 6:1–9, for example, God promises to protect the people Israel so long as they heed God's commands: "Obey, O Israel, willingly and faithfully, that it may go well with you and that you may increase greatly [in] a land flowing with milk and honey, as God, the God of your ancestors, spoke to you." (We discussed this passage at length in chapter 5). According to this theology, the people's future was in their own hands: good things would happen whenever the Israelites obeyed, and bad things would occur whenever they did not. The people could change their ways and thus prevent such terrible things from happening again. The theology of "suffering as retribution for our sins" remained ever-popular with the ancient Rabbis.

The question then naturally arose: what did the Jews do to thus incur God's wrath? Individuals were to weigh their own behavior in this regard:

If he examines and finds nothing [objectionable], let him attribute it to the neglect of the study of the Torah. For it is said: *Happy is the man whom Thou chastenest, O Lord, and teachest out of Thy law* (Ps. 94:12).

The citation is particularly interesting. Psalm 94 opens with a request for the "God of retribution" to judge the wicked. It then suggests that learning Torah can give a person "tranquility in times of misfortune." Its closing line suggests that eventually God will "annihilate" the wicked. This choice is readily understandable, given the lopsided balance of power between Rome and the ancient Rabbis.

The text continues:

If he did attribute it [thus], and still did not find [this to be the cause], let him be sure that these are chastenings of love. For it is said: *For whom the Lord loveth He correcteth* (Prov. 3:12).

This section introduces the idea that misfortune may be God's corrective retribution: just as a loving father will punish his son for misbehavior, adverse events could be opportunities to improve our behavior. The biblical quote comes from the book of Proverbs, in the context of a father's speech to his son.

This next one pushes the idea even further:

Raba, in the name of R[abbi] Sahorah, in the name of R[abbi] Huna, says: If the Holy One, blessed be He, is pleased with a man, he crushes him with painful sufferings. For it is said: *And the Lord was pleased with [him, hence] he crushed him by disease* (Isa. 53:10).

Here suffering is no longer punishment, but instead becomes a sign of divine approval. The biblical quote is from a passage in the book of

Isaiah that describes the Suffering Servant, a person in the Hebrew Bible who suffers mistreatment silently as a servant of God. Isaiah 53:7 states: "He was maltreated, yet he was submissive, / He did not open his mouth; / Like a sheep being led to slaughter, / Like a ewe, dumb before those who shear her, / He did not open his mouth." This suffering is apparently viewed favorably by God.

The *he* in the next sentence refers again to the Suffering Servant, someone whom God crushes with painful sufferings:

> Now, you might think that this is so even if he did not accept them with love. Therefore it is said: *To see if his soul would offer itself in restitution.* Even as the trespass-offering must be brought by consent, so also the sufferings must be endured with consent.

Only if suffering is endured willingly does it merit divine reward.

What does that reward consist of? The subsequent text asks and answers that question:

> And if he did accept them, what is his reward? *He will see his seed, prolong his days.* And more than that, his knowledge [of the Torah] will endure with him. For it is said: *The purpose of the Lord will prosper in his hand.* (Ps. 94:12).[4]

The text concludes: God allows the righteous to suffer so that they might pass the Torah on to generations to follow. This theology helped to provide comfort in the face of Roman persecution. Though the righteous may suffer greatly, at least the world could make sense: the covenant between God and the people Israel was still intact, and the life of the community still had meaning.

This theology is an example of an attempt to give moral coherence to circumstances that apparently defy our moral sense and expectations. Theodicy (the explanation of how God may be good despite the evil in the world) is such an attempt at moral coherence.

From a modern vantage point, the Rabbis' theology looks extremely problematic. It is difficult to create a list of sins that fully justifies the cruelties of war. As far as sins go, the brutality of the Romans in the rabbinic era was considerably worse than the supposed sins they were punishing. Furthermore, most modern thinkers cannot accept its valorization of suffering as evidence of the love of God. After the death of six million Jews in the Holocaust, such a position seems obscene.

7.4. A Medieval View:
Meir ben Baruch Memorializes the Talmud

The liturgical text we read in 7.2 is an example of a martyrological poem that has been used as a prayer. In this next section, we will delve into another martyrological poem to better understand their theological implications.

In the poem "Sha'ali serufah ba-esh" ("Ask, O You Who Are Burned in Fire"), the poet Meir ben Baruch, a young student of the Tosafist school (a medieval school of rabbis united by a common approach to the Talmud) who had witnessed the burning of the Talmud by representatives of the Roman Catholic Church in 1242, protests against the loss of moral coherence: why is it that Jews are persecuted, yet God does not intervene? Some general background: During the medieval period, Jews usually were not citizens of the lands in which they lived. The Jewish communities in Christian Europe normally had a charter enacted by the local monarch that gave them the privilege of settling there. These charters also defined how many Jews could be allowed in a given principality. Sometimes grown children in the Jewish community had to be sent away from the land of their birth, as no space was available for them where they were born. The community's charter could also be revoked, thereby forcing the entire community to relocate. Such events did happen, often when the local prince owed money to community members and did not want to pay it back.

At that time, Jews and Christians lived each within their own universe of meaning; there was no place (metaphorically or literally) to engage in interfaith discussion. Instead of productive dialogue, religious traditions would engage in *polemics*: aggressive arguments made with great conviction in favor of a particular view. Disputations between two religious traditions, therefore, were zero-sum contests: one would win and one would lose, and defeat could be catastrophic.

The poem's translator, Susan Einbinder, explains the specific events precipitating "Ask, O You Who Are Burned in Fire":

When the apostate Nicholas Donin presented his charges against the Talmud to Gregory IX in 1239, "it seemed to have been news to the Pope" that the Jews relied on an extrascriptural book that contained blasphemies against Jesus and Mary as well as numerous other "errors" of belief. . . .

Donin provided Gregory IX with a list of thirty-five charges against the Talmud . . . Moreover, [Donin argued that the Talmud] . . . represented a perversion of the sense of the Bible . . . [to the point that] those who followed its dictates could no longer be considered "Jews," that is, [they could not be considered to be] the surviving remnant of biblical Israel, which . . . Christianity had held itself obligated to preserve as a witness in its midst . . .

For two years, the rabbis [had] managed to stave off the evil decree [that the Talmud had to be burned], but . . . in June of 1242, the Sixth of Tammuz by the Jewish calendar, the Talmud was burned . . .

The attack on the "Talmud" was a blow to the heart of Tosafist education. . . . [The] students . . . had been taught that the Talmud was a sacred corpus of "Oral" Law, revealed to Moses along with the Written Law at Sinai. . . . The burning of the Talmud was thus no less than a burning of the Law itself, a tragedy of unspeakable proportions even in the light of the human losses of those years."[5]

Meir ben Baruch's poem memorializes the burning as a crushing blow. Here is a selection as translated by Einbinder:

> O Sinai, was this why the Lord chose you, disdaining
> Greater mountains to shine within your borders?
> To be a sign of the Law when her glory would dwindle
> And go down? Let me make an analogy:
> You are like a king who wept at his son's feast-day
> Foreseeing his death — so your speech foretold your end.
> O Sinai, instead of your cloak, let your garment be a sack
> Don the garb of widows instead of your dresses.
> I will pour forth tears until like a river they reach
> Unto the tombs of your most noble princes,
> Moses and Aaron, on Mount Hor, and I will ask: Is there
> A new Torah, that your scrolls may be burned? . . .
> My heart will be lifted up when I see the Rock shed light
>   upon you
> Bringing light into your darkness and illuminating your
>   shadows.[6]

The opening lines introduce the idea that God might choose a humble location for delivering messages of universal importance. "Sinai" has a double meaning here: it is the mountain where the Torah was given and it is also a metonym for the people of Israel, who are considered to be a humble people in terms of size and power.

O Sinai, was this why the Lord chose you, disdaining
Greater mountains to shine within your borders?

Given that Judaism was a minority religion, this message was intended to refute the idea that God's truth coincided with what was
largest and grandest (i.e., Christianity). Meir ben Baruch continues:

To be a sign of the Law when her glory would dwindle
And go down?

The original Torah text—the one directly from the hand of God—
is visualized as "black fire on white fire"—black letters illuminating
and burning brightly like fire against the background of white fire.
These lines of the poem, therefore, offer a note of protest: how can
it be that "her glory would dwindle / and go down," that we are
targeted for this kind of abuse? Did God kindle this fire only to let
it burn down to mere embers?

Let me make an analogy:
You are like a king who wept at his son's feast-day
Foreseeing his death—so your speech foretold your end.

When this poem is read in the context of the literature of the ancient
rabbis, then the "king" here is God and the "speech" is the Torah,
which includes predictions of doom and disaster. For example, in
Genesis 15:13, Abraham is told, "Know well that your offspring shall
be strangers in a land not theirs, and they shall be enslaved and
oppressed four hundred years."

O Sinai, instead of your cloak, let your garment be a sack
Don the garb of widows instead of your dresses.

Here again "Sinai" is a metonym for the people Israel. The burning of the Talmud is akin to the death of a loved one. The day is one of mourning.

> I will pour forth tears until like a river they reach
> Unto the tombs of your most noble princes,
> Moses and Aaron, on Mount Hor
> and I will ask: Is there
> A new Torah, that your scrolls may be burned?

The "new Torah" reference here is to a so-called New Testament. Jews have always used the term Hebrew Bible rather than Old Testament, because the latter implies that there is a New Testament superseding the old one, which is what Christians believe. This poem asks God directly: is there a New Testament that would make it acceptable to burn these scrolls? Meir ben Baruch seems to be pointedly questioning God: What good is it to be Your chosen people, if this also includes the martyrdom of the Jewish sages and desecration of the holy texts?

Yet, in the end, he speaks of the Talmud, elsewhere personified in the feminine, as rejoicing at some time in the future:

> My heart will be lifted up when I see the Rock shed light
>   upon you
> Bringing light into your darkness and illuminating your
>   shadows

The "Rock" is another name of God in the literature of the rabbis. The poet maintains that the great loss of the Talmud reinforces the need for the young men of the Tosefist school (who were training to be Torah scholars) to recommit to upholding the Torah, focusing their ardor on Jewish texts.

Other martryological poems of the time also served this dual purpose of remembering those who died and reinforcing the faith of those who lived. As Einbinder explains:

> Successive persecutions and policies of harassment took a brutal toll on once-thriving communities, shattering the self-confidence of learned and common Jews alike. The Tosafist poetry of martyrdom responded to these conditions, crafting images of transcendence in suffering while reflecting the ideological battleground on which Jews and Christians met.
>
> Martyrological poems that commemorated the victims of anti-Jewish violence were designed to present a model of resistance and fortitude in the face of persecution. . . . These poems . . . were also polemical vehicles, embodying in the figures of the martyrs the behaviors and beliefs that reinforced Jewish identity while expressing revulsion for Christian symbols and faith. . . .
>
> Jews who accepted conversion at sword-point, in terror for their lives, were one sort of problem. . . . But not all Jews did convert at sword-point, and it was a terrible blow when a combination of Christian argument and Jewish misery convinced educated young men to abandon their faith. The defection of the Jewish elite was a twofold disaster, both as a loss to the family and community of the apostate and as a weapon in the hands of his new co-religionists.[7]

Along with martyrological poetry, liturgical martyrological works also served this twofold role. For example, in response to the burning of the Talmud twice in 1321, "a fast-day liturgy the Jews recited to save their books still survives in an Italian *mahzor* [High Holiday prayer book] dated to 1420."[8] Einbinder summarizes it as follows:

Unremarkable in most respects, the liturgy is nonetheless touching in its repeated and anxious invocations to *El han-ishkahot*, the Lord of the forgotten. If the expression reflects the petitioners' fear that God has forgotten them, its insistent repetition suggests that without their books, the Jews will no longer remember themselves. What is threatened with the loss of their books is the fragile weave of sacred and social history wrought by learning and memory.[9]

Along with many others, Meir ben Baruch's poem and this surviving fast-day liturgy reinforce the need for deep attachment to God and Torah. The texts express both the theological anguish that God's choice of the Jews has led to suffering and the persistent hope that rededication to Torah will bring about redemption at the hand of God.

7.5. A Modern View: Cohen and the Suffering Servant

In the thinking of Hermann Cohen (1842–1918), a German-Jewish philosopher renowned for his penetrating interpretations of the philosopher Immanuel Kant (introduced in chapter 2), Jewish suffering is "[the Jewish people's] tragic calling, for it proves the heartfelt desire for the conversion of the other peoples, which the faithful people feels." God, he insisted, was not responsible for the Jews' suffering. Non-believers were, and the Jewish people nobly bore the brunt of the suffering in order to create a better world.

By the late nineteenth to early twentieth century, when Cohen was writing, Jews had become citizens of the various nation-states of Europe. This change, known as the *Emancipation*, had occurred as a result of the eighteenth-century *Enlightenment* in Europe, when rationalistic and egalitarian philosophies became dominant. The new idea that human reason transcended all ethnic and religious divisions had suggested (at least in principle) that all of humanity might be equal beneath the outward trappings of difference. On the strength of this idea, citizenship had been extended to Jews throughout Europe.

Within the span of a generation or two, citizenship fundamentally altered what was possible for Jews to achieve within European society. Cohen's own life unfolded in Germany in the midst of ongoing political and academic debates regarding the place—and desirability—of integrating emancipated Jews. From this context, when the cataclysm of the Holocaust was not quite yet on the horizon, it was still possible to speak of a shared commitment to the religion of reason.

In his masterpiece, *Religion of Reason out of the Sources of Judaism*, published posthumously in 1919, Cohen critiqued Christian theology as "mak[ing] the mistake of thinking that suffering is not a means but a final end. Thus, it became possible to represent the divine itself as suffering, as human suffering." Cohen acknowledged that in Christianity, Jesus' suffering on the cross was the path to redemption. While he viewed redemption as a very worthy goal, he considered divine suffering to be deeply problematic, because "through this idea, suffering becomes and is the end." If Christians were distracted from the concept of redemption and focused only on the suffering, then suffering would become its own goal. "Moreover," he wrote, "there is a corrupting attraction in the idea that suffering is a divine end in itself." If the highest example of humanity was made to suffer, what happened to the demand that such suffering be eradicated?

Cohen argued against the Christian view of the Suffering Servant, the traditional Christian interpretation that the Suffering Servant was Jesus on the cross. In response, Cohen was suggesting that the *Jewish people* were the Suffering Servant. Jews took up this mission voluntarily, and their suffering was the awful by-product of attempting to do good in the world. This interpretation eliminates the taunt: If the Jews are God's chosen people, why are they subject to such abuse and mistreatment? God is not the author of this suffering. The rest of humanity is its source, for having spurned the message of monotheism carried forth by the Jews.

In the following passage, Cohen argues that the Jewish people have suffered in service of a messianic goal:

> This historical suffering of Israel gives it its historical dignity, its tragic mission, which represents its share in the divine education of mankind. What other solution is there for the discrepancy between Israel's historical mission and its historical fate? There is no other solution but the one which the following consideration offers: to suffer for the dissemination of monotheism, as the Jews do, is not a sorrowful fate; the suffering is rather its tragic calling, for it proves the heartfelt desire for the conversion of the other peoples, which the faithful people feels.[10]

He notes the people Israel's unique role in the world: to help other nations recognize the need to work toward the messianic age, which will mark the end of suffering:

> This historical suffering of Israel gives it its historical dignity, its tragic mission, which represents its share in the divine education of mankind.

Cohen then asks:

> What other solution is there for the discrepancy between Israel's historical mission and its historical fate?

If the people of Israel are God's chosen people, then why have the Jews suffered such abuse at the hands of others? The Jews must have a special mission to fulfill.

There is no other solution but the one which the following consideration offers: to suffer for the dissemination of monotheism, as the Jews do, is not a sorrowful fate.

Cohen argues that there is something inherently noble in fighting for a just cause. Jewish suffering, therefore, has transcendent meaning.

The suffering is rather its tragic calling, for it proves the heartfelt desire for the conversion of the other peoples, which the faithful people feels.

In other words, for Cohen, Jewish suffering is a badge of honor. The Jewish people are called to bring the nations of the world to the knowledge of God in order to improve the world.

Though it is not obvious in this short passage, Cohen made it clear elsewhere that the "conversion" is to monotheism rather than Judaism. That is, Cohen looked to the day when all peoples would recognize that there is one God in heaven and earth. Each individual monotheistic religion is an expression of that truth.

However, we must ask: does Cohen's valorization of Jewish suffering undermine his critique of Jesus' suffering? Could we not just substitute "the Jews" for "Jesus" when Cohen described the problem with exalting the idea of suffering? In other words, whenever the "Suffering Servant," as he terms it, is given a transcendent meaning, then *suffering for its own sake* may also be given transcendent meaning. Doing so may create a situation in which the suffering of others receives theological sanction—which, in turn, may be misused to excuse oneself from responsibility for addressing the suffering of others.

Also, for all that it makes sense of some parts of Jewish history, this line of thought creates intractable difficulties when it comes to the Holocaust. For one, not all of those killed by the Nazis chose to be the bearers of Judaism's transcendent message to humanity. Some had, in fact, converted to Christianity; some had abandoned religion entirely; and some were ambivalent about their Jewish heritage—yet all were killed on account of their bloodline.

7.6. A Modern View: Rubenstein and the Death of God

When the American rabbi and academic Richard Rubenstein first articulated his "death of God" theology in his 1966 book, *After Auschwitz*, it created a stir, in part for its implicit atheism. Rubenstein's work effectively opened the conversation about the Holocaust in theological terms; he was the first writer in English to seriously grapple with the challenge of the Holocaust and be acknowledged and heard.

In Rubenstein's view, the Holocaust represented a genuine departure or disjunction from what had gone before it. No longer would it work to speak of the covenant with God in the same way. If God was responsive to Jewish suffering (as the book of Exodus suggests) and responsible for the well-being of the Jews (as Deuteronomy 6:1–9 has it), then how can the Holocaust be understood as anything less than a breakdown of the covenant?

The following passage, from a later edition of *After Auschwitz* published in 1992, offers a quietly theistic note, though not in the traditional sense of a philosophy that incorporates the idea of divine activity and care:

It must be stressed at the outset of this essay that the death of God is not something that has happened to God. It is a cultural event experienced by men and women, many of whom remain faithful members of their religious communities. No longer able to believe in a transcendent God who is sovereign over human history and who rewards and punishes men and women according to their deserts, they nevertheless render homage to that God in the rituals and liturgy of the community of their inheritance. . . .

In place of a biblical image of a transcendent Creator God, an understanding of God which gives priority to the indwelling immanence of the Divine may be more credible in our era. Where God is thought of as predominantly immanent in the cosmos, the cosmos in all of its temporal and spatial multiplicity is understood as the manifestation of the single unified and unifying, self-unfolding, self-realizing Divine Source, Ground, Spirit, or Absolute. The names proliferate because we are attempting to speak of that which cannot be spoken of or even named, as mystics in every age have understood. Moreover, the cosmos itself is understood to be capable of vitality, feeling, thought, and reflection, at least in its human manifestation. As the Ground of Being and of all beings, Divinity can be understood as the ground of feeling, thought, and reflection. Human thought and feeling are thus expressions of divine thought and feeling, albeit in a dialectical form.[11]

Rubenstein opens by clarifying his death-of-God theology:

It must be stressed at the outset of this essay that the death of God is not something that has happened to God. It is a *cultural* event experienced by men and women, many of whom remain faithful members of their religious communities.

When Rubenstein first introduced his death-of-God theology, he faced negative professional consequences as a rabbi. It was widely assumed that his position rejected a belief in God. Some even accused him of doing Hitler's work for him by removing the theological underpinnings of Jewish practice. Rubenstein's thought is more nuanced than that accusation would indicate, however. The death-of-God construct does not mean that God has withdrawn from the world. Rather, this "death" refers to the death of our traditional understanding of God. Rubenstein says the Holocaust has destroyed the Jewish people's concept of an all-powerful God who watches over us and metes out rewards and punishments as we deserve.

> [I am] no longer able to believe in a transcendent God who is sovereign over human history and who rewards and punishes men and women according to their deserts.

Rubenstein argues that the idea of *transcendence*—the idea that God is over and above us, remote and supremely powerful, judging us from afar—has been discredited by the experience of the Holocaust. Where was God when we needed redemption? This formula is nonsensical, in fact: if God could redeem, how could God not intervene in response to the horrors of the Holocaust? Clearly an interventionist, redeeming, transcendent god-concept is no longer viable.

> They nevertheless render homage to that God in the rituals and liturgy of the community of their inheritance.

Interestingly, however, Rubenstein did not believe that Jews should abandon observance of Jewish practices in the wake of the death of this purportedly outmoded god-concept. Memory and tradition were still powerful forces within the community. He believed that ritual activity still held vital inherent value.

The concept of God's transcendence may be opposed with the idea of *immanence*, the idea that God is close to us, within the universe, keeping things going. Rubenstein suggests that immanence was still a workable framework for thinking about God:

In place of a biblical image of a transcendent Creator God, an understanding of God which gives priority to the indwelling immanence of the Divine may be more credible in our era.

Rubenstein then articulates such an immanent God-concept:

Where God is thought of as predominantly immanent in the cosmos, the cosmos in all of its temporal and spatial multiplicity is understood as the manifestation of the single unified and unifying, self-unfolding, self-realizing Divine Source, Ground, Spirit, or Absolute.

Rubenstein's position here might best be categorized as *pantheism*: God is within all things in the world, animating them and sustaining them. God is the force behind nature, the ground of being that makes all things possible. Here, Rubenstein appears to be extending Spinoza's original idea of the synonymous aspects of God and nature (see chapter 1) to address the problem of the Holocaust. God is not the commanding God of the covenant narratives and certainly not the interventionist God depicted in the Exodus account.

7.7. A Modern View: Jonas Offers a New Mythic Structure

Recognizing that the god-concept of traditional Judaism presented serious difficulties — God did not appear to be an activist God who engages in a covenantal relationship with the Jews, particularly after the Holocaust — the philosopher Hans Jonas, a former student of the existentialist philosopher Martin Heidegger,[12] offered a new mythic structure for understanding God's relationship to the humans God created.

In the beginning, for unknowable reasons, the ground of being, or the divine, chose to give itself over to the chance and risk and endless variety of becoming. And wholly so: entering into the adventure of space and time, the deity held back nothing of itself: no uncommitted or unimpaired part remained to direct, correct, and ultimately guarantee the devious working-out of its destiny in creation. On this unconditional immanence the modern temper insists. It is its courage or despair, in any case its bitter honesty, to take our being-in-the-world seriously: to view the world as left to itself, its laws as brooking no interference, and the rigor of our belonging to it as not softened by extramundane providence. . . .

God's caring about his creatures is, of course, among the most familiar tenets of Jewish faith. But my myth stresses the less familiar aspect that this caring God is not a sorcerer who in the act of caring also provides the fulfillment of his concern: he has left something for the other agents to do and thereby has made his care dependent on them. He is therefore also an endangered God, a God who runs a risk. Clearly that must be so or else the world would be in a condition of permanent perfection.[13]

Jonas' revised myth draws from that of the mystics. The Lurianic Kabbalah, for example, suggested that God voluntarily contracted (*tzimtzum* in Hebrew) to allow the world to exist. Without this contraction of God's perfection, God's creatures would not have room to change and grow.

However, Jonas works out its implications in a different direction. Key to his formulation is the idea of risk: God took a risk in allowing creation to unfold.

In the beginning, for unknowable reasons, the ground of being, or the divine, chose to give itself over to the chance and risk and endless variety of becoming. And wholly so: entering into the adventure of space and time, the deity held back nothing of itself: no uncommitted or unimpaired part remained to direct, correct, and ultimately guarantee the devious working-out of its destiny in creation.

Specifically, God risked allowing everything in the world to unfold without directing the action. No outcome was predetermined; even God did not know how things would turn out in the end. This theological construct thus answers the question of theodicy, how God can be good and yet evil exist (see chapter 2). Chaos and evil exist in the world because God took a risk in engaging in creation.

On this unconditional immanence the modern temper insists. It is its courage or despair, in any case its bitter honesty, to take our being-in-the-world seriously: to view the world as left to itself, its laws as brooking no interference, and the rigor of our belonging to it as not softened by extramundane providence.

Jonas rules out the possibility of God's providence or intervention in the world. On the contrary, he suggests that God explicitly created the world so as not to know the outcome of events in advance, and in such a way that intervention to change those outcomes would not be possible; therefore, the actions of providence could not possibly have any effect. As a result, our sense of being-in-the-world is actually the sense that we are alone in the world, thrown into a situation that has no transcendent source of help.

And, Jonas continues, since God cannot intervene (God is not a sorcerer), God is dependent upon our actions to enact godliness in the world:

God's caring about his creatures is, of course, among the most familiar tenets of Jewish faith. But my myth stresses the less familiar aspect that this caring God is not a sorcerer who in the act of caring also provides the fulfillment of his concern: he has left something for the other agents to do and thereby has made his care dependent on them.

We are, quite literally, God's hands in the world. We are the ones to enact God's will in creation.

He is therefore also an endangered God, a God who runs a risk. Clearly that must be so or else the world would be in a condition of permanent perfection.

If God were controlling everything, then the world would not have any room to be less than perfect. It is less than perfect, but only because God has given us a part to play, however imperfect we are.

7.8. A Modern View:
Greenberg Senses God's Suffering

The modern Orthodox rabbi Irving (Yitz) Greenberg, an activist in intra-Jewish community building as well as Christian-Jewish dialogue and a key figure behind the establishment of the United States Holocaust Memorial Museum in Washington DC,[14] arrived at his understanding of God's role in the Holocaust all of a sudden. As he wrote in *For the Sake of Heaven and Earth*:

In a flash, it became clear that I had been asking the wrong question: Where was God during the Holocaust? I suddenly understood that God was with God's people—("I will be with him in distress" [Psalm 91:15])—being tortured, degraded, humiliated, murdered. Where else would God be when God's loved ones were being hounded and destroyed? The realization hit how much God had been suffering in the *Shoah* [literally "a catastrophe," also the Hebrew name for the Holocaust], but the pain had been infinite as only an Infinite Consciousness could experience it. Then I burst into tears; a surge of pity for God flowed through me. A sense of compassion, a desire to heal the Divine, breached the wall of polarized anger [at God] and complaint that had arisen between us. . . .

Once my thought moved in this direction, I found many traditional sources that explored God's suffering, alongside the covenantal people, in the midst of historical catastrophe. In time, the true central question came to the fore: Why would God take on such powerlessness in history? I came to interpret this divine self-limitation as a strategy to call humans to greater partnership and responsibility. This insight pointed the way to understanding Israel's torment as that of a suffering servant—the victim of humankind's pathologies and misbehavior—a far more acceptable portrayal of the etiology of Jewish victimization. . . .

In a world where evil forces had access to extraordinary power while God did not intervene to guarantee the safety of the covenantal people, in such a world, any absolute insistence that the people Israel live by a higher standard—or else—was inherently abusive. Such a demand was illegitimate, and therefore null and void, because it only exposed Jews to greater danger. . . .

The fundamental basis of covenant is that out of divine love for humanity, God privileges human dignity and freedom over human obedience. Since the divine goal is to achieve the fullness of human life and capacity, then partnership is essential— because freedom and dignity cannot be bestowed; they must be earned. Therefore, God has self-limited and has invited humans to become partners in the process of perfecting the world.[15]

As we discussed in chapter 2, three fundamental concepts about the nature of God and the nature of the world—(1) God is good (2) God is all-powerful (3) Evil is real—are mutually contradictory. Like Rubenstein and Jonas, Greenberg responds to the challenge of the Holocaust by choosing to deny the second of these, that God is all-powerful. Specifically, he suggests that God suffers alongside the Jews:

> In a flash, it became clear that I had been asking the wrong question: Where was God during the Holocaust? I suddenly understood that God was with God's people—("I will be with him in distress" [Psalm 91:15])—being tortured, degraded, humiliated, murdered. Where else would God be when God's loved ones were being hounded and destroyed?

Greenberg postulates an *anthropopathic* god-concept. God experienced the pain of this trauma much in the way humans do, only on a much grander scale:

> The realization hit how much God had been suffering in the *Shoah*, but the pain had been infinite as only an Infinite Consciousness could experience it.

This awareness of infinite suffering enables Greenberg to consider the world from what he imagines is God's point of view. Greenberg's anger with God subsides, for he concludes that God is feeling the same sense of anguish at the cataclysmic events that have befallen the Jewish people:

> Then I burst into tears; a surge of pity for God flowed through me. A sense of compassion, a desire to heal the Divine, breached

the wall of polarized anger [at God] and complaint that had arisen between us. . . .

Once my thought moved in this direction, I found many traditional sources that explored God's suffering, alongside the covenantal people, in the midst of historical catastrophe.

In support of his conclusions, Greenberg points to many traditional sources that describe God as suffering. Among these sources (not specifically cited by Greenberg here) are rabbinic texts in which God, mourning the destruction of the Temple in Jerusalem, is weeping and refusing to be comforted by the angels. The following example offers a startling counterimage for those who think of God as all-powerful and eternally unmoved by fleeting experiences of human emotion:

My soul shall weep in a secret place for pride" (Jer. 13:17). What is meant by "a secret place"? R[abbi] Samuel bar Unia said in the name of Rav: The Holy One has a place where He weeps — it is called the "secret place." And what is meant by "for [your] pride"? R[abbi] Samuel bar Isaac said: For Israel's pride, which was taken from them and given to the heathen. R[abbi] Samuel bar Nahmani said: For the pride of the kingdom of heaven, which was taken away.[16]

Given such images from traditional literature, Greenberg points out the conundrum:

In time, the true central question came to the fore: Why would God take on such powerlessness in history?

In his answer, the affinities and differences between Greenberg and Jonas become apparent:

I came to interpret this divine self-limitation as a strategy to call humans to greater partnership and responsibility. This insight pointed the way to understanding Israel's torment as that of a suffering servant—the victim of humankind's pathologies and misbehavior—a far more acceptable portrayal of the etiology of Jewish victimization.

For both Greenberg and Jonas, God takes on the role of withdrawing from humanity voluntarily, in order to achieve some higher purpose. To Jonas, God takes on this risk at the start of creation "for unknowable reasons." To Greenberg, God chooses this self-limitation in order to give humans a role in the divine plan.

Yet God's choice also led to the people's martyrdom. Because of this, in Greenberg's view, the era of imposition of covenantal responsibilities upon the people without their own choice to abide by the covenant is over, for Jews cannot be asked to obligate their children to be martyrs:

> In a world where evil forces had access to extraordinary power while God did not intervene to guarantee the safety of the covenantal people, in such a world, any absolute insistence that the people Israel live by a higher standard—or else—was inherently abusive. Such a demand was illegitimate, and therefore null and void, because it only exposed Jews to greater danger.

The covenant, therefore, would become voluntary:

> The fundamental basis of covenant is that out of divine love for humanity, God privileges human dignity and freedom over human obedience. Since the divine goal is to achieve the fullness of human life and capacity, then partnership is essential—because freedom and dignity cannot be bestowed; they must be earned.

Therefore, God has self-limited and has invited humans to become partners in the process of perfecting the world.

The scholar Steven Katz has raised some important questions about Greenberg's formulation. Katz argues that a unique event in history should not necessarily have any impact on the theological structure of the covenant:

> Indeed, I am convinced of the historical uniqueness, both in Jewish and in world-historical terms, of the *Shoah*. Having come to this conclusion, however, which I share, for various reasons, with Greenberg and the other post-Holocaust theologians such as Richard Rubenstein and Emil Fackenheim, I do not see any compelling logical or theological reason for equating this historical judgment with a mandate for halakic change. Historical uniqueness is one thing, the legitimating criteria for halakhic change is something else, and I am yet to see, or to have been shown, the bridge from one to the other.[17]

Commenting directly on the question of whether the experience of the Holocaust mandates the creation of a new, voluntary covenant with God, Katz further wrote: "If Hitler could break God's covenantal promises, God would not be God and Hitler would indeed be central to Jewish belief."[18]

Katz makes an important point here. Should Hitler, of all people, be invoked as the catalyst of a new covenant? In Katz's view, doing so only serves to compound the theological problems presented by the Holocaust. To frame the Holocaust as a wholly unique event in the life of God promotes Hitler into a metaphysical force of evil. Would it not be better, theologically speaking, to argue that Hitler's brutality represented a more mundane form of evil, remarkable only in scale and efficiency, but otherwise continuous with other instances of genocide?

7.9. Summary of Views

The *biblical text* told the story of Joseph's forgiveness for his brothers' abuse of him. Joseph's theological interpretation of the events of his life allowed him to forgive. Meritorious though this may be, the interpretation also presents a theological problem. God, in effect, became the author of the suffering, creating hardships in order to bring about a greater good.

For the *liturgical text*, we read "Eileh Ezkarah" ("These I Remember"), a medieval liturgical poem that memorialized the martyrdom of ten scholars in Roman times. The poem suggested that an evil Roman ruler punished the Jews of his day for the crime of kidnapping Joseph, on the theory that justice had not yet been served. Its refrain — "We have sinned, our Rock; forgive us, our Creator" — may indicate an assumption that God had intervened in history; as much as the Romans were to blame for the persecutions, the Jews of the time also had to bear collective guilt for an event that took place in the biblical era.

In the *rabbinic text*, the ancient Rabbis suggested that when faced with tragedy, one should search one's deeds and find where one has sinned, for such events are assuredly examples of God's retribution. Alternatively, God might have allowed the righteous to suffer to make them worthy of passing on the Torah to future generations.

In the *medieval text*, the poet Meir ben Baruch seemed to be pointedly questioning God: What good is it to be Your chosen people, if this also includes the martyrdom of the Jewish sages and desecration of the holy texts? Why is it that Jews are persecuted and You do not intervene? Yet, by its closing lines, "Ask, O You Who Are Burned in Fire" reinforced the need to defend the Torah against such very attacks. In keeping with the martyrological poetry of the era, the poem served a dual purpose: remembering those who died and reinforcing the faith of those who lived. A surviving fast-day liturgical poem from the subsequent century similarly accentuated the need for the people to maintain their attachment to God and Torah.

In the first *modern text*, Hermann Cohen insisted that God was not responsible for the Jews' suffering. Non-believers were, and the Jewish people nobly bore the brunt of the suffering in order to create a better world. Whereas the Christian view held that the Suffering Servant was Jesus on the cross, in actuality (according to Cohen) the Jewish people was the Suffering Servant. Their suffering was the awful by-product of faithfully upholding their mission to spread monotheism—to bring the nations of the world to the knowledge of God.

In the first *text in response to the Holocaust*, Richard Rubenstein posited a "death-of-God" theological construct. This did not mean that God had withdrawn from the world; rather, in his view, the Holocaust had undermined the human concept of an all-powerful God who watches over us and metes out rewards and punishments. If God could redeem us, where was God when we needed redemption in response to the Holocaust? Clearly an interventionist, redeeming god-concept is no longer viable.

In the second *text in response to the Holocaust*, Hans Jonas offered a new mythic structure for understanding God's relationship to the humans God had created. A key concept within his formulation was the idea of risk: God took a risk in creating the world so as not to know the outcome of events in advance, and so that intervention to change those outcomes would not be possible. Therefore, the actions of God's providence could not possibly have any effect.

In the third *text in response to the Holocaust*, Irving Greenberg concluded that God took on the self-limiting role of withdrawing from humanity voluntarily. Since the divine goal is to achieve the fullness of human life and capacity, then partnership is essential—because freedom and dignity cannot be bestowed; they must be earned. Therefore, God self-limited and invited humans to become partners in perfecting the world. In effect, God chose to be a noninterventionist God. Yet God's choice also led to the people's martyrdom. Because of this, the era of imposition of responsibilities upon the people without their own choice to abide by the covenant is over. The Jewish people's covenant with God should be fully voluntary, for people cannot be asked to obligate their children to be martyrs.

7.10. Why Was God Silent during the Holocaust?

We now take up our second question: why was God silent during the Holocaust?

There are multiple possible answers. In fact, in his essay "Theological Reflections on the Holocaust," Michael Rosenak identifies "five theological orientations" relating to the question of divine silence during the Holocaust:

> The first, the most traditional approach, maintains that nothing is wrong at all. While much is awry with the contemporary world and with Jews who have fallen under its pernicious sway, the classic teachings of Torah concerning divine retribution are, if anything, vindicated by the horrendous events. . . .
>
> The second approach we may characterize as stating "Something seems to be wrong." . . . When the response demanded by the situation is understood, the crisis may be overcome and God's presence may again be clearly perceived, from within the pristine tradition of Torah. . . .
>
> A third approach candidly states, "Something is wrong"; there is a flaw in the present Jewish-divine relationship. . . . For the covenant promises that the commanding God is also the God

of our salvation. In the Holocaust world, this, our saving God, was silent. . . .

A fourth position insists, "There is something radically wrong." God's silence during the Holocaust does in fact threaten the entire structure of Jewish faith. Before there can be the authentic and sincere cultural reaffirmations that contemporary Jewry vitally needs, there must be radical re-thinking of faith questions and positions. . . .

Finally, there is the position that states, "The entire theological enterprise of Judaism is wrong." In this approach, the previous responses and questions are thoroughly radicalized in a nontheistic theology.[19]

In response to these various positions, Rosenak suggests two conclusions. First, this variety in possible responses "should help make it clear to us that 'the lessons' of the Holocaust are by no means self-understood or simply derivative from a grasp of the (historical) facts."[20] Second, he argues, it is possible that this diversity may become an entry-point into greater unity within Judaism. As he writes, "Diverse theological positions, while indeed creating controversy and possibly even enmity among Jews, can also foster, if not understanding, at least empathy among them."[21]

7.11. Suffering and the Human-God Relationship

Let us turn to the last question. Should the experience of great suffering cause us to reconsider our relationship to God?

We saw in the rabbinic passage an attempt to explain suffering within a framework of retribution for sin. However, the medieval text rejected this position, lodging a note of protest when the Talmud was burned. Cohen's formulation, on the other hand, made suffering a natural outcome of the Jewish mission to spread monotheism to the world.

In responding to the Holocaust, however, many of the later thinkers argued that something fundamental had shifted in our relationship to God. On account of this unique event, they argued, we are faced with a new moral imperative. Rubenstein saw in it the death of our traditional god-concepts. Similarly, Greenberg argued that the Holocaust altered the terms of our covenant with God. By contrast, Katz protested that invoking the Holocaust as the catalyst of a new covenant only serves to compound the theological problems presented by the Holocaust by promoting Hitler to a metaphysical force of evil.

What, then, can we say with certainty has changed in the wake of the Holocaust? In my view, it is not that something has changed about God, or in our relation to God. We can name all kinds of heinous events in which God has not intervened; that reality has long been with us. Suffering is part of the human condition, and our free will allows us to misbehave in spectacularly awful ways. I think that what makes the Holocaust unique is the failure of philosophy to prevent it. The Holocaust occurred in a country that was well-acquainted with the ideals of the Enlightenment and its moral standards rooted in reason. The Enlightenment led to the Emancipation of the Jews, yet its ideals of freedom and Existentialism's ideals of authenticity were twisted to support murder in service of the master race.

Joseph Soloveitchik (discussed also in 5.6), too, did not believe that the Holocaust or any other heinous event required the Jewish people to rethink their relationship with God. He wrote that the question of the meaning of suffering appears "in two dimensions: the dimension of fate and the dimension of destiny."[22] In the first dimension, that of fate, suffering has no meaning:

[The sufferer's] agonies are devoid of any clear meaning and they appear as satanic forces, as outgrowths of the primal chaos that pollutes the creation whose destiny it was to be a reflection of the Creator. At this stage of perplexity and speechlessness, of numbness of the heart and confusion of the mind, man does not ask at all about the reason for evil and its essence. He simply suffers in silence and is choked by his anguish, which silences his complaint and suppresses questioning and inquiry.[23]

This description of suffering mirrors many of the responses we saw above.

The other dimension of suffering, however, is that of destiny. Then, Soloveitchik argued:

[One's] approach is halakhic [that is, in accordance with traditional Jewish law] and moral, and thus devoid of any metaphysical/speculative nuance. . . . The problem is now formulated in the language of a simple halakhah and revolves around a quotidian (i.e. daily) task.[24]

Embracing destiny, Soloveitchik argued, the Jew does not need to ask metaphysical questions, and instead finds meaning in the performance of Jewish law. So either suffering has no meaning (the dimension of fate) or it is a question best answered by ignoring it in favor of the performance of the law (the dimension of destiny).

I disagree with Soloveitchik on both counts. First, the dimension of fate ignores our own culpability for our actions. Second, the dimension of destiny, while it may offer a way to avoid the theological problem of suffering, falls short in two major ways.

The first concerns the performance of *halakhah*. This system of Jewish law is intended to prevent egregious behavior, unethical actions, and ungodly appetites. While it is a successful guide, it is not foolproof. It is indeed possible to be a "scoundrel within the four cubits of the law" (as the saying goes). We may be completely lawful yet nonetheless cause suffering. Second, if we cause suffering in the course of our lawful behavior, and our lawful behavior is rooted in our theological commitment to *halakhah*, then we have opened the door to giving theological meaning to the suffering of others—and in so doing, *their suffering becomes acceptable to us.*

It is easy to justify someone else's suffering in the context of one's worldview, particularly if the suffering of someone else is precisely what allows one's worldview to be coherent. That insight ought to scare you; it scares me. I think we each have a responsibility to resist that tendency.

Part 4

Is God a Covenantal Partner and Lawgiver — or Might These Roles Be Rethought in the Modern Age?

Chapter 8

What Is the Relationship
between God and Israel?

- How have different strands of Jewish tradition viewed the
  question of the relationship between God and the Jewish
  people?
- What does it mean to enact a covenant with God?
- Is this covenant a metaphor, or is it to be understood literally?

8.1. A Biblical View:
Enacting a Covenant

In the United States, a home sale often involves a formal closing
ceremony, usually with the buyer and the seller, real estate agents,
a lawyer (at least in some states), and a representative from a title
agency. At this ritualized event, all of the documents are signed and
the keys are passed from seller to buyer.

The ancient Israelites had their own methods for engaging in this
kind of sale. Consider, for example, when Abraham bought the cave
at Machpelah for the burial of his wife Sarah in Genesis 23:3–16. This
transaction occurred at an open-air court by the city gate, where the
elders of the city gathered and where business could be conducted:

Then Abraham rose from beside his dead, and spoke to the Hittites, saying, "I am a resident alien among you; sell me a burial site among you, that I may remove my dead for burial." And the Hittites replied to Abraham, saying to him, "Hear us, my lord: you are the elect of God among us. Bury your dead in the choicest of our burial places; none of us will withhold his burial place from you for burying your dead." Thereupon Abraham bowed low to the landowning citizens, the Hittites, and he said to them, "If it is your wish that I remove my dead for burial, you must agree to intercede for me with Ephron son of Zohar. Let him sell me the cave of Machpelah that he owns, which is at the edge of his land. Let him sell it to me, at the full price, for a burial site in your midst."

Ephron was present among the Hittites; so Ephron the Hittite answered Abraham in the hearing of the Hittites, the assembly in his town's gate, saying, "No, my lord, hear me: I give you the field and I give you the cave that is in it; I give it to you in the presence of my people. Bury your dead." Then Abraham bowed low before the landowning citizens, and spoke to Ephron in the hearing of the landowning citizens, saying, "If only you would hear me out! Let me pay the price of the land; accept it from me, that I may bury my dead there." And Ephron replied to Abraham, saying to him, "My lord, do hear me! A piece of land worth four hundred shekels of silver—what is that between you and me? Go and bury your dead." Abraham accepted Ephron's terms. Abraham paid out to Ephron the money that he had named in the hearing of the Hittites—four hundred shekels of silver at the going merchants' rate.

In biblical times, contractual agreements typically followed this formal structure:

- recording who was included in the contract
- identifying the witnesses
- detailing what each party would do
- specifying consequences if the covenant was broken
- defining a shared ritual

Note that in the exchange between Abraham and Ephron, several elements of this covenant structure are present. The covenant was enacted between the two of them; the Hittites at the city gate served as the witnesses; Abraham took possession of the cave after payment was received; and the shared ritual or formal closing process was the payment, made in view of the elders of the gate, at which point possession of the property changed hands.

Other examples of this kind of transactional covenant appear in the Bible. For example, Genesis 31:43–54 describes the covenant between Jacob and his uncle Laban at the point when tensions between the two are high and they decide to part. They make use of this structure to create an agreement to stay out of each other's way:

> Then Laban spoke up and said to Jacob, "The daughters are my daughters, the children are my children, and the flocks are my flocks; all that you see is mine. Yet what can I do now about my daughters or the children they have borne? Come, then, let us make a pact, you and I, that there may be a witness between you and me." Thereupon Jacob took a stone and set it up as a pillar. And Jacob said to his kinsmen, "Gather stones." So they took stones and made a mound; and they partook of a meal there by the mound. Laban named it Yegar-sahadutha, but Jacob named it Gal-ed. And Laban declared, "This mound is a witness between you and me this day." That is why it was named Gal-ed; and [it was called] Mizpah, because he said, "May God watch between you and me, when we are out of sight of each

other. If you ill-treat my daughters or take other wives besides my daughters—though no one else be about, remember, it is God who will be witness between you and me."

And Laban said to Jacob, "Here is this mound and here the pillar which I have set up between you and me: this mound shall be witness and this pillar shall be witness that I am not to cross to you past this mound, and that you are not to cross to me past this mound and this pillar, with hostile intent. May the God of Abraham's [house] and the god of Nahor's [house]"— their ancestral deities—"judge between us." And Jacob swore by the Fear of his father Isaac's [house]. Jacob then offered up a sacrifice on the Height, and invited his kinsmen to partake of the meal. After the meal, they spent the night on the Height.

Here again we see several elements of the covenant structure present: the agreement is between Laban and Jacob; the witnesses are the pillar and the mound of stones; each party will see the pillar and mound and know that they may not cross; if the agreement is broken, then the other may see that act as indicating hostile intent; and finally, the ritual is sealed by offering a sacrifice and having a meal together.

The biblical text includes multiple examples of covenants enacted with God. One such instance is the covenant enacted between Abraham and God in Genesis 15:7–18. In this text, Abraham is referred to as "Abram" because he has not yet been renamed.

Then [God] said to him, "I am God who brought you out from Ur of the Chaldeans to assign this land to you as a possession." And he said, "O lord God, how shall I know that I am to possess it?" Came the reply, "Bring Me a three-year-old heifer, a three-year-old she-goat, a three-year-old ram, a turtledove, and a young bird." He brought all these and cut them in two, placing each half opposite the other; but he did not cut up the bird. Birds of prey came down upon the carcasses, and Abram drove them away. As the sun was about to set, a deep sleep fell upon Abram, and a great dark dread descended upon him. And [God] said to Abram, "Know well that your offspring shall be strangers in a land not theirs, and they shall be enslaved and oppressed four hundred years; but I will execute judgment on the nation they shall serve, and in the end they shall go free with great wealth.

As for you,
You shall go to your ancestors in peace;
You shall be buried at a ripe old age.

And they shall return here in the fourth generation, for the iniquity of the Amorites is not yet complete."

When the sun set and it was very dark, there appeared a smoking oven, and a flaming torch which passed between those pieces. On that day God made a covenant with Abram: "To your offspring I assign this land, from the river of Egypt to the great river, the river Euphrates."

Let's look closely at this exchange. God has just asked Abram to go forth from his father's house to an unknown land. At this point, God makes a formal agreement, a covenant, with him. These are the first elements of that covenant:

Then [God] said to him, "I am God who brought you out from Ur of the Chaldeans to assign this land to you as a possession." And he said, "O lord God, how shall I know that I am to possess it?" Came the reply, "Bring Me a three-year-old heifer, a three-year-old she-goat, a three-year-old ram, a turtledove, and a young bird."

The agreement fulfills the first requirement for a covenant: it is enacted between God and Abram (though no witnesses are recorded). The terms proceed as follows: in exchange for leaving his father's land, Abram will become the father of a great nation and receive the land as a possession. We also learn that the covenant is enacted through a specific ritual:

> He brought all these and cut them in two, placing each half opposite the other; but he did not cut up the bird. Birds of prey came down upon the carcasses, and Abram drove them away. As the sun was about to set, a deep sleep fell upon Abram, and a great dark dread descended upon him.

By this time we can understand that a ritual was needed to enact the covenant. But, we might ask, why did the ritual have to include cutting up animals?

To better understand how a ritual works, let us use an analogy. How do you typically celebrate your birthday? Children in the United States usually celebrate with some combination of a party with a cake with candles, little party hats, balloons, streamers, and presents. The adult ritual is usually a cake with candles. If you do not have cake and candles, have you celebrated your birthday? Having asked this question of college students over the better part of a decade, I can tell you that the consensus is "no." To truly "celebrate a birthday," one would have a cake with candles. But why? What exactly does *celebrating a birthday* have to do with *lighting pastries on fire*? Objectively speaking, there is no connection between the two actions, and yet people do not conclude it really is a birthday celebration until someone has lit a pastry on fire.

The cake analogy, however, tells us something about the nature of ritual: a ritual does not have to make logical sense in order to be meaningful in context. Yes, you can create "reasons" for these elements: the cake is a wish for sweetness in the new year; its round shape denotes the cycle of the year; the burning candles represent the passing of time. But these explanations are usually created after the fact, to justify what is already in place. Each culture has its own symbolic language by which it conveys these eternal messages: the completion of a year, or the start of a new venture, or a celebration of a harvest—or, in this case, the contraction of a covenantal agreement.

Thus, here we see an example in which the ancient Israelites cut animals in half and passed through the carcasses to enact a covenant, for the same reason Americans set pastries alight to celebrate their birthdays. Rituals require a specific and unusual action to mark their occurrence. A ritual like this one was particularly necessary in a society in which literacy was not universal. The ritual itself helped make the event memorable. And if witnesses were later needed, they would be able to easily testify that they recalled the details of such a memorable transaction.

The text continues:

And [God] said to Abram, "Know well that your offspring shall be strangers in a land not theirs, and they shall be enslaved and oppressed four hundred years; but I will execute judgment on the nation they shall serve, and in the end they shall go free with great wealth.
As for you,
You shall go to your ancestors in peace;
You shall be buried at a ripe old age.
And they shall return here in the fourth generation, for the iniquity of the Amorites is not yet complete."

Interestingly, this passage does not follow logically from what has happened up to this point. Why the sudden interjection regarding the future? Why should God tell Abram that his descendants will experience slavery?

There are (at least) two possibilities here. If you believe that the Hebrew Bible is the word of God given to Moses, then these verses represent a prophecy from God. Abram learns that God's hand is present in history, even in the dark moments of his family's experience. Abram should trust in God's providence and not be afraid for the future. On the other hand, if you believe that the Hebrew Bible was written by humans over the course of centuries, then this text appears to give us clues as to its composite nature. There is reason to think that it might be an interjection by an editor (a redactor) who was stitching together the Genesis and Exodus narratives into one continuous history.

Note, for example, that the book of Exodus makes little mention (just the short narrative about Joseph's bones) of the events in the book of Genesis. As an interjection, this text would have helped tie together the narratives in the two books.

The narrative continues:

When the sun set and it was very dark, there appeared a smoking oven, and a flaming torch which passed between those pieces. On that day God made a covenant with Abram: "To your offspring I assign this land, from the river of Egypt to the great river, the river Euphrates."

Jews point to this as the starting point for the creation of the people of Israel. Having made this covenant, Abram, now renamed Abraham, becomes the father of a multitude.

And so it was that the idea of a covenant arose. The nature of that covenant borrowed from the biblical legal agreements made between human beings. It would also come to serve as a structure by which to explain the relationship between God and Israel. The people

Israel would be faithful to God, as evidenced by observance of the commandments, and God in turn would protect and preserve Israel.

8.2. From the Liturgy:
Shabbat Reenacts the Covenant

Among the covenantal commandments the people of Israel would be required to observe is keeping Shabbat (the sabbath). Our next text is a prayer that thanks God for sanctifying Shabbat. As we will see, the prayer is a process that would unfold as a partnership between the Jewish people and God.

This prayer is the *Kiddush* (literally, "sanctification"), which is recited over wine at the start of Shabbat to set the day apart as holy. Note that the arrival of Shabbat includes an interesting paradox: Shabbat will start at a certain time regardless of whether or not the time is set aside as holy; yet humanity is needed to sanctify the time set aside for Shabbat by lighting Shabbat candles and reciting the blessing over wine. In other words, God created the structure of Shabbat, yet God relies on humanity to make a place for holiness in time.

The prayer text that follows, taken from a traditional prayer book, refers to God as Hashem, literally, "the name," an indication that the prayer invokes the name of God but that this name should not be spoken aloud. Other prayer books will substitute the word *Adonai* ("my Lord") for the four-letter name.

Blessed are You, HASHEM, our God, King of the universe, Who has sanctified us with His commandments, took pleasure in us, and with love and favor gave us His holy Sabbath as a heritage, a remembrance of creation. For that day is the prologue to the holy convocations, a memorial of the Exodus from Egypt. For us did You choose and us did You sanctify from all the nations.

And Your holy Sabbath, with love and favor did You give us a heritage. Blessed are You, HASHEM, Who sanctifies the Sabbath.[1]

The opening line is a standard prayer formula:

Blessed are You, HASHEM, our God, King of the universe, Who has sanctified us with His commandments.

For those who have been taught to recite the traditional Jewish blessings in Hebrew, the first line of the prayer — *Baruch ata Adonai, Eloheinu melekh ha-olam, asher kidshanu b'mitzvotav* — is more identifiable in Hebrew than in English. The basic building-block of the Jewish prayer experience, this opening is used in nearly every Jewish blessing.

The traditional prayer's opening formula is also notable, in part, for its shift from second person ("Blessed are You") to the third person ("Who has sanctified us with His commandments"). This shift in voice reflects the idea of God's *immanence* — the sense that God is present here with us, close to us — as well as God's *transcendence* — the sense that God is greater than us, far beyond our reach. Addressing God as "You" is an example of immanence: God can be addressed closely and directly. Referring to God in the third person ("His commandments") emphasizes the idea of God's remoteness. Ultimately, the text is telling us, we are the subjects of a sovereign will, one that transcends our own will.

This immanent/transcendent prayer formula comes from the ancient Rabbis. They experienced both kinds of relationship with God: they desired to be witness to an immediate, immanent God who hears prayer, yet they also knew first-hand how distant God's assistance could be. Their misfortune could feel like divine judgment — or abandonment. *Perhaps the transcendent God had found them wanting?* Thus, their prayer formula reflects this dual understanding: please, God, the transcendent and awesome God, hear our heartfelt prayer.

By contrast, consider two other renderings of this prayer: one from the Reform *Mishkan T'filah*, and the other from Marcia Falk's *Book of Blessings*. *Mishkan T'filah leaves the traditional Hebrew text in place but the* English translation reads: "Praise to You, Adonai our God, Sovereign of the universe, who finding favor with us, sanctified us with mitzvot."[2] Falk's rewrite of the Hebrew text, *N'vareykh et eyn hahayim matzmihat p'ri hagefen*, is translated as "Let us bless the source of life that ripens fruit on the vine."[3] The Reform movement's version was created in order to avoid using the masculine pronoun for God. As a result, the English removes the explicitly transcendent aspect of the prayer. But the Hebrew text is left intact; thus the shift between the second and third-person pronouns remains a part of the prayer, at least for those learned in Hebrew. In the case of Marcia Falk's *Book of Blessings*, however, the change in language reflects a change in theology. Rather than addressing God as a person, this prayer text uses much more abstract language: the workings of nature, rather than a commanding God, receive the blessing.

All three of these versions reflect a different approach to the question of covenant. In the traditional prayer, the worshippers are reaffirming elements of the covenantal agreement: the people of Israel (*am Yisra'el*) will observe God's commandments in exchange for God's providential care. In the Reform version, that same structure is in place, but the shift in the English translation is indicative of the movement's greater willingness to rethink aspects of the covenantal relationship. In Falk's more universalistic rewrite, the idea of covenant is not invoked at all, and the blessing could conceivably be said by someone who does not affiliate with the Jewish community.

The traditional prayer text continues:

[Who] took pleasure in us, and with love and favor gave us His holy Sabbath as a heritage, a remembrance of creation.

Here we have the third person masculine pronoun again.

For its part, *Mishkan T'filah* removes the third person entirely in the English translation—"In love and favor, You made the holy Shabbat our heritage as a reminder of the work of Creation"—though it is retained in the Hebrew.[4] Thus in the Hebrew version at least, the *Mishkan T'filah* addresses the transcendent aspect of God. By contrast, Falk's version in *The Book of Blessings* has "As we hallow the seventh day—the Sabbath day—in remembrance of creation,"[5] never explicitly invoking God.

Note, too, the linkage of Shabbat and the act of Creation in all three versions of the prayer. This is a common theme in Jewish prayer; the *Kiddush* is far from the only prayer to bear this message. As another example, *Veshamru*, a text also used when sanctifying Shabbat, reads:

> The people of Israel shall keep Shabbat, observing Shabbat throughout the ages as a covenant for all time. It is a sign for all time between Me and the people of Israel. For in six days Adonai made heaven and earth, and on the seventh day God ceased from work and was refreshed.[6]

In the traditional prayer, and in the Reform version as well, we see the relationship between God and Israel unfolding through an explicit connection between the Sabbath and creation: Jews are expected to rest on Shabbat, just as God rested. This kind of idea is known as *imitatio Dei*: the expectation that humans should imitate God's ways. In the Falk version, on the other hand, the covenant is not specifically invoked.

Shabbat bears other meanings that intimate the relationship between God and Israel. For example, it is understood as a foretaste of God's redemption at the end of days, which includes the reminder that God redeems slaves. Returning to the traditional *Kiddush* prayer, we see it addresses this subject:

For that day is the prologue to the holy convocations, a memorial of the Exodus from Egypt.

The "prologue to the holy convocations" is a reference to the end of days, when the Messiah will come. It is juxtaposed with "a memorial of the Exodus from Egypt," a look back to the past, to the redemption from slavery at the hand of God.

Another example, intertwined with the idea of Creation, is the foundational idea of *chosenness*. In a Jewish context, this has often been understood to mean that God chose the Israelites to be God's people, although there are other interpretations. Again, from the traditional prayer:

For us did You choose and us did You sanctify from all the nations.

In this line of thinking, one possible answer to the question, "Why did God create the world?" is "In order to give the Torah to the people of Israel." *Miskan T'filah* includes this idea as well: "You chose us and set us apart from the peoples."[7] By contrast, Falk's version omits the idea of chosenness entirely.

Some of those who endorse the idea that "God chose the people Israel" will point to human love relationships as an analogy. We cannot always say why a person chooses another person instead of someone else. Why should God need a reason for choosing Israel? Perhaps this love has no specific reason.

The traditional closing of this prayer surely invokes God's love for the people Israel:

And Your holy Sabbath, with love and favor did You give us a heritage. Blessed are You, HASHEM, Who sanctifies the Sabbath.

In essence, the traditional *Kiddush* prayer thanks God for setting aside the day of Shabbat as a sign of the partnership between the Jewish people and God.

8.3. A Rabbinic View:
Where Is the Evidence of God's Love?

This next text expresses the idea that the Jewish people are especially beloved by God on account of their exemplary behavior—and, by implication, asks God to reward their fidelity in the midst of persecution. It also directs some bitterness at God, despite the loving covenantal relationship in place. The speaker would like to know: how can it be that unbelievers prosper?

> Rava made the following exposition: What [are the allusions] in the verse, "Come my Beloved, let us go forth into the field," etc. (Song 7:12)? "Come, my Beloved," said the congregation of Israel to the Holy One: O Master of the universe, do not judge me as You judge inhabitants of [heathen] cities who are guilty of robbery, unchastity, and taking vain and false oaths. Rather, "let us go into the field" (ibid.)—Come, and I will show You disciples of the wise who [live in rural areas and] study Torah in poverty. "Let us lodge in the villages" (ibid.)—read not *ba-kfarim*, "in the villages," but *ba-koferim*, "among the unbelievers"—come, and I will show You the descendants of Esau, upon whom You have showered much bounty, yet they refuse to believe in You. "Let us get up early to the vineyards" (Song 7:13), meaning to synagogues and houses of study. "Let us see whether the vine hath budded" (ibid.), budded with students of Scripture; "whether the vine blossoms be opened" (ibid.), opened to students of Mishnah; "and the pomegranates be in flower' (ibid.), flowered with students of Gemara; "There will I give Thee my love"—I

will show You the honor and the greatness that are mine, the glory of my sons and my daughters.[8]

At the outset, the ancient Rabbis comment upon a passage in Song of Songs. The opening line here quotes the first few words of its verse:

Rava made the following exposition: What [are the allusions] in the verse, "Come my Beloved, let us go forth into the field," etc. (Song 7:12)?

The verses are imagined as a conversation that took place between *am Yisra'el* (the Jewish people) and God. The "congregation of Israel" (*am Yisra'el*) spoke to God as a beloved, for God had chosen Israel as a partner in the covenant.

"Come, my Beloved," said the congregation of Israel to the Holy One: O Master of the universe, do not judge me as You judge inhabitants of [heathen] cities who are guilty of robbery, un-chastity, and taking vain and false oaths.

Note that each of the aforementioned sins was prohibited in *hal-akhah* (Jewish law). The covenant has guided the people Israel to do what is right and good in the eyes of God; hence this people should not be judged in the same way as inhabitants of other lands.

Rather, "let us go into the field" (ibid.) — Come, and I will show You disciples of the wise who [live in rural areas and] study Torah in poverty.

In other words, these sages were not living in deluxe apartments in the more wealthy metropolis. Devotion to the Torah had a cost, financially and in lost productivity. How then could God shower bounty on unbelievers?

> "Let us lodge in the villages" (ibid.)—read not *ba-kfarim*, "in the villages," but *ha-koferim*, "among the unbelievers"—come, and I will show You the descendants of Esau, upon whom You have showered much bounty, yet they refuse to believe in You.

These next verses provide the evidence as to why God should behave differently:

> "Let us get up early to the vineyards" (Song 7:13), meaning to synagogues and houses of study. "Let us see whether the vine hath budded" (ibid.), budded with students of Scripture; "whether the vine blossoms be opened" (ibid.), opened to students of Mishnah; "and the pomegranates be in flower' (ibid.), flowered with students of Gemara."

The ancient Rabbis particularly prized early arrival at the house of study. They go on to match each stage in budding with a level of study: the tender new buds are the littlest children studying the Hebrew Bible; the next group up studies the Mishnah (a commentary on the Hebrew Bible); and the oldest students are engaged in the Gemara (a commentary on the Mishnah).

> "There will I give Thee my love"—I will show You the honor and the greatness that are mine, the glory of my sons and my daughters.

The people of Israel have devoted their children, sons and daughters, to keeping the covenant. Where is God's tender mercy in return?

8.4. A Medieval View:
Halevi's Defense of the "Despised Faith"

If the covenant means that the Jews are God's chosen people, Jews would often ask themselves, why then have we held such a lowly position in society? Should it not be true that God's favor translates into some kind of advantage for the Jews?

Judah Halevi (c. 1075-1141), a great rabbi, poet, and philosopher of the medieval Golden Age of Spanish Jewry as well as a physician and businessman,[9] addressed this question in *The Kuzari: In Defense of the Despised Faith*. This masterwork of Jewish philosophy is also one of the better examples of *apologetic literature*: literature that formally defends a system of belief against those who would disparage it.

Halevi's defense of Judaism is structured as a conversation between the king of the Khazars and four people he summons, one after another, to speak with him: a philosopher, a Christian, a Muslim, and a Jew (more specifically, a rabbi). On the basis of his four conversations, the king decides to convert to Judaism.

This passage is taken from the rabbi's response to one of the king's questions. The rabbi is speaking to the king about the annual cycle of ritual observance:

> "The Torah did not leave the details of these services up to the individual; everything was carefully prescribed. This is because man is incapable of determining what is necessary to rectify the faculties of the soul and body, or what measure of rest or activity is necessary, or how long the land should produce before it must rest during the *Shemitah* [every seventh year, when the Land of Israel is to lie fallow and all debts are cancelled] and Jubilee years [capping the cycle of seven sevens] or how one should tithe his produce, and so on. God therefore commanded the

observance of the Sabbath and the Festivals and the agriculture laws of the Sabbatical year.

"All these are in remembrance of our Exodus from Egypt and the act of creation. Those two events are similar in that they were both effected by Divine will and did not happen coincidentally or naturally. This is why Scripture states, 'When you inquire about the earlier days which existed before you. . . . Has a nation ever heard the voice of God [speaking from within a fire as you have and survived?] Or has any other god ever miraculously [extracted one nation from the midst of another?]'.

"Shabbat observance, therefore, is inherently an affirmation of God. Further, it affirms the creation of the universe. For one who accepts the commandment of the Sabbath with the intention that the seventh day marked the end of creation has without a doubt affirmed his belief in an ex nihilo creation. In turn, one who has affirmed the creation has also thereby affirmed the blessed Creator."[10]

In Halevi's place and time (Muslim Spain), the laws concerning the *shemitah* and jubilee years were no longer observed. Halevi was living in the Diaspora (anywhere outside the Land of Israel, from which the Jews were exiled and dispersed after the Second Temple's destruction). All laws specifying practices in the Land of Israel—*shemitah* among them—had been suspended in the Diaspora. Nonetheless, the rabbi's speech proceeds on the assumption that these laws will eventually be reinstated and that they are therefore still valid.

"The Torah did not leave the details of these services up to the individual; everything was carefully prescribed. This is because man is incapable of determining what is necessary to rectify the faculties of the soul and body, or what measure of rest or activity is necessary, or how long the land should produce before it must rest during the *Shemitah* and Jubilee years, or how one should tithe his produce, and so on. God therefore commanded the observance of the Sabbath and the Festivals and the agriculture laws of the Sabbatical year."

The rabbi tells the king that God gave the cycle of ritual observance to the Jewish people. God delivered all of the myriad details relating to these laws to Moses, who transmitted them to Joshua, who transmitted them to the next generation, all on down to the ancient Rabbis.

"All these are in remembrance of our Exodus from Egypt and the act of creation. Those two events are similar in that they were both effected by Divine will and did not happen coincidentally or naturally. This is why Scripture states, 'When you inquire about the earlier days which existed before you. . . . Has a nation ever heard the voice of God [speaking from within a fire as you have and survived?] Or has any other god ever miraculously [extracted one nation from the midst of another?].'"

In the rabbi's speech, God is actively involved in history, guiding the Jewish people to worship the one true God. In this sense, the world was created in order for God to enact the covenant with the Jews.

"Shabbat observance, therefore, is inherently an affirmation of God. Further, it affirms the creation of the universe. For one who accepts the commandment of the Sabbath with the intention that the seventh day marked the end of creation has without a doubt affirmed his belief in an ex nihilo creation. In turn, one who has affirmed the creation has also thereby affirmed the blessed Creator."

The rabbi thus concludes that the Jewish people's performance of the commandments both affirms God's sovereignty over all of Creation and reinforces the special relationship enacted by the covenant with the Jews.

This idea appears in other medieval works as well: Maimonides, for example, argued that the commandments help perfect humanity to enable certain individuals to reach the highest levels of contemplation. Halevi, in turn, suggested that the commandments are the evidence of God's love for Israel. The theology behind these concepts is rather clear: God knows what is best for God's beloved people better than humanity, and thus has seen to it that they have the structure they need for proper observance. In other words, God enacted a covenant with the people Israel out of God's great love for them.

8.5. A Modern View:
Soloveitchik's Mathematical Approach

Does the covenant have any objective reality? That is to say, is it reflected in the world around us? Or is it a metaphor, one that we shape to fit the world we encounter?

As we saw, Joseph Soloveitchik (discussed in 5.6 and 7.12) made a distinction between the dimension of fate and the dimension of destiny, and he identified a similar duality in the realm of the covenant as well. In his view, God concluded two covenants with Israel. The first, the Covenant of Fate, enacted in the Exodus from Egypt, was not at all voluntary. "A Jew cannot banish the God of the Jews from his world. Even if he desecrates his Shabbat, defiles his table and his bed, and tries to deny his identity, he will not escape the dominion of the God of the Jews, which follows him like a shadow."[11]

By contrast, the second covenant, formed at Mount Sinai, was voluntary, required careful preparation, and carried with it the experience of Revelation. As Soloveitchik explains: "When the man of destiny stands before the Almighty, he envisions the God of Israel who reveals Himself only with man's approval and invitation. The God of Israel is united with the finite creature only after man has sanctified and cleansed himself from all pollution and longingly and agitatedly awaits this wondrous encounter."[12]

Soloveitchik argues that this second covenant established an a priori relation between the world and the *halakhah*. Specifically, there exists a halakhic ideal that came to us from God through the Revelation to Moses as interpreted by the Rabbis, and each concrete situation in the present world is to be evaluated against this ideal. While the system has grown and changed over time, it nonetheless reflects an unbroken chain of tradition, one faithfully transmitted from one generation to the next.

Soloveitchik delves into this in *Halakhic Man*:

When halakhic man approaches reality, he comes with his Torah, given to him from Sinai, in hand. He orients himself to the world by means of fixed statutes and firm principles. An entire corpus of precepts and laws guides him along the path leading to existence. Halakhic man, well furnished with rules, judgments, and fundamental principles, draws near the world with an a priori relation. His approach begins with an ideal creation and concludes with a real one. To whom may he be compared? To a mathematician who fashions an ideal world and then uses it for the purpose of establishing a relationship between it and the real world. . . . The essence of the Halakhah, which was received from God, consists in creating an ideal world and cognizing the relationship between the ideal world and our concrete environment in all its visible manifestations and underlying structures. There is no phenomenon, entity, or object in this concrete world which the a priori Halakhah does not approach with its ideal standard. When halakhic man comes across a spring bubbling quietly, he already possesses a fixed, a priori relationship with this real phenomenon: the complex of laws regarding the halakhic construct of a spring. . . . When halakhic man approaches a real spring, he gazes at it and carefully examines its nature. He possesses, a priori, ideal principles and precepts which establish the character of the spring as a halakhic construct, and he uses the statutes for the purpose of determining normative law: does the real spring correspond to the requirements of the ideal Halakhah or not?[13]

Here, Soloveitchik has built upon Maimonides' and Halevi's philosophy. According to Maimonides, Moses reached the highest levels of human perfection, and understood how the law and the natural world were in accord. According to Halevi, the commandments were a gift from God reflecting God's special love for the Jewish people. For Soloveitchik, the commandments represent the highest possible understanding of the world, for they give a schema by which to judge events in the world.

Analyzing this passage in parts, from the outset we also see Hermann Cohen's influence on Soloveitchik's work:

Halakhic man, well furnished with rules, judgments, and fundamental principles, draws near the world with an a priori relation. His approach begins with an ideal creation and concludes with a real one.

The idea that the real world is always filtered through preexisting ideals, and must be when determining how to act, is a neo-Kantian formulation Soloveitchik adapted from Cohen (for more on Cohen, see 2.5 and 7.5). However, Soloveitchik's interpretation is also significantly un-Kantian. For Soloveitchik, the Revelation of the *Halakhah*, with its "rules, judgments, and fundamental principles," exists prior to the world and serves as the ideal by which the world may be measured. By contrast, for Kant this Revelation could not be a source of a priori ideals because it was a unique historical event that took place at a certain time and locale; ideals, on Kant's view, were necessarily eternal and unchanging.

Soloveitchik continues:

> To whom may he [Halakhic man] be compared? To a mathematician who fashions an ideal world and then uses it for the purpose of establishing a relationship between it and the real world.

Note Soloveitchik's comparison of *Halakah* to mathematics. This is not the messy process of evaluating legal cases against precedents; rather, the process is much more scientific and precise. Soloveitchik explains:

> The essence of the Halakhah, which was received from God, consists in creating an ideal world and cognizing the relationship between the ideal world and our concrete environment in all its visible manifestations and underlying structures. There is no phenomenon, entity, or object in this concrete world which the a priori Halakhah does not approach with its ideal standard.

Since the Halakhah came directly from God, the world must necessarily line up with it. We should not expect to find areas in which the law falls short. If such an area exists, it is because humanity has failed to discern the divine will.

> When halakhic man comes across a spring bubbling quietly, he already possesses a fixed, a priori relationship with this real phenomenon: the complex of laws regarding the halakhic construct of a spring.

Here, Soloveitchik's view stands in opposition to that of Buber. In 3.5, we saw Martin Buber describe two modes in which one might encounter a tree: *I-It* and *I-You*. Approaching the tree from the perspective of *I-It* was to describe it, to measure it, or to make use of it. This type of relation was the way of the everyday world. Being in an *I-You* relation, on the other hand, is to be fully in the presence of the tree, to be completely aware of it without analyzing it or speaking of it. This moment of standing in front of the tree in all of its "treeness" is like standing before God. Both kinds of being in the world are needed, but only one of them (*I-You*) involves a sense of the Divine.

For Soloveitchik, in contrast, *the I-It relation is actually the pathway to the Divine*. Halakhic man is continually evaluating reality in light of the ideal, to gauge and to analyze how well the concrete world measures up to halakhic ideals.

> When halakhic man approaches a real spring, he gazes at it and carefully examines its nature. He possesses, a priori, ideal principles and precepts which establish the character of the spring as a halakhic construct, and he uses the statues for the purpose of determining normative law: does the real spring correspond to the requirements of the ideal Halakhah or not?

Note that this approach does not include any kind of pragmatic adjustment to the changeable nature of reality; rather, every situation is measured against the ideal of the *Halakhah*. In the case of the spring, for example, halakhic man is evaluating whether it has the proper qualities to be used for immersion for the sake of purification (such as whether it is large enough). Once the covenant at Mount Sinai bestowed upon the Israelites the unique knowledge of God's ideal, they—and we—became obligated to enact that ideal, as closely as possible, through observance of the covenant.

8.6. A Modern View:
Borowitz's Metaphorical Covenant

Perhaps the covenant might be negotiable? Eugene Borowitz (1924–2016), a rabbi who taught for most of his career at the Reform seminary Hebrew Union College, where he influenced generations of Reform rabbis, argued that the commandments were guidelines. The Reform movement itself held that the *Halakhah* is a guideline rather than a binding requirement. To Borowitz, the covenant could be amended and renewed.

Mixed into his Reform identity and ideology was Borowitz's traditional yet multifaceted Jewish upbringing. According to his obituary in the *New York Times*, "He liked to say he was a product of intermarriage—that of his paternal great-grandparents—between two great traditions of Judaism: the cerebral Lithuanian tradition and the more emotional Hasidic tradition."[14] Hasidism, a mystical Jewish movement that originated in Poland in the eighteenth century, was opposed by the *Mitnagdim*, those who disavowed Hasidism and followed the Lithuanian tradition of rationalism. Borowitz incorporated elements of both mysticism and rationalism in his thought.

Here is Borowitz's text, from *Renewing the Covenant: A Theology for the Postmodern Jew* (1991):

> But if Jews could confront their Judaism as Jewish selves and not as autonomous persons-in-general, I contend that they would find Jewish law and lore the single best source of guidance as to how they ought to live. Rooted in Israel's corporate faithfulness to God, they would want their lives substantially structured by their people's understanding of how its past, present, and future should shape daily existence. But as autonomous Jewish selves, they would personally establish the validity of every halakhic and communal prescription by their own conscientious delib-

eration. We would then judge their Jewish authenticity less by the extent of their observance than by the genuineness of their efforts to ground their lives, especially their actions, in Israel's ongoing Covenant with God. The more fully they integrate their Jewish selves, the more fully will every act of theirs demonstrate their Jewishness.[15]

Note that Borowitz has a very different understanding of the structure of the commandments than Soloveitchik. To him, the commandments are not the divine instruction of how to respond to our daily reality; rather, they are "the single best source of guidance as to how [Jews] ought to live." Rather than revealed law, the commandments are useful counsel.

> But if Jews could confront their Judaism as Jewish selves and not as autonomous persons-in-general, I contend that they would find Jewish law and lore the single best source of guidance as to how they ought to live.

Several points here are worth noting. First, observe Borowitz's juxtaposition of the "Jewish self" against the "autonomous person-in-general." In this context, *autonomous* refers to an idea in Kantian thought that a person should act independently, without the structure of external law or the pull of human emotion; rather, one should choose a course of action on the basis of one's own rigorous sense of moral duty. For example, one is to give to the poor out of a sense of duty rather than out of pity for the individual or on account of the laws of one's religion. The "Jewish self" reflects the particular: it is the sense of belonging to a specific people. The "autonomous person-in-general" is the universal: it is the concept of humanity as a whole.

As we saw above, Borowitz drew his language of autonomy from the philosophy of Kant. Kant argued that genuinely ethical behavior could not arise from external laws; one must self-legislate. Therefore, an autonomous self would self-legislate what right behavior looks like, on the basis of a set of duties.

Also, pay attention to the linkage of "law and lore." Here, Borowitz places the two concepts on equal footing. This is a very different formulation from Soloveitchik's mathematical depiction of the *Halakhah*.

Borowitz continues:

> Rooted in Israel's [the Jewish people's] corporate faithfulness to God, they would want their lives substantially structured by their people's understanding of how its past, present, and future should shape daily existence. But as autonomous Jewish selves, they would personally establish the validity of every halakhic and communal prescription by their own conscientious deliberation.

Rather than building a communal consensus regarding practice, Borowitz suggests that each person is to "personally establish the validity of every halakhic and communal prescription." He leaves it to the individual to decide independently what appropriate Jewish practice might look like.

> We would then judge their Jewish authenticity less by the extent of their observance than by the genuineness of their efforts to ground their lives, especially their actions, in Israel's ongoing Covenant with God. The more fully they integrate their Jewish selves, the more fully will every act of theirs demonstrate their Jewishness.

Borowitz's idea of authenticity was likely influenced by the German philosopher Martin Heidegger, who argued that authenticity is being true to one's self rather than listening to what the world has to say about the matter. It has encouraged Jews to follow their own idiosyncratic paths to discover their own sense of covenant. Empowering though this may be, Borowitz's individualism is in tension with Judaism's long history of creative adaptation and reinterpretation at the communal level. If each person decides individually about what is appropriate Jewish practice, then how can the congregation or the community know what constitutes *authentic* Judaism, and in so doing, establish normative behavior? Are there any limits to what qualifies as Jewish practice?

In Borowitz's view, in fact, the covenant now has a threefold aspect. Specifically, as his student Rabbi Dr. Rachel Sabath beit-Halachmi explains, "A Jewish self lives in covenant with God, with the Jewish people (past, present, and future), and with one's self, because of the absolute aspect of autonomy for the modern/postmodern Jew."[16] Rather than being the response to a commanding voice first heard at Sinai, the covenant represents a flexible framework for understanding our responsibility to God, to other Jews, and to ourselves.

8.7. A Modern View: Fishbane's Hermeneutical Theology

It could be that the covenant represents a joining of human action and divine concern. Such is the thinking of the American scholar Michael Fishbane, an eminent contributor to numerous areas of Jewish literature, theology, and philosophy.[17] The connecting thread between these fields is the study of *hermeneutics*: the question of how texts are interpreted.

In early adulthood, Fishbane was affiliated with the Conservative movement and was a founding member and core teacher of Havurat

Shalom, an experimental community cofounded by Arthur Green (see 1.5), but he later made his religious home in Orthodoxy. The scholar and educator Sam Berrin Shonkoff explains: "This shift was fueled by [Fishbane's] ever-deepening faith in traditional Jewish praxis, and his increasing sense that theological sensibilities must be embodied in concrete practices in order to be maximally transformative for the individual and transmissible for the community."[18]

The following passage is drawn from Fishbane's 2008 work, *Sacred Attunement*:

> Through the language of blessings, the inner self is guided to a twofold consciousness; of the fullness, vast and sovereign, *and* the particular occasion, specific and personal. The fullness is the illimitable transcendence of Divinity, the Life of all life, ever exceeding human knowledge and grasp; the particular is the experience of God's immanent actuality as the Life of the life we find in the world we know and intuit. As religious persons, the ideal is to try to live at this crossing point and keep both theological dimensions in mind. The vector moves from the universal whole to specific concrescences of existence, and it keeps one centered on the particulars of naturalness, experienced as the gift of God's all-unnamable "Shall-Be." Such a responsive and dutiful "joining" of heaven and earth with spiritual awareness is the core of Jewish religious praxis, of *mitzvah* [commandments from God], understood here fundamentally as *tzavta* (or "bonding" of human consciousness with Divinity).[19]

One practice of traditional Judaism involves the regular intonation of blessings to respond to the events of everyday life. Blessings exists for all sorts of phenomena, from eating fruit to wearing new clothing to seeing a rainbow. It is in this context that we read the first line of this paragraph:

Through the language of blessings, the inner self is guided to a twofold consciousness; of the fullness, vast and sovereign, *and* the particular occasion, specific and personal.

Fishbane is drawing attention to how the language of blessings invokes God's transcendent reality and God's immanent actuality. As we saw earlier in the chapter (8.2), the standard prayer-formula also includes both transcendent and immanent aspects of the Divine. Fishbane continues:

The fullness is the illimitable transcendence of Divinity, the Life of all life, ever exceeding human knowledge and grasp;

The transcendence of God exceeds human consciousness—great and awesome, larger than we can imagine, more powerful than we can say, and beyond language. And this, in turn, is linked to another, different experience of God:

The particular is the experience of God's immanent actuality as the Life of the life we find in the world we know and intuit.

This immanence is the knowledge of God that is intimate and close to our hearts. God is as near to us as breathing, and experienced in nature as well. Fishbane explains that

As religious persons, the ideal is to try to live at this crossing point and keep both theological dimensions in mind.

To Fishbane, both aspects of God are needed, which means that Jews must stay ever aware of both dimensions.

We have discussed scholars who don't agree with this. Later thinkers, among them Fishbane's contemporaries Richard Rubenstein and Irving Greenberg (both discussed in the last chapter), tend to emphasize God's immanence and reject the idea of God's transcendence. To most post-Holocaust writers, a transcendent, commanding, and redeeming God-concept is no longer tenable. They emphasize instead how God is in the hearts and minds of Jews, as a source of comfort and guidance. Michael Fishbane's insistence on retaining both poles of the traditional god-concept is notable in the postmodern period.

The next sentence introduces the notion of *concrescences*. This term, drawn from biology to describe living organisms that start out as separate beings but eventually grow together, is used in a philosophical sense to mean "a process of becoming, a process of weaving together the 'prehensions' [a primitive form of 'apprehension' meant to indicate 'taking account of' or 'feeling', devoid of conscious awareness] of the actual occasions that are in the immediate past."[20]

> The vector moves from the universal whole to specific concrescences of existence, and it keeps one centered on the particulars of naturalness, experienced as the gift of God's all-unnamable "Shall-Be."

As we become conscious of our experiences, we become aware of the intersection of divine transcendence (in the sense of majesty) and of divine immanence (in the sense of love).

> Such a responsive and dutiful "joining" of heaven and earth with spiritual awareness is the core of Jewish religious praxis, of *mitzvah* [commandments from God], understood here fundamentally as *tzavta* (or "bonding" of human consciousness with Divinity).

To Fishbane, a personal sense of commandedness emerges out of our intuitive awareness of the axial nature of our experience, living as we do at the intersection of God's transcendence and immanence.

8.8. A Modern View:
Hartman's "Autoimmune Disease"

According to the covenant, God is obligated to interact with the people Israel in certain prescribed ways, and the people in turn have a specific set of responsibilities to God. What happens when these ideas get misused?

Donniel Hartman argues that religion can develop an "autoimmune disease" in which the very things that allow a religion to do good in the world (such as enforcing an ethical system or articulating the meaning of our lives) also can attack the foundations of the religion itself, so as to produce negative behaviors (such as ignoring the pain of others or engaging in violence).

In *Putting God Second*, Hartman identifies two types of "monotheistic religions' autoimmune disease": God Intoxication and God Manipulation.

> For the God-Intoxicated person, the awareness of living in the presence of the one transcendent God demands an all-consuming attention that can exhaust one's ability to see the needs of other human beings. This religious personality is defined by strict non-indifference to God. The more we walk with God, the less room we have to be aware of the human condition in general, and consequently, our moral sensibilities become attenuated.
>
> A second manifestation of religion's autoimmune disease, God Manipulation, aligns the identity and the will of the One with the interests and agendas of those who lay claim to God's

special love. Antithetical to God Intoxication, in which God's transcendence shifts our vision away from humanity toward the transcendent One, here the passionate yearning to be loved by the transcendent One unleashes a sinful impulse to control the transcendent. In a paradoxical manner, monotheism, which sought to uproot idolatry, gives birth to perhaps the greatest idolatry of all, the idolatry of human self-intoxication, an idolatry in which God is drafted in the service of human self-interest. Within this way of thinking, we may embrace the obligation to love our neighbors as ourselves, while redefining neighbors to include not those among whom we live but rather the much smaller circle of those who share our particular set of religious beliefs. God Manipulation extends a blanket exemption from truly seeing anyone outside of our religious community.[21]

Hartman avers that God-Intoxicated people ignore the suffering of others. Since they generally view others who are not part of their religious group as "sinners," such people's pain does not register with them as needing a response. Those with this "diseased" understanding are able to walk past "sinners" with eyes turned toward heaven. Hartman impugns this position as a perversion of religious values.

In another passage, Hartman speaks further of the second kind of autoimmune disease, God Manipulation:

This form of auto-immune disease creates a circle of believers that engages in the persecution of non-believers. One is able to inflict all kinds of terror and hurt upon them as a result. Again, it is a perversion of religious ideals to think in these terms.

What is the best defense against these two kinds of autoimmune disease? Hartman proposes the following:

If the exclusive ideal of religious life were to live in a divinely endowed Garden of Eden in which everything we need is bestowed upon us by grace, then gratitude and humility are the sole defining features that a life with God would seem to require, indeed permit. While most monotheistic faiths include a desire to return to a version of this mythic garden at an unspecified end of days, that is not the reality in which we currently reside. The essence of a life with God is thus to effectuate, through our actions and deeds, as close an approximation as possible to a Garden of Eden in this world. Religious life, then, is both a call to humility and a call to *tikkun olam* [repairing the world] by empowered agents fully aware of our responsibility, capacity, and ultimate purpose.[22]

Hartman suggests here that there are three ways to address this problem of religion's autoimmune disease: humility, gratitude, and repair.

First, religious people ought to have a sense of humility, recognizing that it is not possible to replace God's understanding with human understanding. No interpretation of God's law is absolute, and no interpretive enactment of the rules of religious living has the unquestionable endorsement of God behind it. Humanity can get the details wrong. At the same time, religious people need to act with confidence and determination in order to reduce suffering.

Second, religious people ought to express gratitude for those who have something critical to say. As Hartman admonishes: "Do not cast all external critics as hostile enemies. If you do, you will lose a profound resource for moral self-renewal. To the contrary, actively cultivate the voices and embrace the judgments of outsiders who articulate an independent moral standard."[23]

Third, there is a need "to recognize that the tradition itself is flawed and in need of repair, that it permits immoral behavior, practices of the impious and unwise. The tradition thus faces a difficult educational challenge, for is not sufficient merely to declare the primacy of the ethical, which is difficult to assimilate in light of prevailing religious assumptions and norms." Contending that the religious tradition itself must be repaired through the careful work of education, he explains: "The educational system must be geared to cultivate people committed to the standard of the pious, the wise, the just, and the right, and who insist that the tradition live up to this standard as well."[24]

In this context, Hartman argues that the covenant between God and Israel needs to be treated in a very nuanced way. It must be viewed as something more than a metaphor; rules and guidelines are needed to structure Jewish communal living so as to avoid the chaotic state of "anything-goes" (this idea is an implicit critique of the liberal movements within Judaism). At the same time, the covenant should also be treated strictly as a metaphor; otherwise the religious community will decide that they are in possession of exclusive truth and thereby become too rigidly dogmatic in its fulfillment of the commandments (this idea is an implicit critique of the ultra-Orthodox movements). Thus Hartman's critique strikes a balance. The covenant, finally, must be a dynamic concept, one that allows God and Israel to adjust their understanding over time, so as to bring the world closer to the perfection of Eden.

8.9. Summary of Views

In the *biblical text*, we saw that the covenant between God and Israel borrowed from the formal structure of legal agreements made between human beings in biblical times. These agreements recorded who was included in the contract, identified witnesses, detailed what each party would do, specified consequences if the contract was broken, and defined a shared ritual. This structure would come to serve as a framework by which to explain the relationship between God and Israel. The people Israel would be faithful to God, as evidenced by observance of the commandments, and God in turn would protect and preserve Israel.

Among the covenantal commandments the people of Israel were required to observe was keeping Shabbat. We saw how the *liturgical text*, a prayer that thanks God for sanctifying Shabbat, is part of a process that unfolds as a partnership between the Jewish people and God. We noted an interesting paradox: Shabbat will start at a certain time regardless of whether or not the time is set aside as holy; yet humanity is needed to sanctify the time set aside for Shabbat by lighting Shabbat candles and reciting the blessing over wine. In other words, God created the structure of Shabbat, yet God relies on humanity to make a place for holiness in time. In short, the covenant between God and the people requires regular action by the Jews in the form of observance of the commandments.

The *rabbinic text* asks God to reward fidelity. The people of Israel are exemplary; they have devoted their sons and daughters to keeping the covenant. Why, then, are they being treated so brutally by the Roman authorities? Where is God's tender mercy in return? In essence, if the Jews are asked to engage in difficult and dangerous work to keep the covenant, then God ought to be responsible for protecting and caring for them in return.

The *medieval text*, Halevi's masterwork of Jewish philosophy, the *Kuzari*, is structured as a conversation between the king of the Khazars and the four people he summons, one after another, to speak with him: a philosopher, a Christian, a Muslim, and a Jew (more specifically, a rabbi). On the basis of his conversations, the king decides to convert to Judaism. In this text, the rabbi argues that God knows what is best for the people better than humanity, and has seen to it that the beloved people have the structure they need for proper observance. The covenant given to the Jewish people is evidence of God's love for them.

In the first *modern text*, we saw that for Joseph Soloveitchik, the covenant represented the highest possible understanding of the world. A halakhic ideal had come to the Jewish people from God through the Revelation to Moses as interpreted by the Rabbis, and each concrete situation in the present world was to be evaluated against this ideal. Since the *halakhah* came directly from God, by necessity it had to line up with the real world; if the law seemed to fall short, it was because humanity had failed to discern the divine will. As recipients of this divine gift of law, Jews have both a responsibility and an opportunity to enact God's will on earth. Once the covenant at Mount Sinai bestowed upon the Israelites the unique knowledge of God's ideal, they—and we—became obligated to enact that ideal, as closely as possible, through observance of that covenant.

In the second *modern text*, we saw that to Eugene Borowitz, the commandments are not the divine instruction of how to respond to our daily reality; rather, they are "the single best source of guidance as to how [Jews] ought to live." Rather than revealed law, the commandments are useful counsel. Rather than building a communal consensus regarding practice, Borowitz suggested that each person "personally establish the validity of every halakhic and communal prescription"—thus deciding independently as to what appropriate Jewish practice might look like. In this understanding, the covenant becomes threefold: between the Jew and God, between the Jew and fellow Jews, and between the Jew and him or herself.

In the third *modern text*, Michael Fishbane characterizes the transcendence of God as exceeding human consciousness—great and awesome, larger than we can imagine, more powerful than we can say, and beyond language—and links it to the immanence of God—the knowledge of God that is so intimate and close to our hearts, God is as near to us as breathing, and experienced in nature as well. As we become conscious of our experiences, we become aware of the intersection of divine transcendence (in the sense of majesty) and of divine immanence (in the sense of love).

In the fourth *modern text*, Donniel Hartman argued that religion can develop an "autoimmune disease" in which the very things that allow a religion to do good in the world (such as enforcing an ethical system or articulating the meaning of our lives) can also attack the foundations of the religion itself, so as to produce negative behaviors (such as ignoring the pain of others or engaging in violence). Hartman's critique rests on a valorization of balance: too much laxity in observance may create chaos and too much dogmatism may pervert religious values. He presents three antidotes: humility to recognize that one's interpretation of the tradition is not the only possible answer, gratitude in response to those who would raise their voices in protest against unethical religious behavior, and resolution to repair the religious tradition through the careful work of education. The covenant, therefore, must be a dynamic concept, one that allows God and Israel to adjust their understanding over time, so as to bring the world closer to the perfection of Eden.

8.10. Meaning of Enacting the Covenant

Let us return to our second question: what does it mean to enact a covenant with God? It means, at the very least, that there is some sort of framework for the relationship. The covenant specifies what is demanded and what will occur in return. In a sense, it defines the nature of reality itself: is the world tractable in response to our efforts? Is God obligated to us in any meaningful sense? The covenant is an expression of *moral coherence*: the idea that the universe is not completely random, an agglomeration of events without meaning or justice. A covenant represents the reassurance that the world does have a larger structure, a framework of meaning.

It happened once that I served as a teacher at a Jewish day school in a classroom where the previous teacher had left abruptly. The students were distraught, and I needed a way to convince them that they could trust my leadership of the classroom and settle back into learning. We used the covenant structure as a way to formulate our obligations to each other. The covenant-idea worked well in this context: they needed me to guarantee certain behaviors (such as staying as their teacher through the end of the year), and I needed them to guarantee certain behaviors (such as fulfilling their assignments). Having created a covenant document together, we then formulated a ritual to mark the occasion in front of witnesses, which in this case were the principal and the vice-principal. As I recall, the ritual involved passing a chocolate sheet cake between two rows of students and then cutting it into pieces and eating it together.

That said, whereas in this situation the cocreated "covenant" ultimately served as an effective framework for the teacher-student relationship, with regard to the covenant between God and the Jewish people, we have seen several texts argue that God has not been delivering on the divine end of the bargain. Consider, for example, Greenberg's assertion (discussed in 7.10) that the covenant must now be considered voluntary, given that its establishment did not rule out the possibility that a Holocaust could happen. In effect, if the meaning of enacting a covenant is to bind the Jewish people, then God, too, must be bound.

There is another alternative, however: the covenant might become a metaphor, one that asserts that our relationship with God continues to have structure and meaning.

8.11. Covenant as Metaphor

Is the covenant a metaphor? When it is understood as the literal word of God, the commandments become a Jew's indisputable obligation, irrespective of context. It is difficult to justify changing them in any way. How can we presume to alter what is eternal and transcendent? For this reason, it is not surprising that the liberal movements often remove the transcendent aspects of the prayer language. For them, God is an encounter, immediately felt and experienced, rather than a transcendent lawgiver who speaks and commands for all time. The liberal movements prefer the *I-You* relation over Soloveitchik's valorization of the *I-It*.

In my classroom, the covenant I made with my students was indeed real. We cocreated it to be binding on both parties. The students had an active partner with genuine authority over them. It was clear who was in the position to voice commandments. The covenant was also tacked up on the wall of the classroom.

When the covenant is understood as a metaphor, however—which is often the case when the commandments are seen to come from a source other than God, such as the tradition, or human insight—it is generally viewed as malleable. Furthermore, if the covenant is a metaphor, the meaning of that metaphor may shift over time.

In the case of the classroom covenant, the structure offered some flexibility; though the covenant itself did not change, we could agree to a specific interpretation of its precepts. We had created, for example, a series of punishments if either side did not carry out the prescribed duties, and on a few occasions I had to threaten to implement these punishments (more homework) when the students were not fulfilling their requirements (cogent participation in class). This, for its part, led to long discussions of what did and did not constitute breach of covenant.

As a metaphor, the purpose of the classroom covenant was to establish that the students could trust that the classroom experience would be both predictable and meaningful. It became the vehicle for creating that sense of meaning. As a metaphor, it linked our (local, situational) relationship to the (theological, historical) experience of the Jewish people.

Chapter 9

Is It a Binding Covenant?

- How have different strands of Jewish tradition viewed the question of whether God's covenant with the Jewish people is binding for all time?
- Is the covenant binding if the Bible was not revealed by God?
- How can Jews who believe that God gave a binding covenant specifically to the people of Israel exist peacefully in a pluralistic world?

9.1. A Biblical View: Preparing for Revelation

In the opening chapters of the book of Exodus, God redeems the Israelites from their slavery in Egypt. After wandering in the desert, the Israelites are asked to prepare themselves for the Revelation of the Torah at Mount Sinai. Exodus 19:7–17 details the process of preparation necessary for encountering God. Eventually, the people will conquer the Land of Israel in order to settle there and build a community founded on this Revelation.

> Moses came and summoned the elders of the people and put before them all that God had commanded him. Those assembled answered as one, saying, "All that God has spoken we will do!" And Moses brought back the people's words to God. And God

said to Moses, "I will come to you in a thick cloud, in order that the people may hear when I speak with you and so trust you ever after." Then Moses reported the people's words to God, and God said to Moses, "Go to the people and warn them to stay pure today and tomorrow. Let them wash their clothes. Let them be ready for the third day; for on the third day God will come down, in the sight of all the people, on Mount Sinai. You shall set bounds for the people round about, saying, 'Beware of going up the mountain or touching the border of it. Whoever touches the mountain shall be put to death without being touched — by being either stoned or shot; beast or person, a trespasser shall not live'. When the ram's horn sounds a long blast, they may go up on the mountain."

Moses came down from the mountain to the people and warned the people to stay pure, and they washed their clothes. And he said to the people, "Be ready for the third day: [the men among] you should not go near a woman."

On the third day, as morning dawned, there was thunder, and lightning, and a dense cloud upon the mountain, and a very loud blast of the horn; and all the people who were in the camp trembled. Moses led the people out of the camp toward God, and they took their places at the foot of the mountain.

Throughout this passage, Moses is depicted as working as an emissary for the two sides in the agreement. He takes the words of God to the Israelites and the words of the Israelites back to God, as if he were engaged in shuttle diplomacy. Here, he begins by summoning the elders, relaying God's words to them and then relaying their responses to God:

Moses came and summoned the elders of the people and put before them all that God had commanded him. Those assembled answered as one, saying, "All that God has spoken we will do!" And Moses brought back the people's words to God.

The text prompts the question: if God is all-knowing, why does Moses meet with God to communicate the people's wishes?

And God said to Moses, "I will come to you in a thick cloud, in order that the people may hear when I speak with you and so trust you ever after."

Apparently, the people's response, "All that God has spoken we will do!," is pleasing to God, as God is persuaded to come down to the people.

The next step will be for the people to engage in a ritual of purification or sanctification, to purify their souls before their encounter with God. Since the Hebrew Bible did not distinguish between body and soul, in the biblical era a "pure soul" would have been understood as one who had not come into physical contact with a chaotic element such as life-blood or a deathly thing like a corpse. Participating in a purifying ritual would have made sense for a people about to receive Revelation. One would not want chaotic elements to come into contact with the divine energy; that might produce unpredictable and dangerous results.

Then Moses reported the people's words to God, and God said to Moses, "Go to the people and warn them to stay pure today and tomorrow. Let them wash their clothes. Let them be ready for the third day; for on the third day God will come down, in the sight of all the people, on Mount Sinai.

As we saw in 2.2, the biblical word in Hebrew for "pure," *tahorah*, referred to the concept of ritual purity. The root of *tahorah* (*tet-hey-*

resh) means "to be clean, be pure."[1] In the passage here, however, a different word is used. The text states "v'kidashtam hayom," meaning "you shall sanctify yourselves today." The root of this word, *kof-dalet-shin*, means "to be holy, be sacred"; the best-known word with this root is *kodesh*, "holy." This root originally meant "to separate,"[2] implying that holiness involves some kind of separation. In other words, this moment of Revelation includes the idea that the Israelites will not be like all the other peoples, each with their own pantheon of gods. They will be "set apart" in the sense that they will have a special relationship with the Creator of heaven and earth.

The text continues:

> "You shall set bounds for the people round about, saying, 'Beware of going up the mountain or touching the border of it. Whoever touches the mountain shall be put to death without being touched—by being either stoned or shot; beast or person, a trespasser shall not live'. When the ram's horn sounds a long blast, they may go up on the mountain."

Something about God may not be touched: there is this sense of physical separation between the Israelites and the divine presence. The people are to remain at the base of the mountain until the all-clear blast is given. Interestingly, to this day synagogues use a ram's horn as part of the High Holiday services. But its use is not specifically tied to this text. Rather, it recalls the ram Abraham used in place of offering his son Isaac as a sacrifice.

Once again, in what follows, the English "pure" is translating what might better be rendered "holy." Moses warns the people to remain holy:

> Moses came down from the mountain to the people and warned the people to stay pure, and they washed their clothes. And he

said to the people, "Be ready for the third day: [the men among] you should not go near a woman."

The procedures for remaining holy are similar to those for remaining pure. "You should not go near a woman" has been understood to mean that the Israelites are to avoid seminal emissions and menstrual blood. The generative fluids of life belong to the realm of the profane.

On the third day, as morning dawned, there was thunder, and lightning, and a dense cloud upon the mountain, and a very loud blast of the horn; and all the people who were in the camp trembled. Moses led the people out of the camp toward God, and they took their places at the foot of the mountain.

The stage is set for what will happen next: the Israelites will receive a direct Revelation from God.

However, in Exodus 20 (where the Ten Commandments are given) it is not clear what part of the Revelation is said out loud, at what time, where, and to whom. Do the Israelites *directly* hear the whole thing, just part of it, or none of it? Do they, in their fear, send Moses up to talk to God and only hear the commandments from Moses at a later time? Try reading Exodus chapters 19 and 20 and outlining what happens from moment to moment. You will quickly discover that it is not entirely clear.

Nonetheless, in this encounter, the Israelites take on a legal obligation, one that binds the future generations as well to act according to the precepts of Jewish law.

9.2. From the Liturgy: With Great Love

From the perspective of Jewish tradition, God gave the laws and commandments out of a special love for Israel, to show the people the proper way to live. The fact that Jews traditionally viewed the revealed laws as God's gift of love is evident in many Jewish prayers. One such example is the *Ahavah Rabbah* ("Deep is Your Love") prayer from the daily morning service, which stresses the importance of studying Torah and observing its commandments.

The following translation is from the Conservative prayer book *Siddur Sim Shalom for Shabbat and Festivals*:

> Deep is your love for us, Adonai our God,
> boundless Your tender compassion.
> *Avinu Malkenu*, You taught our ancestors life-giving laws.
> They trusted in You;
> for their sake graciously teach us.
> Our Maker, merciful Provider, show us mercy;
> grant us discernment and understanding.
> Then will we study Your Torah, heed its words,
> teach its precepts, and follow its instruction,
> lovingly fulfilling all its teachings.
>
> Open our eyes to Your Torah;
> help our hearts cleave to Your mitzvot.
> Unite all our thoughts to love and revere You.
> Then we will never be brought to shame,
> for we trust in Your awesome holiness,
> and will delight in Your deliverance.
> Bring us safely from the four corners of the earth,
> and lead us in dignity to our holy land,
> for You are the Source of deliverance.
> You have called us from all peoples and tongues,
> constantly drawing us nearer to You,
> that we may lovingly offer You praise,

proclaiming Your Oneness.
Praised are You Adonai, who loves the people Israel.[3]

A series of interlocking ideas—all of them core concerns—are presented here. The first of these is that God loves the people Israel:

Deep is your love for us, Adonai our God,
boundless Your tender compassion.

The second idea is that the commandments, as summarized in Jewish law, are the manifest expression of God's love.

Avinu Malkenu, You taught our ancestors life-giving laws.
They trusted in You;
for their sake graciously teach us.

As Rabbi Reuven Hammer has noted in his commentary on this prayer: "The love that God expresses to us by granting us the Torah is returned as we study and fulfill it in love. This is the worthiest and highest motivation."[4] In other words, the people are to reciprocate God's love by observing God's laws.

The third idea is that God might teach these laws. The prayer requests that God grant the worshipers the capacity to understand God's laws, in order that they might observe them faithfully and correctly.

Our Maker, merciful Provider, show us mercy;
grant us discernment and understanding.
Then will we study Your Torah, heed its words,
teach its precepts, and follow its instruction,
lovingly fulfilling all its teachings.

As a fourth point, the commandments are not merely an expression of God's love; they also provide a way to salvation. In fact, some mystical prayers express the hope that by performing the commandments uniformly and with intentionality, Jews may bring to pass the redemption of the world.

> Open our eyes to Your Torah;
> help our hearts cleave to Your mitzvot.
> Unite all our thoughts to love and revere You.
> Then we will never be brought to shame,
> for we trust in Your awesome holiness,
> and will delight in Your deliverance.

At this juncture, the tie between the commandments and the end of days becomes clearer: the hope is that in time, the performance of the commandments will bring the Messiah.

> Bring us safely from the four corners of the earth,
> and lead us in dignity to our holy land,
> for You are the Source of deliverance.

Several of the prayers in the weekday morning service include this request for the "ingathering of the exiles," as identified by the phrase, "bring us safely from the four corners of the earth." According to this idea, a Messiah will come and end the Jewish people's exile, gathering all of the Jews in the Land of Israel once more. Even after the creation of the State of Israel, the requests remain, because these messianic hopes have not yet been brought to fruition.

The closing section of this prayer also thanks God for having chosen the people Israel to receive the commandments.

You have called us from all peoples and tongues,
constantly drawing us nearer to You,
that we may lovingly offer You praise,
proclaiming Your Oneness.
Praised are You Adonai, who loves the people Israel.

This particular translation of the prayer plays down the aspect of chosenness, however, which is more apparent in the Hebrew. A more literal translation of the final phrase would be "who chooses Israel in love." In essence, the Jews are distinguished from other peoples by having God's "laws of life" to structure and guide them and give their lives meaning.

Because this prayer appears in a Jewish prayer book, there is no consideration of whether other peoples have revealed laws of their own. Rather, this prayer (along with others in the prayer book, such as the Torah blessing) is (subtly, at least in this translation of the prayer) asserting that the Jews are God's chosen people. As Hammer wrote more definitively in his commentary, "'Chosen' is another term for 'love', which was shown by God's designation of the Patriarchs and their descendants to be the people of the covenant."[5] To this way of thinking, the Torah itself is evidence of God's love.

9.3. A Rabbinic View:
God Holds Sinai over Their Heads

The following rabbinic text from the Gemara (commentary on the Mishnah, a discussion of legal questions and pithy sayings redacted in the second to third centuries CE) includes a surprise. In contrast to the prayer above, this passage suggests that the Israelites had to be coerced into accepting the yoke of the commandments:

And they stood under the mount (Exodus 19:17): R[abbi] Abdimi b[en] Hama b[en] Hasa said: This teaches that the Holy One, blessed be He, overturned the mountain upon them like an [inverted] cask, and said to them, "If ye accept the Torah, 'tis well; if not, there shall be your burial." R[abbi] Aha b[en] Jacob observed: This furnishes a strong protest against the Torah. Said Rabba, Yet even so they re-accepted it in the days of Ahasuerus, for it is written [*the Jews*] *confirmed, and took it upon them* [etc.] (Esther 9:27) [i.e.,] they confirmed what they had accepted long before.[6]

Let us take this in pieces to see how to understand it.

And they stood under the mount (Exodus 19:17).

The rabbinic text responds to a small detail in the biblical passage: the word *b'tachtit* can mean "at the foot of" or, possibly, "underneath." Working with the first definition, the Israelites stood "at the foot of" Mount Sinai when they received the Ten Commandments. But if one stretches the meaning a bit and the text is read as "underneath," then the Israelites stood "underneath" Mount Sinai when they received the Ten Commandments. The ancient Rabbis offer an explanation based on this second understanding: the Israelites stood *underneath* Mount Sinai when they were asked to accept the Torah:

> R[abbi] Abdimi b[en] Hama b[en] Hasa said: This teaches that the Holy One, blessed be He, overturned the mountain upon them like an [inverted] cask, and said to them, "If ye accept the Torah, 'tis well; if not, there shall be your burial."

In other words, God lifts up the mountain and holds it over the people's heads. God threatens to drop the mountain on them if they do not accept the Torah! It is an astonishing image.

The text continues:

R[abbi] Aha b[en] Jacob observed: This furnishes a strong protest against the Torah.

Rabbi Aha ben Jacob makes a strong point here: if the Torah was accepted under duress, then it is not actually in force. An agreement made under duress is not a binding agreement. One could use this event to excuse the Israelites (and their descendants, the Jews) from fulfilling the precepts of the Torah. But the Rabbis conclude it is not that simple. They argue that the Jewish people have reaffirmed the covenant since that time, so it nonetheless remains in force.

Said Rabba, Yet even so they re-accepted it in the days of Ahasuerus, for it is written [*the Jews*] *confirmed, and took it upon them* [etc.] (Esther 9:27) [i.e.,] they confirmed what they had accepted long before.

Rabba suggests that this ostensible "out" is not actually an "out," for the Jewish people had reaffirmed the covenant in the days of Queen Esther. Here is Esther 9:26–28:

In view, then, of all the instructions in the said letter and what they had experienced in that matter and what had befallen them, the Jews undertook and irrevocably obligated themselves and their descendants, and all who might join them, to observe these two days in the manner prescribed and at the proper time each year. Consequently, these days are recalled and observed in every generation: by every family, every province, and every city. And these days of Purim shall never cease among the Jews, and the memory of them shall never perish among their descendants.

Note that this passage is actually explaining the origins of the observance of the Jewish holiday of Purim. In that light, one could make the case that the Jews of Shushan (an ancient city in Persia, modern-day Iran, where the Purim story unfolds) are not taking upon themselves the responsibility of observing all the precepts of Judaism. They have merely agreed to celebrate Purim every year.

Rabba, however, argues that the acceptance of Purim is also an acceptance of all of Judaism, for it requires the self-conscious choosing to be associated with the Jews of Shushan in the context of a larger history. Thus, the language of "what they had experienced in that manner and had befallen them" refers not only to the events of the Purim story, but rather to all of Jewish history. An apt analogy might be to how potential converts to Judaism are instructed that Judaism has often been the target of scorn; they must choose to take on that burden if they are to become Jewish.

Despite its neat resolution, the initial suggestion that the Israelites were not entirely free to choose against the Torah might cause us to protest. Given that the Purim story includes a example of how antisemitism can turn deadly, accepting the Torah may well be a death sentence in its own right.

Note too that while Rabba chose the Purim narrative as the example of covenantal rededication, this was not the only possible prooftext. For one, Rabba might have selected the more direct affirmation of the covenant in Deuteronomy 29:9–14:

> You stand this day, all of you, before your God—your tribal heads, your elders, and your officials, all the householders of Israel, your children, your women, even the stranger within your camp, from woodchopper to water drawer—to enter into the covenant of your God, which your God is concluding with you this day, with its sanctions; in order to establish you this day as God's people and in order to be your God, as promised you and

as sworn to your fathers Abraham, Isaac, and Jacob. I make this covenant, with its sanctions, not with you alone, but both with those who are standing here with us this day before our God and with those who are not with us here this day.

Rabba might also have pointed to the more straightforward text of Nehemiah 8:1–18, which relays the details of a rededication ceremony during the rebuilding of the Temple in Jerusalem:

The exiles return to the Land of Israel, read once again from the Torah scroll, and rededicate themselves to the observance of the Jewish holidays. Ezra opened the scroll in the sight of all the people, for he was above all the people; as he opened it, all the people stood up. Ezra blessed the Lord, the great god, and all the people answered, "Amen, Amen," with hands upraised. Then they bowed their heads and prostrated themselves before the Lord with their faces to the ground. (Neh. 5–6)

Perhaps Rabba chose the Purim story because its narrative is set outside the Land of Israel. The Rabbis may have wished to convey that the covenant is operative even outside the boundaries of the Land, even in eras outside the timeframe of the Bible.

9.4. A Medieval View:
Ibn Pakuda and the Duty to Obey

We first met Bachya Ibn Pakuda in chapter 1, noting that he lived in Muslim Spain during a period of fruitful interaction between Jews and Muslims. There, Ibn Pakuda was concerned with reconciling the scientific view of the world with the account of creation in Genesis. We also saw, in chapter 6, how he argued on behalf of predetermination: God directs all things that happen in the world.

Here, Ibn Pakuda argues that the covenant is binding and it is our duty to obey God.

> Whoever meditates upon those of God's graces which are bestowed equally upon him and upon the rest of the creatures realizes his obligation to obey Him in all the different intelligible duties. And whoever contemplates God's special favors to his people and his tribe, His preference for them over the other nations, realizes his obligation to obey God in all the duties imposed by revelation. Whoever reflects upon God's special favors to his kin, which distinguish them from the others, as in the case of the Priests and Levites, realizes his obligation to obey God in all the duties special to his kin. . . . Analogously, whoever is endowed with a special grace of God which distinguishes him among the rest of the people should also bind himself to obey in a special way, different from the obedience of others. This is in addition to his efforts devoted to the general obedience that is common to him and the rest of the people. He should endeavor to do this to the utmost of his ability and power, as an expression of his gratitude to God for the special favor given him. . . .
>
> Whoever fails in his obedience for a special favor done to him is driven to fail further in the special obedience accorded to his kin, and then his tribe, and then he may go on to neglect the Law altogether. And once he deserts the Law, he is no longer bound even by the intelligible duties. When he does not bind himself by the persuasion of the mind, although he is aroused by it and able to understand it, then he loses completely the image of man and he is worse than beasts . . .[7]

First, note that Ibn Pakuda recognizes that it is possible to deduce a set of ethical obligations for all peoples. These obligations exist prior to the specific commandments the Jews have received through Revelation.

> Whoever meditates upon those of God's graces which are bestowed equally upon him and upon the rest of the creatures realizes his obligation to obey Him in all the different intelligible duties.

These are the ethical responsibilities that transcend one's specific religious community. Underlying this portion of the text is the ancient Rabbis' determination that the peoples of the earth are bound by seven Noahide commandments constituting the basic requirements for morality and ethics. The seven ethical obligations include creating a court system and six prohibitions: worshiping idols, using God's name in vain, engaging in sexual immorality, murdering fellow human beings, stealing property, and eating a limb torn from a living animal.

However, in Ibn Pakuda's view, God has shown special love for the Jewish people, by revealing a more extensive system of laws and precepts:

> And whoever contemplates God's special favors to his people and his tribe, His preference for them over the other nations, realizes his obligation to obey God in all the duties imposed by revelation.

Ibn Pakuda grounds the requirement for observance of these laws in the recognition that these laws are a gift of love. Obedience flows from a sense of gratitude. Furthermore, those who are additionally blessed have additional obligations as well:

Whoever reflects upon God's special favors to his kin, which distinguish them from the others, as in the case of the Priests and Levites, realizes his obligation to obey God in all the duties special to his kin.

In ancient Israel, the priesthood was hereditary, from father to son. It was considered an honor to be a priest. Even after the destruction of the Second Temple, families kept track of their lineage, and to this day some Jews maintain the family tradition of tracing their heritage back to the ancient priesthood.

Ibn Pakuda also links intellectual gifts to this obligation to obey God. In his view, those who are particularly gifted in their intelligence and capability have a particular responsibility to go out of their way to distinguish themselves in their obedience to God:

Analogously, whoever is endowed with a special grace of God which distinguishes him among the rest of the people should also bind himself to obey in a special way, different from the obedience of others. This is in addition to his efforts devoted to the general obedience that is common to him and the rest of the people. He should endeavor to do this to the utmost of his ability and power, as an expression of his gratitude to God for the special favor given him.

What happens if someone ignores this responsibility? Are there any consequences for this failure? Ibn Pakuda says yes, there are:

Whoever fails in his obedience for a special favor done to him is driven to fail further in the special obedience accorded to his kin, and then his tribe, and then he may go on to neglect the Law altogether. And once he deserts the Law, he is no longer bound even by the intelligible duties.

Ibn Pakuda is offering a "slippery slope" argument: this small thing leads to that small thing, which leads to something truly awful. This assertion has some warrant from the rabbinic literature; in *Pirkei Avot* 4:2 ("The Sayings of the Forefathers") we are told that one sin leads to another, just as one good deed in response to the commandments leads to another.

But Ibn Pakuda offers something new here as well: the idea that abandoning the revealed Law will also lead a person to abandon the ethical duties that can be derived through reason.

> When he does not bind himself by the persuasion of the mind, although he is aroused by it and able to understand it, then he loses completely the image of man and he is worse than beasts.

In other words, a person's religious obligations will buttress a person's ethical obligations as well. Through observing the smaller, less obvious requirements (such as praying in a specific direction), one learns to temper one's behavior in pursuit of a higher morality.

For Ibn Pakuda, the covenant is indeed binding. Because God has shown the Jewish people such beneficence in bestowing the laws, Jews have an obligation to obey them. Turning away from this heritage is the way of lawlessness.

9.5. A Modern View: Rosenzweig's Universal Love

Franz Rosenzweig (1886–1929), a student of Hermann Cohen, wrote in his masterwork, *The Star of Redemption*, that Judaism's role was to be eternally other—to be a separate people with a unique role to play in the unfolding of world history. Yet at the same time, Rosenzweig did not consider the commandments to be part of a binding covenant.

Revelation does not know of any father who is universal love; God's love is always wholly in the moment and at the point where it loves; and it is only in the infinity of time, step by step, that it reaches one point after the next and permeates the totality with soul. God's love loves whom it loves and where it loves; no question can touch it, for each question will one day have its answer in that God loves, too, even the questioner who thinks he is forsaken by God's love. God always loves only whom and what he loves; but what separates his love from an "all-love" is only a "not-yet"; it is only "not yet" that God loves everything besides what he already loves. His love traverses the world from an always new impulse. It is always in the today and entirely in the today, but every dead yesterday and tomorrow are one day swallowed into this triumphant today; this love is the eternal victory over death; the Creation which death finishes and completes cannot resist it; it must surrender to it at every moment and thus also ultimately in the plenitude of all moments, in eternity.

So apparently there is a narrowness in the concept of God's love as faith understands it: that unlike light, this love does not shine forth in all directions as an essential attribute would do; rather, in a mysterious seizing, it seizes individuals — men, peoples, times, things — unforeseeably in this seizing except for the one certainty that the love will one day seize even that which has not yet been seized. . . . If it seized everything all at once, how would it differ from Creation? For Creation, too, created everything all at once, and so became the everlasting past; a love which would have seized everything to begin with would only be "to-begin-with," only a past, and not what alone transforms love into love present, pure unalloyed present.[8]

Revelation, Rosenzweig is arguing, is a specific incident in the history of a particular people. Therefore, it is not yet an event with universal meaning.

> Revelation does not know of any father who is universal love; God's love is always wholly in the moment and at the point where it loves; and it is only in the infinity of time, step by step, that it reaches one point after the next and permeates the totality with soul.

Furthermore, Rosenzweig is saying, God's love is always just in the present moment. That love is experienced as an event in a moment in time. The very moments of experiencing God's love are potentially infinite in number, but the content of each moment does not spill into the next. What distinguishes and separates the "loved-now" community (the Jews) and the "not-yet-loved" community (the Christians) is the unfolding of time. Not yet, but eventually, at the end of days, the two will merge into a universal love; the whole of creation will be "permeated" with God's soul.

Notice that Rosenzweig does not speak of the content of Judaism as a system of law and observance. Rather, he is addressing the larger, more universal question as to the nature of God, explaining how God could be manifest in multiple religious traditions at once.

> God's love loves whom it loves and where it loves; no question can touch it, for each question will one day have its answer in that God loves, too, even the questioner who thinks he is forsaken by God's love.

The repetitiveness of the language may make this text hard to follow, but the idea itself is fairly straightforward. This sentence answers the question of chosenness: it explains why the Jews are so loved by God as to receive Revelation from God. At this juncture, God loves whom God loves. "One day," however, all will be loved.

Notably, whereas in traditional Judaism (as we saw in this chapter particularly in our liturgical example), the content of God's love is the Revelation of the commandments, for Rosenzweig, there is no content of God's love. This love is apparent only in the Revelation of the presence of God.

> God always loves only whom and what he loves; but what separates his love from an "all-love" is only a "not-yet"; it is only "not yet" that God loves everything besides what he already loves.

The idea of "not-yet" is core to Rosenzweig's philosophy. Elsewhere he wrote: "This existence of the Jew forces upon Christianity in all times the thought that it has arrived at neither the goal nor the truth, but always remains on the way."[9] Eventually, he reiterates here, Christianity will be included in the love that God demonstrates for the people Israel. But at this point, it is a "not-yet."

> His love traverses the world from an always new impulse. It is always in the today and entirely in the today, but every dead yesterday and tomorrow are one day swallowed into this triumphant today; this love is the eternal victory over death; the Creation which death finishes and completes cannot resist it; it must surrender to it at every moment and thus also ultimately in the plenitude of all moments, in eternity.

God is eternally in the present moment, as a presence right now rather than a continuing event. That is to say, an "always new impulse" is God's presence in the world, which enlivens the world (as in

Creation) but has nothing specific to say. And being in the moment means that there is no death.

What, you might ask, does death have to do with this? Rosenzweig fashioned his own synthesis of Jewish and Christian thought: the chosenness of Judaism in the moment meets the Christian idea of God's love overcoming death. He borrowed from Christianity the idea that death may indeed be conquered, but did so without also adopting the Christian belief that following the teachings of Jesus will allow a person to achieve eternal life. For Rosenzweig the covenant is not simply a moment in the history of the Jews; it is the archetype of how redemption will come for all peoples. It is part of the larger synthesis of the world religions yet to come. In the future, God's love will include all peoples:

> So apparently there is a narrowness in the concept of God's love as faith understands it: that unlike light, this love does not shine forth in all directions as an essential attribute would do; rather, in a mysterious seizing, it seizes individuals—men, peoples, times, things—unforeseeably in this seizing except for the one certainty that the love will one day seize even that which has not yet been seized.

Ultimately, God will love all peoples, including the "not-yet" of Christianity.

Here, Rosenzweig explains why the love of Christianity was delayed so that it is presently a "not-yet":

> If it seized everything all at once, how would it differ from Creation? For Creation, too, created everything all at once, and so became the everlasting past; a love which would have seized everything to begin with would only be "to-begin-with," only

a past, and not what alone transforms love into love present, pure unalloyed present.

In this view, Creation and Revelation are closely tied together; both are expressions of God's love. In the case of Creation, God's love seized everything all at once, causing the world to come into being. Revelation, on the other hand, was selective, seizing only a single people rather than all things at all times. Had Revelation seized everything, it would be synonymous with Creation. The unfolding of time would not be able to proceed forward.

Rosenzweig's notion that Judaism's core idea is the intuition of the immediacy of the immanent presence of God (rather than the observance of the structure of the commandments) became a source of inspiration for other Jewish thinkers, particularly Martin Buber and Emmanuel Levinas. For these thinkers, too, the content of the covenant is not the Revelation of laws, but the Revelation of God's presence.

9.6. A Modern View: Novak's Concern for Human Rights

David Novak, an American rabbi who studied under Abraham Joshua Heschel at the Jewish Theological Seminary, affirms that God engaged in a binding covenant with the Jewish people. In this section, we will read from two of his writings, the first explaining how the concept of covenant works and the second elucidating how God's covenant with the Jews creates the basis for universal human rights.

Novak asserts in *The Jewish Social Contract* that the idea of covenant in the Bible has five possible meanings. Two of these types of covenant are much more important than the others:

The term *berit* [covenant] is used in Scripture to designate five kinds of interpersonal relationships: (1) a relationship between

God and humans; (2) a relationship between humans themselves; (3) a relationship between God and Israel or the Jewish people; (4) a relationship between Jews themselves; (5) a relationship between Jews and gentiles. . . .

Despite the fact that the term *berit* is used to designate all five of the relationships mentioned above, there are only two such covenants that could be termed *"the* covenant" (*ha-berit*) in the pure sense of that term. First there is the *Noahide covenant*, which is God's perpetual relationship with humankind after its near destruction in the Flood, from which only Noah and his family survived as the progenitors of humankind restored. That relationship is consummated by the perpetual human acceptance of what can be seen as God's universal law (and what some have called "natural law"). Then there is the *Sinaitic covenant*, which is God's relationship with Israel, consummated by the revelation of the Torah at Mount Sinai. Conversely, the other three covenants—those between humans, between Jews, and between Jews and non-Jews—all require one of these *master covenants* as their past or background, their foundation or ground, and their future or foreground. Both of these master covenants are seen as being perpetual (*berit olam*), so that the Noahide covenant is called "everlasting" (Genesis 9:6) and the Sinaitic covenant is called "everlasting" (1 Chronicles 16:17). . . .

As for the relation of the two master covenants themselves, the Noahide covenant and the Sinaitic covenant, one could arguably assert that the Sinaitic covenant presupposes the Noahide covenant, not as its ground but as a necessary precondition for its acceptance by humans. That is, if Israel had not considered itself bound by the universal law of God perpetuated by the Noahide covenant with humankind on earth, it would have been in no position to conscientiously accept the more singular law of God revealed at Sinai to it and for it.[10]

Let's look at this text in greater detail:

> The term *berit* [covenant] is used in Scripture to designate five kinds of interpersonal relationships: (1) a relationship between God and humans; (2) a relationship between humans themselves; (3) a relationship between God and Israel or the Jewish people; (4) a relationship between Jews themselves; (5) a relationship between Jews and gentiles. . . .

As noted in the last chapter, the idea of covenant appears in multiple forms in the biblical text. In Novak's view, the covenant is a lot like a contract, yet it also requires a shared universe of meaning in order to be enacted. Specifically, he suggests that a covenant presupposes monotheism: "From the scriptural evidence," Novak writes, "we see that Abraham could enter a covenant with some people but not with others. This means that at least some people in his world were worshipers of this one universal God, too."[11]

According to Novak, two of the covenants described in the Bible, the *Noahide* and the *Sinaitic*, are particularly important:

> Despite the fact that the term *berit* is used to designate all five of the relationships mentioned above, there are only two such covenants that could be termed *"the* covenant" (*ha-berit*) in the pure sense of that term. First there is the *Noahide covenant*, which is God's perpetual relationship with humankind after its near destruction in the Flood, from which only Noah and his family survived as the progenitors of humankind restored. That relationship is consummated by the perpetual human acceptance of what can be seen as God's universal law (and what some have called "natural law"). Then there is the *Sinaitic covenant*, which is God's relationship with Israel, consummated by the revelation of the Torah at Mount Sinai.

The first of these two covenants, the *Noahide covenant*, which specifies that God will not destroy the earth ever again, is with all peoples. The second of these two covenants, the *Sinaitic covenant*, is with a specific people that God has singled out from among all the other nations. Novak argues that these two covenants provide the context for all the other covenants:

> Conversely, the other three covenants — those between humans, between Jews, and between Jews and non-Jews — all require one of these *master covenants* as their past or background, their foundation or ground, and their future or foreground.

That is to say, these two covenants function as the past, present, and future of all other covenantal agreements. They are the *past*, because they necessarily came first; they are the *present*, because they define how the covenant is enacted at the time that it is enacted; and they are the *future*, because they define how the covenant will be understood. Consequently, these two types of covenant are perpetually binding:

> Both of these master covenants are seen as being perpetual (*berit olam*), so that the Noahide covenant is called "everlasting" (Genesis 9:6) and the Sinaitic covenant is called "everlasting" (1 Chronicles 16:17).

Which of these two covenant agreements serves as the foundation of the other?

> As for the relation of the two master covenants themselves, the Noahide covenant and the Sinaitic covenant, one could arguably assert that the Sinaitic covenant presupposes the Noahide covenant, not as its ground but as a necessary precondition for

its acceptance by humans. That is, if Israel had not considered itself bound by the universal law of God perpetuated by the Noahide covenant with humankind on earth, it would have been in no position to conscientiously accept the more singular law of God revealed at Sinai to it and for it.

The Noahide covenant made the Sinaitic covenant possible.

In an earlier piece, "Religious Rights in Judaic Texts," Novak builds the argument that the particularistic Sinaitic covenant was a necessary precursor to the emergence of the concept of universal human rights.

> The Noahide covenant and its law are the minimal conditions for the emergence and development of this more specific covenant [the Sinaitic covenant], but they are not rich enough in detail and intensity to suffice for the fuller life with God on earth required by the historicity of the human condition. That historicity consists of singular events and their celebration that can only be the subject of the memory of a singular community among others in the world. The Noahide covenant involves the generality of nature; it does not supply content. It presents negative limits but not the positive claims that can only be made by persons historically situated in a community. Nevertheless, this covenant is considered to be ultimately for all of humankind. Thus God informs Abraham at the very moment of his initial call to him that "all the families of the earth shall be blessed through you" (Genesis 12:3). The covenant is of universal significance, even if at present it is only a matter of local experience and practice. Minimally, this means that the moral standards of this community are defensible as being in the interest of universally valid human rights.[12]

This first covenant is the background by which the covenant with the Israelites may be understood. The narrative history in the Bible and its interpretation provide the structure by which Jews are to understand their ethical obligations. These, in turn, are God's response to the needs of a specific community—that is, Abraham and his descendants—for rules and laws.

Let us look more closely.

> The Noahide covenant and its law are the minimal conditions for the emergence and development of this more specific covenant, but they are not rich enough in detail and intensity to suffice for the fuller life with God on earth required by the historicity of the human condition.

As we saw in 9.4, the ancient Rabbis held that all other peoples were expected to follow the seven Noahide commandments. While these commandments, in the context of a covenant with God, provided the basic outline for ethics, in and of themselves they were not enough. To move from ideas of basic decency toward the creation of "a kingdom of priests," a more detailed covenant was needed. Thus, God singled out a people for a greater commitment:

> That historicity consists of singular events and their celebration that can only be the subject of the memory of a singular community among others in the world.

God engaged in a covenant with the Jewish people so that the community could create reinforcing social structures for observing the holidays related to historical events. By reenacting each event through the holiday (as is done at Passover with the Seder and at Shavuot with study), the community reaffirms its commitment to the commandments gained through this historical revelation. Note too Novak's claim: what is universal *must first* come from the particular; it must arise in a specific time and place.

Novak then elaborates on why the Noahide commandments were not sufficient:

> The Noahide covenant involves the generality of nature; it does not supply content. It presents negative limits but not the positive claims that can only be made by persons historically situated in a community.

The "negative limits" define what may not be done, but they do not create a structure for understanding and enforcing human rights. On the other hand, "positive claims . . . made by persons historically situated in a community" may be treated as actionable, enforceable rights. This shift from a general idea of ethics to a fully formed, clearly defined legal system is only possible in the context of repeated relational interactions; that is to say, it only happens in a community.

> Nevertheless, this covenant is considered to be ultimately for all of humankind. Thus God informs Abraham at the very moment of his initial call to him that "all the families of the earth shall be blessed through you" (Genesis 12:3).

In other words, the smaller, tightly defined space of a covenantal community served as the incubator for the idea of universal human rights. Note Novak's repeated reference to the biblical text. Eventually, Abraham's covenant will become the guideline for all of humanity.

> The covenant is of universal significance, even if at present it is only a matter of local experience and practice. Minimally, this means that the moral standards of this community are defensible as being in the interest of universally valid human rights.

Novak is proposing that human rights are built upon the foundations of the biblical text, made valid by it even for those who do not accept its authority. Even if the other peoples of the world do not follow these laws now, the way to their universalization is modeled by the Abrahamic covenant. It is, in a sense, another (yet different) way of expressing Rosenzweig's "not-yet": the Jewish people's role is to serve as an example of how human rights grow out of religious community. The pull of the binding covenant is God's demand upon the Jews to create the context for universal human rights.

9.7. Summary of Views

In the *biblical text*, we learned how the Israelites in the Sinai desert prepared themselves for encountering God and experiencing the Revelation of the Torah. This moment of Revelation includes the idea that the Israelites will not be like all the other peoples, each with their own pantheon of gods. They will be "set apart" in the sense that they will have a special relationship with the Creator of heaven and earth. Essentially, the Israelites will take on a legal obligation, one that binds the future generations as well: to act according to Jewish law.

The *liturgical text* thanked God for having chosen the people Israel (*am Yisra'el*) to receive the commandments, and requested that God grant the worshipers the capacity to understand them. The Torah itself is evidence of God's love. The laws are a gift, providing the structure by which the people can live life in accordance with God's will. Since the people are to reciprocate God's love by observing the laws, the prayer entreats God to help the worshipers comprehend them so they may be observed faithfully. Furthermore, the binding covenant is also a pathway to salvation. Some mystical prayers express the hope that by performing the commandments uniformly and with intentionality, Jews may bring to pass the redemption of the world.

The *rabbinic text* included a surprise: in contrast to the prayer above, it suggested that the Israelites had to be coerced into accepting the yoke of the commandments. Each generation thereafter has faced a similar compulsion, so to speak. The mountain of the history of the Jews has been held over each Jew's head: would you accept the Torah or be buried here?

In the *medieval text*, Ibn Pakuda argued that while certain ethical responsibilities transcend one's specific religious community, God demonstrated special love for the Jewish people by revealing the system of laws and precepts to the Jews. Ibn Pakuda grounded the requirement for observance of these laws in the recognition that they are a gift of love. The people's obedience is to flow from a sense of gratitude.

In the first *modern text*, Rosenzweig disavowed the idea that the commandments were part of a binding covenant, the product of a direct revelation from God. Rosenzweig did not speak of the content of Judaism as a system of law and observance. Rather, he addressed the larger, more universal question as to the nature of God, explaining how God could be manifest in multiple religious traditions at once. In the case of Creation, God's love seized everything all at once, causing the world to come into being. Revelation, on the other hand, was selective, seizing only a single people — the Jews — rather than all things at all times.

In the second *modern text*, Novak argued that two of the covenants described in the Bible, the Noahide and the Sinaitic, are particularly important, because they constitute the ground on which all other covenant agreements are rooted. Consequently, these two types of covenant are perpetually binding. Originally, all peoples were expected to follow the seven Noahide commandments, but in and of themselves these were not enough. To move from ideas of basic decency toward the creation of "a kingdom of priests," a more detailed covenant was needed. Therefore God singled out a people—Abraham and his descendants—for a greater commitment that would be binding for all time. Even if the other peoples of the world do not follow these laws now, the way to their universalization is modeled by the Abrahamic covenant. The pull of the binding covenant is God's demand upon the Jews to create the context for universal human rights.

9.8. Is the Covenant Binding if the Bible Was Not Revealed by God?

Returning to the second question posed at the outset, is the covenant binding if the Bible was not revealed by God?

Even before the time of the Enlightenment, a number of secular philosophical arguments have been made against the authority of the Bible and its claim of a binding covenant. In 1.8, for example, we noted that Benedict Spinoza argued against the Bible's claim to authority on the basis of Revelation. He suggested, rather, that Moses was the author of the Torah, and that Moses had a specific set of social and political goals in mind. Therefore, the Torah's authority is confined to a certain time and place.

Another philosopher, Immanuel Kant, argued that Revelation itself cannot be the source of binding authority, because it is experienced as a historical event. To Kant, faith is either true faith, grounded in universal, eternal ideals unrelated to time and place (in which case a historical narrative is not necessary) or it is historical faith, grounded in particular events (in which case it is not universal). The Bible may well suggest ethical laws (such as "do not murder") which are consonant with reason, but its authority is nonetheless insufficient on its own to compel compliance.

Instead, Kant argued, we human beings are to employ the moral ideal autonomously. We are to take on the role of lawgiver, acting in the manner of God and legislating for ourselves the best response, which is to act from a sense of duty. An individual should freely choose to do his or her duty, and should feel compelled to do so without needing the incentives and disincentives of historically given law, such as is found in the *halakhah*.

How do modern and postmodern Jewish thinkers respond to this challenge? We saw, in 9.6 above, Novak's response to this philosophical tradition. Novak argues for universal ethics grounded in the provisions of the biblical text. In his view, in fact, the very idea of universal ethics emerges out of a particular historical situation: the covenant between God and Israel. For Novak, that covenant, including the structure of the *halakhah*, is still fully binding.

Other modern Jewish thinkers, such as the neo-Kantian German-Jewish philosopher Hermann Cohen (see s 2.5 and 7.5), also contend that a religiously derived system of ethics is needed to define moral rules and behaviors. Like Novak, Cohen believes that Judaism is the source of the idea of a universal ethics, but in Cohen's case, it is an ethics grounded in reason rather than Jewish religious law. In essence Cohen distinguishes the ritual and civil laws of the Bible, which he considers not to be binding, from those laws that specifically relate to ethics, the true binding elements of the covenant.

Thus, when it comes to whether the covenant is binding even if the Bible was not revealed by God, some thinkers reaffirm that it was in fact revealed, while others believe it (or at least portions of it) must be upheld because of its essential contribution to universal ethics.

9.9. Existing Peacefully in a Pluralistic World

How can Jews who believe that God gave a binding covenant specifically to the people of Israel exist peacefully in a pluralistic world? Can we maintain that other nations have received commandments from God as well?

Personally, I believe that other religious traditions do have a genuine sense of God's will, regardless of whether or not it is expressed as a series of commandments or rules, and it is important to communicate this understanding when the context is right for such an exchange. For example, when I served a previous congregation, an imam at a local mosque in our town once asked me whether Jews believe that other nations may be in possession of prophecies from God. I thought for a moment, and then replied, "Yes, our foundational texts do mention prophets of other lands. We are aware of the possibility of prophecy among all nations."

I said this because in Jewish tradition the Torah is not the only source of revealed law. Although the Five Books of Moses are considered to hold the greatest authority, all books of the Hebrew Bible are valid sources of halakhic or legal material. Other prophets, appearing in the later biblical books, can therefore be a source of new legal material; it does not all have to come from Moses. In addition, the Torah mentions prophets who are non-Israelite peoples. For example, Numbers 22:5 speaks of "Balaam, son of Beor in Pethor, which is by the Euphrates." Balaam is clearly not an Israelite, yet he speaks with God, uses the Tetragrammaton when referring to God, and makes true pronouncements of the future—all of which are consistent with the practices of Israelite prophecy.

Meanwhile, the imam nodded, and then asked a second question: "Why, then, do you not follow the instructions of the prophet Mohammed?" Again, I thought for a moment before responding: "Our texts tell us that we should not follow the prophets of other nations."

One example of this would be the following Midrash: "Should a person tell you that there is wisdom among the nations believe it. . . . That there is Torah among the nations—do not believe it."[13] The Jewish tradition acknowledges that other nations possess wisdom, but the Torah, that unique body of God's laws, is ours alone.

My second response to the imam delighted him as well: it was the very answer he was seeking. In wondering why Jews did not heed the message of Mohammed, I think he was concerned that we had rejected these teachings as false (which in essence would be a rejection of him and his beliefs), rather than as foreign (which is to embrace our tradition without rejecting him or his beliefs).

Such discussions are potentially very fruitful. In this case, our two congregations started a regular exchange, with events such as a Ramadan break-the-fast at the mosque and a Passover festival service at the synagogue, that continued after I had left that pulpit. I have engaged in similar work in my new congregation as well: we have rejoiced together with Muslim friends at Thanksgiving services and cried together at vigils after violence has been committed against our coreligionists.

It is both useful and helpful to find ways to read our tradition so that we can exist peacefully in a pluralistic world. Furthermore, we have a responsibility to find and communicate these kinds of "theological shorthand" positions. They allow us to support genuine tolerance, as well as engage with the deeper thought of other religious traditions.

Chapter 10

How Should the Revealed
Law Be Understood?

- How have different strands of Jewish tradition understood how to interpret the revealed law?
- When did a literal understanding of the revealed law become normative for many ultra-Orthodox Jews?
- Can we strike a balance between tradition and innovation in our approach to the Torah?

10.1. A Biblical View: It Is Not in Heaven

In Deuteronomy 30:11–20, Moses reassures the Israelites that they are up to the task of interpreting the revealed laws:

> Surely, this Instruction which I enjoin upon you this day is not too baffling for you, nor is it beyond reach. It is not in the heavens, that you should say, "Who among us can go up to the heavens and get it for us and impart it to us, that we may observe it?" Neither is it beyond the sea, that you should say, "Who among us can cross to the other side of the sea and get it for

us and impart it to us, that we may observe it?" No, the thing is very close to you, in your mouth and in your heart, to observe it.

See, I set before you this day life and prosperity, death and adversity. For I command you this day, to love your God, to walk in God's ways, and to keep God's commandments, God's laws, and God's rules, that you may thrive and increase, and that your God may bless you in the land that you are about to enter and possess. But if your heart turns away and you give no heed, and are lured into the worship and service of other gods, I declare to you this day that you shall certainly perish; you shall not long endure on the soil that you are crossing the Jordan to enter and possess. I call heaven and earth to witness against you this day: I have put before you life and death, blessing and curse. Choose life—if you and your offspring would live—by loving your God, heeding God's commands, and holding fast to [God]. For thereby you shall have life and shall long endure upon the soil that God swore to your fathers Abraham, Isaac, and Jacob, to give to them.

In this text, the laws' intelligibility is an important point. The laws must be understandable, and their fulfillment attainable. Otherwise, if the commandments are not easily understood, once Moses is no longer available to elucidate them, the question of authority will arise: to whom should the Israelites turn when they need to have them explained? Furthermore, how will they go about extending the laws' reach to new situations?

Note that this text, taken in isolation, appears to suggest that any one of the Israelites can engage in interpretation. However, when it is read alongside the rest of the Torah narrative, it turns out that the vast majority of individual Israelites are *not* granted the power to determine the meaning of this law. Exodus 18:25–26 describes the court system Moses created for adjudicating cases arising from the laws:

> Moses chose capable deputies out of all Israel, and appointed them heads over the people—chiefs of thousands, hundreds, fifties, and tens; and they judged the people at all times: the difficult matters they would bring to Moses, and all the minor matters they would decide themselves.

The laws are intended to be intelligible for the *magistrates*. Their intellect will be more than sufficient for the task.

Note: it is possible that Exodus 18 and Deuteronomy 30 have two different authors, and that the two did not know one another. In that case, Exodus 18 is intentionally hierarchical whereas Deuteronomy 30 is explicitly democratic. The composite document, however, makes it clear that the magistrates were to perform the role of interpreting the revealed laws.

The next portion of our passage details what each party was to do, as well as some of the consequences:

> See, I set before you this day life and prosperity, death and adversity. For I command you this day, to love your God, to walk in God's ways, and to keep God's commandments, God's laws, and God's rules, that you may thrive and increase, and that your God may bless you in the land that you are about to enter and possess.

God would be the people's ruler, and the Israelites, in turn, would follow God's commandments. Here, the covenant is structured as a choice: one may choose whether or not to fulfill its terms. However, it appears that the stakes were stacked fairly high in favor of compliance. If the Israelites obeyed the laws, there would be blessings, such as the ability to thrive in the land that had been promised. Disobedience, on the other hand, carried with it a heavy penalty of curses.

Earthly covenants of the Ancient Near East reflected a profoundly lopsided balance of power: the sovereign lord dictated the terms to the population of the vassal states. Similarly, this covenant is offered as a choice, but is also presented as an expression of the divine will:

> But if your heart turns away and you give no heed, and are lured into the worship and service of other gods, I declare to you this day that you shall certainly perish; you shall not long endure on the soil that you are crossing the Jordan to enter and possess.

The Israelites were not to worship other gods; the covenant was intended to be an exclusive contract.

If this stipulation seems surprising, keep in mind that in the context of Israelite history, this outcome was not a given. In fact, some biblical scholars maintain that the Israelite religion started out as *monolatrous*, meaning that the people were worshiping one God above all other gods that were worshiped. Eventually, the Israelite religion became *monotheistic*: the people worshipped the singular God and denied the reality of all others. As the biblical scholar Bernard Levinson explains: "The religion of Israel reflected by Deuteronomy in the pre-exilic period [w]as in many ways a 'Near Eastern' religion. This applies preeminently to the original theology of the text, which like all religions of its time and place, viewed its god as presiding over a 'divine council' of lesser deities. . . . But once radical monotheism became the Jewish norm in the Second Temple period . . . the original 'Israelite' view gradually became 'foreign' and unintelligible."[1] Thus in its original context, the text of Deuteronomy likely reflected a monolatrous rather than a monotheistic worldview.

Why are the heaven and earth called as witnesses, when in fact they cannot witness events?

> I call heaven and earth to witness against you this day: I have put before you life and death, blessing and curse.

Calling the heaven and earth as witnesses may have been a way for a newly monotheistic people to ensure that the great powers of nature could not be taken for other gods. In this light, "heaven and earth" may be interpreted as an all-inclusive term to indicate "all of the things that God created," in the sense of Genesis 1:1, "when God began to create the heaven and the earth." Thus, the text fulfills the requirements of the covenant structure (witnesses are named) but it does not admit the existence of other gods (for the witnesses are actually a metonym for all of Creation).

Returning to our text, the next two sentences reaffirm the positive consequences of upholding the revealed law:

> Choose life—if you and your offspring would live—by loving your God, heeding God's commands, and holding fast to [God]. For thereby you shall have life and shall long endure upon the soil that God swore to your fathers Abraham, Isaac, and Jacob, to give to them.

Here we are told yet again that the revealed law involves a choice: one may choose to heed the commandments or choose to ignore them. But this choice is also presented as profoundly consequential: it is the choice between life and death. Therefore, it becomes imperative that the given commandments are comprehensible, interpretable by the magistrates, and translatable into a legal system. This system will become the organizing principle upon which communal Jewish life is founded.

10.2. From the Liturgyv This Is the Torah

In one seemingly small moment at the end of the Torah service on Monday, Thursday, and Shabbat, the community of worshipers makes a profound theological statement: the text of the Torah scroll is directly linked to the experience of Revelation at Mount Sinai.

A congregation's reading of the *sefer Torah* (hand-sewn parchment scroll with the first five books of the Bible handwritten in block Hebrew letters) usually includes considerable ceremony; in many congregations, it is paraded through the congregation as a sign of honor. After the scroll has been read, but before it is returned to the ark, the congregation rises and someone is called up to the *bimah* (the pulpit) to lift it. That person holds the scroll overhead to show the assembled congregation the handwritten text, and then brings it back down to allow it to be rolled tightly and dressed in its ceremonial coverings.

In many Conservative congregations, at the time the Torah is held aloft, the following text from *Siddur Sim Shalom* is sung in Hebrew:

This is the Torah that Moses set before the people Israel: The Torah, given by God, through Moses.

In these moments, a foundational experience is being reenacted by the congregational community, as Rabbi Reuven Hammer explains in his companion commentary to *Siddur Sim Shalom*:

This is the Torah. Deuteronomy 4:44 As the Torah is lifted, these words are spoken. In many places it is customary to point at the scroll with the little finger or with the *tzitzit* [tassels typically affixed to the prayer shawl], emphasizing that *this* is the Torah.

...*given by God.* From Numbers 9:23. Added to Deuteronomy 4:44 in order to express our belief in the divine nature of the Torah. It was presented by Moses, but represents God's will. We express our belief in the divine nature of the Torah.

... *Through Moses.* Although the Torah is divine, it is often called ... *Torat Moshe,* the Torah of Moses. It is through Moses that the word of God came to us. The Torah is God's word as filtered through the consciousness of Moses and other prophets.[2]

The statement the community sings when the Torah is held aloft is actually a composite text drawn from the Bible. In context of the first quoted text, from Deuteronomy 4:44, Moses is giving a series of speeches before his death, recapping the history of the Israelites' wandering and admonishing them to stay faithful. "This is the Torah" in this context refers to the series of laws he is about to restate.

The second text, drawn from Numbers 9:23, reads in full: "On a sign from God they made camp and on a sign from God they broke camp; they observed God's mandate at God's bidding through Moses." In context, the quote is indicating that the Israelites moved when God told them to move and encamped when God told them to encamp. The liturgy quotes the last clause, which could alternatively be translated as "from the mouth of God, by the hand of Moses," essentially asserting that God dictated the text to Moses the scribe.

Thus it is that in one seemingly small moment at the end of the Torah service, the congregational community makes a profound theological statement: the text of the Torah scroll is directly linked to the experience of Revelation at Mount Sinai.

In effect, the "This is the Torah" ritual renders the abstract theological concept (Moses received Revelation from God) into a concrete object: *this object here* is the Torah that Moses received from the mouth of God. A visual representation of that moment is thereby reenacted over and over, in every Torah service, before the congregation.

In addition, the symbol of this Revelation from God is given profound reverence. The Torah becomes a placeholder for the role of God within the community. Although the Torah is not worshiped—for that would be idolatry—it is given a role of honor, as the representative of God's love for the Jewish people.

10.3. A Rabbinic View:
Halakhah according to the Rabbinic Majority

After receiving the Ten Commandments in the presence of the Israelites, the Bible says that Moses climbed Mount Sinai to spend forty days alone with God. According to rabbinic tradition, during this time Moses learned both the *written Torah*, the text of the first five books of the Hebrew Bible, as well as the *oral Torah*, the rabbinic commentary on those books, which appears in sources like the Mishnah. As the Midrash states: "When the Holy One came to give the Torah to Israel, he uttered it to Moses in its order, Scripture and Mishnah, Talmud and *Aggadah* [midrashic stories], as is said 'The Lord spoke all these words' (Exod. 20:1)."[3]

The *halakhah* (system of Jewish law), growing out of the intersection of the written and oral Torah, is the product of nearly two millennia of discussion and scholarship. As such, *halakhah* has become so specialized that it is often exceedingly difficult to pinpoint the principles by which it is decided. As the talmudic scholar Rabbi Adin Steinsaltz notes: "Hundreds of principles are employed in halakhic Decision Making. Some are general principles that apply in all cases, and some apply only to isolated instances. . . . One major principle, in arriving at a halakhic decision, is that the Babylonian Talmud takes precedence over the Jerusalem Talmud or any other rabbinic source . . . but there are exceptions.[4]

The ancient Rabbis, for their part, believed that the *halakhah* should be determined according to rabbinic majority ruling. By means of the following talmudic story, drawn from the Babylonian Talmud, the Rabbis assert this right—and claim that God is pleased with their approach to halakhic decision-making:

It has been taught: "On that day, Rabbi Eliezer used (lit., "replied") all the arguments (lit., "replies") in the world, but they did not accept [them] from him. He said to them: "If the Halakhah is in accordance with me, let this carob tree prove [it]." The carob tree was uprooted from its place one hundred cubits—and some say four hundred cubits. They said to him: "One does not bring proof from a carob tree."

He then said to them: "If the Halakhah is in accordance with me, let the channel of water prove [it]." The channel of water turned backward. They said to him: "One does not bring proof from a channel of water."

He then said to them: "If the Halakhah is in accordance with me, let the walls of the House of Study prove [it]." The walls of the House of Study leaned to fall. Rabbi Yehoshua rebuked them, [and] said to them: "If Talmudic Sages argue with one another about the Halakhah, what affair is it of yours (lit., 'what is your nature')?" They did not fall, out of respect for Rabbi Yehoshua; but they did not straighten, out of respect for Rabbi Eliezer. And they still remain leaning.

He then said to them: "If the Halakhah is in accordance with me, let it be proved from Heaven." A [heavenly] voice went forth and said: "Why are you [disputing] with Rabbi Eliezer, for the Halakhah is in accordance with him everywhere?" Rabbi Yehoshua rose to his feet and said: "It is not in heaven."

What does "it is not in heaven" [mean]?

Rabbi Yirmeyah said: That the Torah was already given on Mount Sinai [and] we do not pay attention to a [heavenly] voice, for You already wrote in the Torah at Mount Sinai: "After the majority to incline."

Rabbi Natan met Elijah [and] said to him: "What did the Holy One, blessed be He, do at that time?" He said to him: "He smiled and said: 'My sons have defeated Me, My sons have defeated Me.'"[5]

As our narrative opens, the ancient Rabbis have been arguing about the purity of the oven of Akhnai, which had come into contact with a dead thing. The specifics of this debate are not our concern here. Rather, our focus is on how the Rabbis dispute the broader question: "the Halakhah is in accordance with me." As we reread the opening text, note that the ancient Rabbis knew full well that carob trees could not uproot themselves. Nor could water flow backwards, or the walls of the rabbinic academy lean upon command. Rather, this story is structured along the lines of a folktale. Like the three bears or the three wishes or any other group of three in the folktale genre, here we have three proofs: the carob tree, the stream, and the academy walls.

It has been taught: "On that day, Rabbi Eliezer used (lit., 'replied') all the arguments (lit., 'replies') in the world, but they did not accept [them] from him. He said to them: "If the Halakhah is in accordance with me, let this carob tree prove [it]." The carob tree was uprooted from its place one hundred cubits—and some say four hundred cubits. They said to him: "One does not bring proof from a carob tree."

Rabbi Eliezer appears to be a minority of one in this argument. All the other Rabbis seem to be taking the opposite side, as Rabbi

Eliezer always speaks by himself, mostly trying to convince "them," the group of mostly unnamed Rabbis.

The uprooted tree's movement indicates that heaven—i.e., the original source of Revelation—agrees with Rabbi Eliezer. Unfazed, the other Rabbis counter that the miracle of the carob tree is not adequate proof.

> He [Rabbi Eliezer] then said to them: "If the Halakhah is in accordance with me, let the channel of water prove [it]." The channel of water turned backward. They said to him: "One does not bring proof from a channel of water."

We might admire the other Rabbis' tenacity in this debate, as the first two events occurring in the natural world support Rabbi Eliezer. So does the third event:

> He [Rabbi Eliezer] then said to them: "If the Halakhah is in accordance with me, let the walls of the House of Study prove [it]." The walls of the House of Study leaned to fall. Rabbi Yehoshua rebuked them, [and] said to them: "If Talmudic Sages argue with one another about the Halakhah, what affair is it of yours (lit., 'what is your nature')"? They did not fall, out of respect for Rabbi Yehoshua; but they did not straighten, out of respect for Rabbi Eliezer. And they still remain leaning.

Rabbi Yehoshua's rebuke of the walls indicates that the Sages interpreted all three miracles as supporting Rabbi Eliezer's position. Now we reach the climax of the story:

> He then said to them: "If the Halakhah is in accordance with me, let it be proved from Heaven." A [heavenly] voice went forth and said: "Why are you [disputing] with Rabbi Eliezer, for the

Halakhah is in accordance with him everywhere?" Rabbi Yehoshua rose to his feet and said: "It is not in heaven."

Finally, a heavenly voice weighs in on this dispute, making it clear that Rabbi Eliezer is correct in his assessment of the *halakhah*. Note that Rabbi Yehoshua's response line, "It is not in heaven," comes from Deuteronomy 30:12 (which we read in section 10.1). Rabbi Yehoshua is claiming that God agreed to let humans decide these matters; therefore, God should stay out of the dispute.

The text then asks itself the very question underlying Rabbi Yehoshua's interpretation:

What does "it is not in heaven" [mean]?
Rabbi Yirmeyah said: That the Torah was already given on Mount Sinai [and] we do not pay attention to a [heavenly] voice, for You already wrote in the Torah at Mount Sinai: "After the majority to incline."

Rabbi Yirmeyah's statement appears to be a rebuke to the heavenly voice: no meddling allowed! The Torah is now in the hands of the Rabbis, the majority of whom clearly disagree with Rabbi Eliezer's assessment. Thus, even if his ruling is in keeping with *halakhah* in its most ideal, purest form, the final judgment will not be made on that basis. For their supporting proof, the Rabbis say, "You already wrote in the Torah at Mount Sinai: 'After the majority to incline.'"
In conclusion:

Rabbi Natan met Elijah [and] said to him: "What did the Holy One, blessed be He, do at that time?" He said to him: "He smiled and said: 'My sons have defeated Me, My sons have defeated Me.'"

The testimony of the prophet Elijah indicates that God was pleased with their insistence that the *halakhah* will be determined according to majority ruling.

In effect, the ancient Rabbis were making a theological statement about human agency in response to Revelation. They seemed to have recognized that some of their interpretations challenged the plain meaning of the texts in fundamental ways. Arguing with the voice from heaven, they insisted that decisions concerning the revealed law should be made by majority rule of their own rabbinic body.

Consider another story found in the Babylonian Talmud.:

Rab Judah said in the name of Rab. When Moses ascended on high, he found the Holy One, blessed be He, engaged in affixing coronets to the letters. Said Moses, "Lord of the Universe, Who stays Thy hand?" [i.e., is there anything wanting in the Torah that these additions are necessary?] He answered, "There will arise a man, at the end of many generations, Akiba b. Joseph by name, who will expound upon each tittle heaps and heaps of laws." "Lord of the Universe," said Moses; "permit me to see him." He replied, "Turn thee round." Moses went and sat down behind eight rows [and listened to the discourses upon the law]. Not being able to follow their arguments, he was ill at ease, but when they came to a certain subject and the disciples said to the master, "Whence do you know it?" and the latter replied, "It is a law given unto Moses at Sinai," he was comforted.[6]

We may be amused by the narrative of Moses' ego getting bruised and then assuaged. Nonetheless, the ancient Rabbis were aware that it is a difficult business to remain true to a foundational text such as the Torah while also adapting to the concrete cases that will arise in the course of making use of such a document. American government faces the same problem: the founders of the United States of America could not have imagined that their Constitution would eventually be used as a source text for rulings on questions of Internet privacy. It does, though, as modern determinations are rooted in the language of the original text.

The story of Moses in Akiba's academy illustrates how the law grows and changes over time. As a result, decisions made in Rab Judah's era would not be intelligible to earlier generations, even to a figure as great as Moses. In both narratives, the specific text of the revelatory event (i.e., the voice from heaven, or the Revelation that Moses received directly) is refracted through the interpretative lens of the later Rabbis who may reframe it or otherwise change its meaning.

By including these stories in the Talmud, the ancient Rabbis were trying to balance continuity and change in the context of a revelatory tradition. Presumably, they were very aware of what was at stake in this process. On the one hand, innovation must necessarily be discouraged, for how can one improve upon the word of God? Even those who don't agree with the idea that the Torah is "from the mouth of God" might still feel the weight of tradition and have trouble conceiving of its being changed by ordinary individuals like us. In changing it, the tradition would no longer be what was received, but rather become some new hybrid thing. On the other hand, how can it adapt to current circumstances? Ideas are the technology of the mind: just as our tools change over time to become more effective and precise in creating the outcomes we seek, so, too, do our ideas become more effective and more precise: how to rule, how to administer justice, how to communicate, and the like. That is not to say that the progress of humanity is assured or that it always climbs upward, but once an idea is invented, it becomes an option to choose. Indeed, we see an example in Moses' own administration of the laws. At first, Moses hears every case himself. Later, in Exodus 18, his father-in-law Jethro gives him some management advice: create a system of magistrates.

Not surprisingly, Moses heeds his father-in-law's advice: a superior technology drives out the inferior one.

The ancient Rabbis faced this challenge, in fact one we all face: what happens when we learn a new truth, one that changes how we understand our past? How do we adapt a received tradition, particularly one with the force of Revelation behind it, while at the same time conserving it?

In these passages, the revealed law is subject to the interpretative process and subject to majority will. Elsewhere the Talmud similarly states: "Where there is a controversy between an individual and a group, the *Halachah* follows the group."[7] The minority voice is also preserved, however, on the understanding that it may later prove to be correct. (The United States judicial system likewise records and preserves dissenting opinions, which may be used as support in later cases.) The Rabbis thus instituted a system by which the *halakhah* could grow and change (since they gave themselves permission to interpret it), but could also retain its authority and be kept consistent (since majority decision-making would ostensibly weed out idiosyncratic rulings).

Adin Steinsaltz identifies other interesting aspects of "halakhic Decision Making." For one: "The *halakha* is in accordance with the opinion of Rabbi Yehoshua in disputes with Rabbi Eliezer"[8]—apparently, the oven question was not their only argument, and Rabbi Yehoshua was consistently the victor in their disputes. Steinsaltz points to various halakhic exceptions to the rabbinic majority rule, among them: "The authoritative version of the Bible, from which Torah scrolls as well as scrolls of the Prophets and the *Megillot* are copied, is the Masoretic tradition consolidated in tenth-century Tiberias, even where it contradicts the Talmud."[9] Here we additionally see that certain specific texts have come to receive greater weight than other texts. All in all, the tradition has been flexible enough to adapt to shifting values but conservative enough to resist rapid change.

10.4. A Medieval View:
Saadia on Why Prophecy Is Needed

Saadia Gaon ("Saadia the Genius," the usual title given to leaders of academies in his era, 882–942), argued that Revelation was necessary for humankind. There were "two ways to religious truth"—reason and Revelation—and "both ways [were] essential: reason because without it superstitious ideas will proliferate; Revelation because not everyone can arrive at the truth by speculation."[10] In the following text, from his seminal philosophical work, *The Book of Beliefs and Convictions*, Saadia explained specifically why Revelation was imperative:

> There are people who contend that [humanity does] not need prophets, and that their Reason is sufficient to guide them aright according to their innate cognition of good and evil. I, therefore, subjected this view to the test of true reasoning, and it showed me that if things were as they make out, God would know it better and would not have sent us prophets, for He does not do things which have no purpose. Then I reflected still more deeply and found that mankind is fundamentally in need of the prophets, not solely on account of the revelational laws, which had to be announced, but also on account of the rational laws, because their practice cannot be complete unless the prophets show us how to perform them. Thus, for instance, Reason commands gratitude towards God for the blessings received from Him, but does not specify the form, time, and posture appropriate to the expression of such gratitude. So we are in need of prophets. They gave it a form which is called "Prayer"; they fixed its times, its special formula, its special modes and the special direction which one is to face when praying.[11]

If you think long and hard about what is the right thing to do, would you, by virtue of your own reasoning skills, be able to figure out what is good and what is evil without having to resort to prophecy? If you would say yes to this question, then you might be among the "people who contend that humanity does not need prophets":

> There are people who contend that [humanity does] not need prophets, and that their Reason is sufficient to guide them aright according to their innate cognition of good and evil.

Saadia fundamentally disagreed with this position. In his estimation, some questions require prophecy to resolve. The next part of the text details why:

> I, therefore, subjected this view to the test of true reasoning, and it showed me that if things were as they make out, God would know it better and would not have sent us prophets, for He does not do things which have no purpose.

His first reason has to do the nature of God. If God is a perfect being, and as such does not engage in unnecessary activities, then God would not have sent prophets if they were not needed. There must be some aspect of ethics that is not readily discerned.

> Then I reflected still more deeply and found that mankind is fundamentally in need of the prophets, not solely on account of the revelational laws, which had to be announced, but also on account of the rational laws, because their practice cannot be complete unless the prophets show us how to perform them.

Here Saadia makes a different kind of claim: though we can deduce some things by our reason, we cannot map out the entire structure of religious ethics on our own. Some parts are unknown to us in the absence of Revelation:

> Thus, for instance, Reason commands gratitude towards God for the blessings received from Him, but does not specify the form, time, and posture appropriate to the expression of such gratitude.

He makes an assumption: offering a prayer of thanksgiving to God is in fact a rational act. In his view, we encounter the world as a gift, and it is therefore rational—and therefore knowable without instruction--to think we have an obligation to express gratitude for the blessings of that encounter. What form that gratitude should take, however, is not given by reason.

> So we are in need of prophets. They gave it a form which is called "Prayer"; they fixed its times, its special formula, its special modes and the special direction which one is to face when praying.

Prophecy, Saadia concludes, helps fill in those gaps for us. In his view, the prophets settled questions that could not be discovered through reasoning. Through their teachings, it is possible to know God's will.

Furthermore, Moses, the prophetic lawgiver, is clearly not deemed to be the only source of Revelation. Saadia agrees with the ancient Rabbis that God revealed both the written and the oral Torah. In other words, in his concept of Revelation, Saadia invokes the most expansive meaning of "Torah," including the full corpus of Jewish canonical texts.

The receipt of Revelation does not mean, however, that there is no need for reason. For Saadia, Revelation is not merely a dictation of rules to follow blindly without understanding. Rather, Revelation fills in the gaps in humanity's knowledge, providing the information we would not be able to deduce without the benefit of prophecy.

10.5. A Modern View:
Steinberg on Who Is Fit to Interpret Revealed Law

Milton Steinberg (1903–50), the preeminent Conservative rabbi who authored *Basic Judaism* and *As a Driven Leaf* (the best-selling Jewish novel about the heretical ancient rabbi Elisha ben Avuya), took issue with the ancient Rabbis' fiats concerning who was fit to interpret the revealed law.

Before we get into the particulars of his views, we need to know the rather startling conclusion of the oven of Akhnai story we read in section 10.3, in which Rabbi Eliezer's opinion had been vindicated by heaven but rejected by the majority.

> They said: "That day they brought all the objects that Rabbi Eliezer had declared ritually pure and burned them in a fire, and they voted (lit., "were counted") about him and they excommunicated (lit., "blessed") him.

After deciding the fate of the oven, the ancient Rabbis excommunicated Rabbi Eliezer for his views! Excommunication is rare in Jewish practice, but it does exist, as a form of shunning. It may be reversed; the excommunicated individual may be readmitted to the community upon repenting for the alleged misbehavior.

Keep in mind that here these rabbis *knew* that Rabbi Eliezer was correct, at least from the standpoint of the heavens. Why, especially then, did they take this drastic measure? Did they think the heavenly voice was a trick? Were they convinced that they were right? Were they concerned that Rabbi Eliezer would continue to argue, and thereby refuse to allow the majority to make its ruling? At this point in the narrative, the Talmud does not elaborate on these or any other possible explanations. Rather, the text continues:

> And they said: "Who will go and inform him?" Rabbi Akiva said to them: "I will go, lest someone who is unsuitable will go and inform him, and as a result he will destroy the entire world."

Rabbi Akiva, one of the leading scholars of his day, wished to communicate the results of the Rabbis' decision in a dignified manner, to minimize Rabbi Eliezer's outrage.

> What did Rabbi Akiva do? He dressed in black [garments] and wrapped himself in black, and sat before him at a distance of four cubits.

Rabbi Akiva kept his distance on account of the fact that Rabbi Eliezer had been excommunicated. All that remained now was to gently inform him of this.

> Rabbi Eliezer said to him: "Akiva, what is [the difference between] today and any other day (lit., 'what is one day from two days')"? [Akiva] said to him: "Rabbi, it seems to me that [your] colleagues are staying away from you." [Eliezer], too, rent his garments and took off his shoes, and he slipped down and sat on the ground. His eyes streamed with tears.

It is a poignant scene: the two Rabbis sitting on the ground, both crying, because one of them has been removed from the community for his refusal to budge on a matter of conscience. The text continues, with pathos:

The world was smitten: one-third of the olives, and one-third of the wheat, and one-third of the barley. And some say [that] even the dough in a woman's hands swelled. [A Tanna] taught: There was a great calamity on that day, for every place upon which Rabbi Eliezer laid his eyes was burnt.

Since the Rabbis were ruling *against* the wishes of the heavenly voice, the natural world responded. Olives, wheat, and barley were the staples of the ancient world; one could scarcely have a meal without them. Each of these consequences could have resulted from a heat wave: the olives, wheat, and barley all depended on rain; so, too, excessive heat could cause dough to swell and areas to burn. In the Jerusalem Talmud (*Moed Katan* 3:1), however, a parallel version of the story clarifies that Rabbi Eliezer is actually burning the wheat with his eyes. His actions are a direct retaliation for the Rabbis' actions: just as they burnt all the items Rabbi Eliezer declared clean, so too, he burnt the necessary ingredients for sustenance. Finally, the crisis comes to a head:

And Rabban Gamliel, too, was coming on a ship, [and] a wave rose up against him to drown him. He said: "It seems to me that this is only because of Rabbi Eliezer ben Hyrcanus." He rose to his feet and said: "Master of the Universe, it is revealed and known before You that I did not do [this] for my [own] honor, nor did I do [it] for the honor of my father's house, but for Your honor, so that controversies will not multiply in Israel." The sea rested from its wrath.[12]

Here, at last, we see the reason behind the excommunication: Rabbi Eliezer's unwillingness to concede the point was considered a challenge to the majority rule. It could have caused a major rift in the community.

The Rabbis needed a methodology for deciding difficult cases. That is to say, they were aware that the perfect (the precisely right ruling in every case) could be the enemy of the good (the ability to make decisions in a collegial manner, on the basis of majority vote). In their view, this was such a case. In order to uphold a higher truth—the established framework for interpreting the revealed law—it was necessary to make a less than ideal decision. And so, much as Rabbi Eliezer was deeply respected in his community, he had to be excommunicated, in order to preserve the process of maintaining majority rule. (In the Jerusalem Talmud's version of the story, there is a happy ending: Rabbi Eliezer is reinstated and his rulings get recorded in the Talmud without attribution, to ensure they are followed.)

At this point, we introduce Milton Steinberg's discussion of the story of the oven of Akhnai, which includes his own paraphrasing of the Babylonian Talmud narrative:

> And finally, on the obligation to stand by the truth as one sees it against, if need be, Almighty God Himself, the following revealing legend from the Talmud:
>
>> Tradition has it on that day Rabbi Eliezer advanced every conceivable argument without persuading his fellows.
>>
>> Whereupon he said to them, "If the law be according to my opinion, then let yon carob tree prove it." And a carob tree moved one hundred cubits from its place!
>>
>> To which they responded, "What sort of demonstration does a carob tree afford?"
>>
>> Whereupon he said to them a second time, "If the law be according to my opinion, let yon stream prove it." And the stream flowed backward!

To which they responded, "What sort of demonstration does a stream afford?"

Whereupon he said to them, "If the law be according to my opinion, let the walls of this academy prove it."

And the walls bent to the point of falling until Rabbi Joshua rebuked them saying, "When scholars contend with one another, what business have ye among them?"

And so they did not fall out of respect for Rabbi Joshua, and they did not straighten out of respect for Rabbi Eliezer but remain slanting to this day.

Whereupon Rabbi Eliezer persisted and said to them, "If the law be according to my opinion, let them prove it from on high."

And a heavenly voice sounded forth and said, "What have ye against Rabbi Eliezer after whose opinion the law is always to be framed?"

At which Rabbi Joshua arose and said, "The Torah declares concerning itself, 'It is not in heaven'; that is to say, once the Torah was given on Mount Sinai, we pay no heed to heavenly voices but, as the Torah ordains further, we follow the opinion of the majority."

Through which tale it becomes clear that the magnificent impudence of Job was no freak in Judaism, that as he advocated the requirements of conscience against God Himself, so the Jewish religion expects its faithful to defend reason not only against men and human error but, if such a contingency can be imagined, against the very hosts of Heaven.[13]

Note that Steinberg's rendering of the talmudic narrative emphasizes the aspects of the story he wished to bring to the fore. Perhaps the most notable is the compact conclusion by Rabbi Joshua: "The

Torah declares concerning itself, 'It is not in heaven'; that is to say, once the Torah was given on Mount Sinai, we pay no heed to heavenly voices but, as the Torah ordains further, we follow the opinion of the majority." From this, Steinberg proceeds to assert: "The Jewish religion expects its faithful to defend reason not only against men and human error but, if such a contingency can be imagined, against the very hosts of Heaven." In other words, reason takes precedence even over Revelation: one should not abandon a reasoned position, even if challenged by a voice from heaven, until a better-reasoned argument is in fact presented.

Interestingly, Steinberg's own teacher and mentor, Rabbi Mordecai Kaplan, had been excommunicated for somewhat similar reasons as Rabbi Eliezer. Where Rabbi Eliezer argued in favor of adopting a new (oven) technology, Rabbi Kaplan created a prayer book that removed some of the traditional prayer rubrics, arguing that Judaism had to change anew. However, Kaplan (unlike Rabbi Eliezer) was not expecting the hosts of Heaven to weigh in favor of his proposed changes; rather, he expected these changes to be adopted on the basis of reason. Steinberg's comments could therefore conceivably be applied to Kaplan: "The Jewish religion expects its faithful to defend reason not only against men and human error but, if such a contingency can be imagined, against the very hosts of Heaven."

10.6. A Modern View:
Heschel's Understanding of Revelation

For Abraham Joshua Heschel (see 6.5), Revelation was quite real. To attempt to interpret it correctly, however, one needed to accept that God spoke in metaphors.

Heschel elaborated on the nature of Revelation as he saw it in *Between God and Man.*

"God spoke." Is it to be taken symbolically: He did not speak, yet it was as if He did? The truth is that *what is literally true to us is a metaphor compared with what is metaphysically real to God.* And when applied to Him our mightiest words are feeble understatements. The speech of God is not less but more than literally real. The nature of revelation, being an event in the realm of the ineffable, is something which words cannot spell, which human language will never be able to portray. . . .

The words in which the prophets attempted to relate their experiences were not photographs but illustrations, not descriptions but songs. A psychological reconstruction of the prophetic act is, therefore, no more possible than the attempt to paint a photographic likeness of a face on the basis of a song. The word "revelation" is like an exclamation; it is an *indicative* rather than a descriptive term. Like all terms that express the ultimate, it points to its meaning rather than fully rendering it.

We must not try to read chapters in the Bible dealing with the event at Sinai as if they were texts in systematic theology. Its intention is to celebrate the mystery, to introduce us to it rather than to penetrate or to explain it. As a report about revelation the Bible itself is *a midrash.*[14]

To Heschel, the Hebrew Bible was *not* a written account of events in the Ancient Near East millennia ago. It did not record the dictated word of God, taken down by Moses, atop Mount Sinai. At the same time, however, the Hebrew Bible was not a work of pious fiction. Rather, the text metaphorically recorded the prophets' encounter with God:

"God spoke." Is it to be taken symbolically: He did not speak, yet it was as if He did? The truth is that *what is literally true to us is a metaphor compared with what is metaphysically real to*

God. And when applied to Him our mightiest words are feeble understatements.

Inherent in the text was the problem of speech: how could any text possibly communicate what to us is unknowable? How could the infinite be expressed in a finite text? Some ideas are greater than our human capacity to understand them.

The speech of God is not less but more than literally real.

There exists a realm beyond our everyday world that has a greater reality. It is *more real* in the sense that it is *more important* and *more lasting*. In this next sentence, Heschel speaks of the ineffable, a term denoting what cannot be expressed in words:

The nature of revelation, being an event in the realm of the ineffable, is something which words cannot spell, which human language will never be able to portray.

Heschel subsequently links prophetic Revelation to artistic achievement, a common analogy in his works. Both prophecy and artistry are attempting to express what cannot easily be rendered.

The words in which the prophets attempted to relate their experiences were not photographs but illustrations, not descriptions but songs. A psychological reconstruction of the prophetic act is, therefore, no more possible than the attempt to paint a photographic likeness of a face on the basis of a song.

There are truths that run deeper than what can be said.

Indicative in the next sentence means acting as a sign or a symbol. For example, the rainbow at the end of the Noah story would be indicative of God's promise not to destroy humanity again.

> The word "revelation" is like an exclamation; it is an *indicative* rather than a descriptive term. Like all terms that express the ultimate, it points to its meaning rather than fully rendering it.

Thus, Heschel avows, the Hebrew Bible is the *indicative* rather than the literal word of God. It should not be read as a transcript of God's speech, but as an artistic rendering of an encounter that cannot be fully articulated. Furthermore:

> We must not try to read chapters in the Bible dealing with the event at Sinai as if they were texts in systematic theology. Its intention is to celebrate the mystery, to introduce us to it rather than to penetrate or to explain it. As a report about revelation the Bible itself is *a midrash*.

The biblical text points to something greater than can be articulated, and does not make its meaning explicit. The reader's task is to recognize this mystery, which Heschel understands to be the numinous experience of the divine presence. One is to become aware of its presence, not to define it.

Heschel's final comment, "As a report about revelation the Bible itself is *a midrash*," conveys his view that the biblical text provides an *explanation of the text* of Revelation rather than direct Revelation itself. If the Bible is like a painting, then its *source* is like the human being holding the paint brush and its sometimes inscrutable *subject* is God's essence. In that case, the Bible should not be taken literally. If the text is essentially indicative, then there is room to interpret it according to the needs of the present, through the halakhic process of interpretation, undertaken in a spirit of humility.

10.7. Summary of Views

In the *biblical text*, we saw that the revealed law involves a choice: one may choose to heed the commandments or ignore them. But this choice is also presented as profoundly consequential: it is the choice between life and death. Therefore, it becomes imperative that these commandments are comprehensible, interpretable (by the magistrates), and translatable into a legal system. This system, in fact, will become the organizing principle upon which communal Jewish life is founded.

Through the *liturgical text*, we saw how in one moment at the end of the Torah service, the text of the Torah scroll is directly linked to the experience of Revelation at Mount Sinai. The ritual in which the Torah is held aloft ("This is the Torah") renders the abstract theological concept ("Moses received Revelation from God") into a concrete object: *this object here* is the Torah that Moses received from the mouth of God. The Torah becomes a placeholder for God within the community. Although the Torah is not worshiped directly—for that would be idolatry—it is given a role of honor, as the representative of God's love for the Jewish people.

In the *rabbinical text*, we saw that the ancient Rabbis faced the challenge of how to adapt a received tradition, particularly one with the force of Revelation behind it, while at the same time conserving its content. They decided that a heavenly voice no longer decided matters of law; the task of interpreting the Torah was now in their hands, to be adjudicated by their own majority rule. As proof they told the story of Rabbi Eliezer, who it seemed had heaven on his side of a dispute, though the majority of sages disagreed with his assessment.

It was determined that even if his (or any) ruling was in keeping with the purest and most ideal form of *halakhah*, as evidenced by a voice from heaven, the final judgment would not be made on that basis. Even if the majority was mistaken, the majority's decision on how to interpret the *halakhah* would prevail.

In the *medieval text*, Saadia Gaon argued that Revelation was necessary for humankind, and that the prophetic text helps fill in gaps in our knowledge so that we may discern God's will. For Saadia, Revelation is not merely a dictation of rules to follow blindly without understanding. Rather, Revelation fills in what reason alone cannot ascertain, providing the information we would not be able to deduce without it.

In the first *modern text*, Milton Steinberg paraphrased the Babylonian Talmud narrative to emphasize how reason takes precedence over Revelation. In his view, the story could be interpreted as a defense of reason "against the very hosts of Heaven," by which he meant one should not abandon a reasoned position, even if challenged by a voice from heaven, until a better-reasoned argument can in fact be presented.

In the second *modern text*, Abraham Joshua Heschel asserted that we should not interpret the Hebrew Bible as recording the word of God as a form of dictation, taken down by Moses atop Mount Sinai. The Torah's Revelation can only be understood metaphorically, for how could the infinite be expressed in a finite text? We would best conceive of the text as an artistic rendering of an encounter that cannot be fully articulated. And if so, if the biblical text is an *explanation of the text* of Revelation rather than direct Revelation itself, then the Bible should not be used as a source text for fundamentalist thinking. If the text is *indicative* rather than literal, then there is room to interpret it according to the needs of the present, through the halakhic process of interpretation, in a spirit of humility.

10.8. Accounting for the Rise of Literalism

Let us return, then, to the second opening question: When did a literal understanding of the revealed law—essentially, "it is not possible to change one jot or tittle"—become normative for many ultra-Orthodox Jews?

The scholar of Jewish intellectual history Leora Batnitzky explains in *How Judaism Became a Religion* that this kind of literalism arose as a response to the nascent Reform movement of nineteenth-century Germany. Reform, in turn, was a response to the Enlightenment and Emancipation of the Jews:

> In March 1812, the status of Jews in Prussia changed. Jews were declared citizens of the Prussian state. . . . Special taxes and occupational restrictions for Jews were abolished. . . . The question now was: What value is there to Judaism in an age in which Jews don't have to be defined as Jews, at least from the perspective of the modern nation-state?[15]

In Prussia and elsewhere in the German principalities, the Jewish response to this newly changed status included the development of a Reform movement dedicated to modernizing Judaism. In the reformers' view, it should not be necessary to choose between being a Jew and being a modern citizen of the nation-state.

> [Abraham] Geiger (1810–74), the intellectual founder of the [R] eform movement, equates what he claims is Judaism's world-historical essence with its role as a religion. . . . Understood historically, Geiger maintains Jewish law has always changed as its historical circumstances have changed. Based on Greek and Aramaic translations of the Bible, Geiger's *The Original Text and Translations of the Bible in their Dependence on the Inner*

Development of Judaism, published in 1857, attempts to show
that the interpretations of biblical passages changed over time,
and then illustrate from these changes the earlier and later
layers of accepted religious interpretation of Jewish law. Geiger
concludes that freeing contemporary Jews from what to many
of his coreligionists appear to be the unchanging authority of
Jewish law is not only consistent with but also most appropriate
to Judaism's historical development.[16]

Note that, in broad strokes, much of what Geiger suggests here is
now widely accepted by academic researchers in Jewish intellectual
history: interpretations of biblical passages have changed over time,
and it is possible to discern layers of accepted religious interpretation
of Jewish law. Geiger was a rabbi who also held a PhD for his work
in comparative religion, which would have provided the necessary
training for engaging in this kind of scholarly research. But his more
traditional contemporaries challenged his work:

> The traditionalists who responded to Geiger and the reformers
> laid the foundations for what today is called Jewish orthodoxy.
> [Samson Raphael] Hirsch (1808–88), the foremost intellectual
> proponent of what is now labeled Orthodox Judaism, denies
> exactly what Geiger affirms: that Judaism and Jewish law in
> particular are subject to historical change. . . .
>   Hirsch contends that the reformers and especially Geiger have
> attempted to transform divine revelation, an eternal, metaphys-
> ical fact, into a religion created by humans that can be changed
> according to human whim and desire. He responds to Gei-
> ger's claim that Judaism has changed throughout history with
> a simple but firm declaration that Judaism and Jewish law have
> not changed historically. At "all times and in every situation,"
> Judaism and Jewish law are "an untouchable sanctuary which

must not be subjected to human judgment or subordinated to human considerations."[17]

This position was something new. Batnitzky explains how this process further resulted in a departure from the tradition:

> Hirsch in fact established the modern phenomenon of Jewish sectarianism by highlighting the necessity of *correct belief*. Based on his conception of the genuine Jew and the true Jewish congregation made up of such individuals, he petitioned for a Prussian bill, eventually passed in 1876, that allowed Orthodox Jews to establish a separate community by seceding from the Jewish community recognized by the state. To defend his separatist stance toward non-orthodox Jews, Hirsch transform[ed] what had been simultaneously a Jewish political and theological concept—heresy—into a purely theological category by separating heresy from the heretic. The heresy that most concerns Hirsch is not one related to the practice of Judaism but rather to Jewish belief, and specifically the *belief* that "the law, both written and oral, was closed with Moses at Sinai."[18]

Scholars of Jewish intellectual history agree that the interpretation of the oral and written Torah did in fact change over time. Hirsch's unchanging literalism is thus an anomaly, a late nineteenth-century phenomenon created in response to the nascent Reform movement, specifically the academic research of Reform rabbi-scholars such as Abraham Geiger. Nonetheless, the literalist ultra-Orthodox position continues to have sway to this day.

10.9. Reimagining a Foundational Document

Can we strike a balance between tradition and innovation in our approach to the Torah?

Significantly, while the Torah itself cannot be amended, its interpretation is an ongoing project. As we saw in section 10.3, according to the tradition, when Moses spent forty days receiving God's Revelation on Mount Sinai, he learned both the written and the oral Torah. The talmudic tractate *Mishnah Avot* relates what happened next: "Moses . . . handed it down to Joshua, and Joshua to the elders, and the elders to the prophets, and the prophets handed it down to the men of the Great Assembly."[19]

The talmudic scholar Philip Blackman detailed this chain of transmission for traditional Jews:

> The "elders" were the "Judges" [we read of in the Bible] of whom Eli was the last . . . Samuel was the first [prophet] and Haggai, Zechariah and Malachi were the last of these prophets. . . . [and the Great Assembly] or *Great Synagogue*, [was] a body of one hundred and twenty elders, judges, prophets, sages, teachers, and scribes who returned from exile with Ezra [and] whose spiritual regeneration of the people they continued by drawing up and enacting new rules and regulations and restrictions and laid the foundation of the *Liturgy*.[20]

The tradition suggests that Moses gave both the written Torah and the oral Torah he had received from God to Joshua, his successor. Joshua gave it to the judges such as Eli (whom we read about in the book of Judges), the judges transmitted it to the prophets (Samuel, Haggai, Zechariah, Malachi among them), the prophets handed it down to the elders of the Great Assembly, and they, in turn, handed it down to the ancient Rabbis.

Given this context, it becomes especially clear why the Rabbis recognized that Moses would not comprehend the Torah as it was read in their era (as discussed in section 10.3). Not only had they reinterpreted various aspects of the written text; the process of interpretation had also become more complex over time. Moreover, the Rabbis did not see these changes as at all haphazard, but rather as part of a larger project of study, discussion, and education in a communal setting.

Finally, and perhaps most importantly, according to the Rabbis the original Revelation itself provided the authority for these interpretations, for the very process of adaptation itself was "a law given unto Moses at Sinai." The biblical text reads: "It is not in the heavens, that you should say, 'Who among us can go up to the heavens and get it for us and impart it to us, that we may observe it?'" (Deut. 30:12). With this in hand, we can conclude that the text itself allows for our creative interpretation and reinterpretation according to the needs of the time.

There are rules to this process of interpretation. The system of rabbinic law is built on the assumption of coherence: the rabbinic literature makes sense when considered as a whole, even if it includes directly contradictory statements within it. New, unanticipated, or unresolved problems are not evidence of a breakdown in coherence. Rather, they are like the oddities and extra words in the Bible: a source of exegetical creativity, an invitation to participate in solving the endless puzzles of text. It is understood that these puzzles cannot all be resolved for all time. Rather, the process of legal reasoning involves the illumination of a landscape, to develop the awareness of how the various elements stand in relation to each other.

In the modern and postmodern periods, however, this traditional approach to Jewish law, an approach that assumed that coherence might be discerned in the multiplicity, has broken apart into a multiplicity of approaches that are not easily reconciled. The Reform movement, for example, has introduced the idea of personal autonomy with respect to the law: a person may critique the precepts of the *halakhah* for ethical or even aesthetic reasons (as we saw in Eugene Borowitz's take on autonomy and the law in chapter 8). In this spirit, feminism takes issue with the nonegalitarian treatment of women under the *halakhah* and seeks to remedy this situation through innovations in liturgy and theology (as we saw in chapter 4). And, as we saw in section 10.8, following the thought of Samson Raphael Hirsch, a literalism about the text has become a dominant thread in ultra-Orthodoxy. Each of these adaptations has its own logic and its own reasons. And in each case, its proponents argue that their own methodology best expresses the desired balance between tradition and innovation within Judaism.

Conclusion

The questions raised in this book about the nature of God are not easily answered, but hopefully we have developed awareness of how the various elements stand in relation to one another.

1. Is God the Creator and Source of All Being—Including Evil?

In the first part, "Is God the Creator and Source of All Being—Including Evil?," we asked what it means to say that God created the world and, if God is good, why evil exists. While, as we saw, strands of Jewish tradition through the ages have come to decidedly different conclusions, it is illuminating to recognize that Judaism encourages this kind of diversity of thought. The common Jewish saying, "two Jews, three opinions," concisely expresses this valorization of multiple viewpoints; similarly, in the rabbinic literature, it is common to encounter the phrase *davar acher*, which means, colloquially, "another thought." Usually, it introduces an idea that takes the discussion in an entirely new direction.

Beyond this, however, we do find commonalities in perspective on the aforementioned questions about God and Creation. Most Jewish thinkers believe that there is purpose and order to the world, and that we seem to be here for a reason, even if we don't always know (or agree) what it is. Evil, on the other hand, appears to be a necessary by-product of our free will: if we have the ability to choose to do good, we must also have the ability to choose to do evil.

In fact, some of our baser yearnings—such as our desire to be something in the world—motivate our highest achievements. Recognizing this, and rather than spurning the shadow side of our psyche, the Rabbis embraced it. Thus, the Rabbis suggested that the *yetzer ha-ra* (the urge to do what is bad or evil) can also be a motivating force: it can lead us to take risks and move forward with some of the most challenging decisions in our lives.

2. Does God Have a Personality— or Is God an Impersonal Force?

The book's second part, "Does God Have a Personality—or Is God an Impersonal Force?," looked at how imagining a personal God is different from imagining God as something unlike a person. It also took up the question of gender in relation to God and the meaning of declaring God's oneness.

Writing in the twelfth century, Moses Maimonides articulated the foundations of Jewish thought with regard to anthropomorphism; nearly all that follows is a response to him. Maimonides argued that since God is so profoundly different than the world, positive statements about God (such as that "God is powerful and knowing and willing") do not adequately explain God's essence. Rather than imperfectly apprehend God's essence, it would be better to admit what we do *not* know; it would be preferable to use negations to describe God (including double negations in place of positive statements, such as "God is not not merciful" in place of "God is merciful").

For many of us, however, it is much easier to address prayer to a person—or to a person-like Being—than to address prayer to, say, a force that causes nature to endlessly create, or any other of the multiple abstract ways Jews understand God. But as we saw, when we attribute human qualities to God, we do little more than magnify human ideals. In so doing, we conceive God as upholding the values peculiar to our society and our time, rather than imagining God as the force that moves us to break apart the unrecognized injustices within it. That's one reason why many feminist thinkers object to speaking about God in hierarchical terms, that these terms preserve regressive ideals inconsistent with the transcendent justice of God.

As it turns out, the question of gender is more complicated than deciding which pronouns to use for God. There is the question of how gender is expressed, and what assumptions we bring to a given role: do we only see women as nurturers, for example, and men as warlike? Additionally, there is the question of gender itself: how do we relate to the multiplicity of gendered forms, such as the five categories of gender found in the Talmud? Is gender really binary or something more fluid? Does God encompass all gendered forms or transcend them? On all these matters, the tradition remains divided.

All the Jewish thinkers introduced in this part affirmed the desirability of reciting the *Shema* twice daily as part of the prayer service, but differed on the questions of its purpose and effects. Some and not others believed that reciting the *Shema* involves an encounter with God. For Maimonides, contemplation of God is the end goal of reciting the *Shema*. For Schneerson, and Hasidic worship in general, recitation of the *Shema* allows a person's own sense of separateness from God to dissolve into the greater unity. To Soloveitchik, this recitation in the midst of a worship service is intended to remind us that God remains God and humanity remains humanity. In Schachter-Shalomi's view, the *Shema* is more than a prayer; it becomes the point at which it is possible to recognize the fundamental unity of God behind the illusion. Still, there is consensus that affirming the singularity and uniqueness of God helps us to recognize that God is much bigger, and grander, than our comprehensions.

3. Does God Redeem — or Might God Not Redeem?

In the third part, "Does God Redeem — or Might God Not Redeem?," we saw that God's apparent willingness to respond to suffering on the national scale, as retold each year at Passover, raises questions. Does God's providence extend to every generation, or only to certain ones, such as the generations of the Exodus? And, if this narrative unfolds according to God's will, why does the Israelites' liberation require the Egyptians' suffering? A rabbinic Midrash expresses this tension particularly well:

When the Holy One was about to drown the Egyptians in the sea, Uzza, heavenly prince of Egypt, rose up and prostrated himself before the Holy One, saying: Maser of the universe, You created the world by the measure of mercy. Why then do You wish to drown my children? The Holy One gathered the entire heavenly household and said to them: You be the judge between Me and Uzza prince of Egypt. At that, the heavenly princes of the other nations began to speak in behalf of Egypt. When Michael [Israel's heavenly prince] perceived this, he gave the sign to Gabriel, who in one swoop darted down to Egypt, where he pulled out a brick with its clay enclosing a [dead] infant who had been immured alive in the structure. He then came back, stood before the Holy One, and said: Master of the universe, thus did the Egyptians enslave Your children. Whereupon the Holy One sat in judgment over the Egyptians in accord with the measure of justice and drowned them in the sea.

In that instant the ministering angels wished to utter song before the Holy One, but He rebuked them, saying, "The works of My hands are drowning in the sea, and you would utter song in My presence!"[1]

Here the suffering of the Egyptians is framed as retribution for the systematic murder of Israelite children. Those deaths require a response. Yet the Egyptians' humanity is also acknowledged; God refuses to listen to songs of victory from the ministering angels as the perpetrators drown. Further, every year, as a reminder of the suffering of the innocent in Egypt, each participant in a seder takes ten drops out of a wine glass to symbolize each of the ten plagues that afflicted Egypt.

The attempt to answer the question of how God might be good yet still allow evil to exist is known as theodicy. Theodicy grows out of our human need to make sense of the world. We would like to be able to make the following three assertions regarding God:

1. God is good.
2. God is all-powerful (omnipotent).
3. Evil is real.

But we can't affirm all three of these at once; they appear to contradict each other. Moral coherence would seem to require that we deny one of these three. Thus we might reinterpret the first statement, questioning what is meant by the phrase, "God is good." If God's will is inscrutable to us humans, it is possible that what we see as evil is actually good. As for the second assertion, we might declare that God is not all-powerful. That is to say, for whatever reason, God cannot prevent tragedies from happening. In terms of the third, we might affirm that God is good and all-powerful, but deny the reality of evil. In that formulation, evil is merely an illusion, for the world is a veil that obscures the view of the Divine.

Yet we cannot resolve this tension, not entirely. The strength of the rabbinic text above is its awareness that each of these events requires its own response: the retribution for the murder of the Israelite infants does not mean that it is acceptable to rejoice over the deaths of the Egyptian first-born. Each tragedy has its own separate sense of loss; we do not get to brush aside the sufferings of others even when they occur as a result of our own redemption.

The suffering of the people Israel presents another problem. The liturgical poem "*Eleh Azkerah*" suggested that God had caused suffering as a form of punishment for the earlier sins of the community. Similarly, a rabbinic passage attempted to explain the people's suffering within a framework of God's retribution for the nation's sin. However, the medieval text rejected this position, lodging a note of protest to God when the Talmud was burned. Hermann Cohen's formulation, on the other hand, made suffering a natural outcome of the Jewish mission to spread monotheism to the world. Tying these various threads together is our human need to find purpose and meaning in our lives.

But that sense of meaning can be elusive. In responding to the Holocaust, many of the later thinkers argued that something fundamental had shifted in our relationship to God. On account of this unique event, they argued, we are faced with a new moral imperative. Richard Rubenstein saw in it the death of our traditional god-concepts. Similarly, Irving Greenberg argued that the Holocaust altered the terms of our covenant with God. By contrast, Steven Katz protested that invoking the Holocaust as the catalyst of a new covenant only serves to compound the theological problems presented by the Holocaust, by promoting Hitler into a metaphysical force of evil. The question remains, then: what is the theological meaning of the Holocaust? We might want a simple answer, yet it could be that no single formulation wholly makes sense of it.

We also saw that it is very easy to justify someone else's suffering in the context of one's worldview, particularly if the suffering of someone else is precisely what allows one's worldview to be coherent. Perhaps the human challenge, and responsibility, is to resist this tendency.

4. Is God a Covenantal Partner and Lawgiver—or Might These Roles Be Rethought in the Modern Age?

Our fourth and final part, "Is God a Covenantal Partner and Lawgiver—or Might These Roles Be Rethought in the Modern Age?," explored the tradition's responses to essential questions of our ongoing responsibilities in light of Israel's covenant with God. Borrowing from legal agreements made between human beings, the covenant as it appeared in the Bible set forth the relationship between God and Israel on these terms: the people Israel would be faithful to God, as evidenced by observance of the commandments, and God in turn would protect and preserve Israel. Joseph Soloveitchik argued that once the covenant at Mount Sinai bestowed upon the Israelites the unique knowledge of God's ideal, they—and we—became obligated to enact that ideal, as closely as possible, through scrupulous observance of the covenant. Others, however, such as Eugene Borowitz, argued that rather than a response to a commanding voice first heard at Sinai, the covenant represents a flexible framework for understanding our responsibility to God, to other Jews, and to ourselves.

Later in the discussion, a dichotomy was introduced: when the covenant is understood as literal, as the word of God, the commandments become a Jew's direct obligations to God. Understood this way, it is less desirable and more difficult to change them in any way. How can we presume to alter what is eternal and transcendent? For certain thinkers, such as Bachya Ibn Pakuda, the covenant is indeed binding. Because God has shown the Jewish people such beneficence in bestowing the laws, Jews have an obligation to obey them. Turning away from this heritage is the way of lawlessness. In our own day, this position is upheld by David Novak, who sees the particular Jewish covenant as the basis for creating universal human rights.

On the other hand, when the covenant is understood as a metaphor—which often is the case when the commandments are seen to come from a source other than God, such as the tradition, or human insight—it is generally viewed as malleable. Furthermore, if the covenant is a metaphor, the meaning of that metaphor may shift over time. For Franz Rosenzweig, for example, the content of the covenant is not the Revelation of laws, but the Revelation of God's presence. He disavowed the idea that the commandments were part of a binding covenant, the product of a direct Revelation from God. For Abraham Joshua Heschel, the biblical text provides an *explanation of the text* of Revelation, rather than a recording of the word of God as dictated to Moses atop Mount Sinai. The Torah's Revelation can only be understood metaphorically, for how could the infinite be expressed in a finite text?

Regardless of how Jews understood the biblical commandments, it was agreed that the Bible itself did not address every life situation. Thus the question arose: who is fit to interpret the biblical laws? For their part, the ancient Rabbis decided that the task of interpreting Torah was in their hands, to be adjudicated by their own majority rule. In their eyes, the perfect (the precisely right ruling in every case) could be the enemy of the good (the ability to make decisions in a collegial manner, on the basis of majority vote). Furthermore, according to them, the original Revelation itself provided the authority for these decisions; the very process of adaptation itself was "a law given unto Moses at Sinai." In line with that tradition, in the modern era Milton Steinberg, for one, espoused the imperative for future generations to forcefully advocate for needed adaptations so that the *halakhah* would continue to reflect changing times.

The system of law the Rabbis constructed is built on the assumption of coherence: the world as a whole is a coherent text when read in full. This brings us back to a question of moral coherence:

how do we understand God? At the heart of it, all the theologies in this book—and our own—are actually personal explanations for the world, defining what could be meaningful, what might become possible, and how everything we experience or imagine might be understood.

Notes

INTRODUCTION

1. Stein, *Contemporary Torah*.
2. Heschel, *Man Is Not Alone*, 13.
3. Heschel, *Man Is Not Alone*, 27.
4. Heschel, *Man Is Not Alone*, 13.
5. Heschel, *Man Is Not Alone*, 27.

1. GOD CREATED THE WORLD

1. Stein, *Contemporary Torah*. All references to the Torah will be from this translation.
2. Blackman, *Mishnayot*, vol. 3, *Mishnah Yevamoth* 6:6.
3. Epstein, *Babylonian Talmud: Yebamoth* 65b.
4. The Hebrew Bible also specifies that when consuming animals, one should not eat or drink the animal's blood. For example, Deut. 12:20–25, states: "When the Lord enlarges your territory, as He has promised you, and you say, 'I shall eat some meat', for you have the urge to eat meat, you may eat meat whenever you wish. If the place where the Lord has chosen to establish his name [i.e., the Temple sanctuary] is too far from you, you may slaughter any of the cattle or sheep that the Lord gives you, as I have instructed you: and you may eat to your heart's content in your settlements. Eat it, however, as the gazelle and the deer are eaten: the unclean may eat it together with the clean. But make sure that you do not partake of the blood; for the blood is the life, and you must not consume the life with the flesh. You must not partake of it; you must pour it out on the ground like water: you must not partake of it, in order that it may go well with you and with your descendants to come, for you

will be doing what is right in the sight of the Lord." Blood, in fact, seems to have had some kind of special power in the biblical imagination, as it was kept away from what was holy. The structure of the Temple in Jerusalem included a series of courtyards by which persons with bodily flux of some kind, such as menstrual flow, would be prevented from reaching the center-point of the building.

5. Harlow, *Siddur Sim Shalom*, 97. The majority of Conservative congregations in America use this prayer book; this version includes extensive page-by-page commentary on each prayer.

6. Bialik and Ravnitzky, *Book of Legends*, 12–13.

7. In the rabbinic literature, there is a saying, *ain mukdam v'ain meuchar*, which means that "there is no 'early' and no 'late'" in the Torah. The key idea here is that the Torah text may not be arranged chronologically; events mentioned earlier may have happened later.

8. Bell, *Bloomsbury Companion*, 109.

9. Jacobs, *Jewish Religion*, 44.

10. This excerpt is not truly representative of Ibn Pakuda's full work. His writing also demonstrates profound emotion and deep piety.

11. Ibn Pakuda, *Book of Direction*, 116–18.

12. Green, *Seek My Face*, 61.

13. To my knowledge, Green has not commented on the question of how to categorize his work. It is worthwhile, however, to browse the collection of essays he has linked to his faculty profile at hebrewcollege.edu/about/faculty. One gets a sense from it that, ever curious, he is continually revising and rethinking as he goes.

14. E. Klein, *Comprehensive Etymological Dictionary*, 455.

15. Kushner, *Eyes Remade for Wonder*, 94–95.

16. Jacobs, *Jewish Religion*, 480.

17. Spinoza, *Theologico-Political Treatise*, 76.

18. Bialik and Ravnitzky, *Book of Legends*, 6.

19. Levy and Levy, *JPS Rashi Discussion Torah Commentary*, 3.

20. Waskow, *Down-to-Earth Judaism*, 19.

21. Heschel, *Man Is Not Alone*, 215.

2. HOW DOES EVIL EXIST?

1. E. Klein, *Comprehensive Etymological Dictionary*, 213.

2. In the *Contemporary Torah* text, the Tetragrammaton is left untranslated and is printed in Hebrew letters. In this work, when quoting the

Contemporary Torah, the Tetragrammaton is dropped if it is part of a compound name; otherwise, it is translated simply as "God."

3. E. Klein, *Comprehensive Etymological Dictionary*, 486.

4. It is conjectured (and not proven) that this prayer may have been written as a counter-argument against the Christian idea of Original Sin.

5. Frishman, *Mishkan T'filah*, 196.

6. An example of how blood could be used for purification is the ritual of cleansing after a skin eruption in Lev. 14:3–7. Similarly, ashes may be used for purification. The ashes from the sacrifice of a red heifer would be used to purify someone who had come into contact with a corpse, as detailed in Num. 19:17–19.

7. E. Klein, *Comprehensive Etymological Dictionary*, 237.

8. Bialik and Ravnitzky, *Book of Legends*, 543.

9. Maimonides, *Guide of the Perplexed*, 1:2, 24–25.

10. Maimonides, *Guide of the Perplexed*, 1:14, 40.

11. Maimonides, *Guide of the Perplexed*, 3:12, 444.

12. Maimonides, *Guide of the Perplexed*, 3:12, 444.

13. Maimonides, *Guide of the Perplexed*, 3:12, 444.

14. Maimonides, *Guide of the Perplexed*, 2:5, 259

15. Cohen, *Religion of Reason*, 182.

16. Kushner, *When Bad Things Happen*, 53.

17. Kushner, *When Bad Things Happen*, 68–69.

18. Bialik and Ravnitzky, *Book of Legends*, 23.

19. Jonas, *Mortality and Morality*, 139.

3. IS GOD LIKE A PERSON?

1. Bialik and Ravnitzky, *Book of Legends*, 559.

2. Epstein, *Babylonian Talmud: Rosh Hashanah*, 16b.

3. Epstein, *Babylonian Talmud: Rosh Hashanah*, 16b.

4. Epstein, *Babylonian Talmud: Rosh Hashanah*, 17b.

5. According to the German-Jewish scholar Ismar Elbogen, who produced his still-relevant masterwork, *Jewish Liturgy*, in 1913, the practice of reading this passage as part of the Torah service during Yom Kippur has its origins in the practices of the medieval mystics: "From the influence of the Kabbalists comes the custom of saying the Thirteen Attributes of God (Ex. 34:6) on certain days when the Torah is taken out of the ark. Luria's followers introduced it at first for the month of Elul [the Hebrew month that precedes the High Holidays]; from here it was transferred to

the New Year and the Day of Atonement, and finally to the three pilgrim festivals" (Elbogen, *Jewish Liturgy*, 160)."

6. Goldberg et al., *Mishkan Hanefesh*, 2:256.

7. Bialik and Ravnitzky, *Book of Legends*, 503.

8. Maimonides, *Guide of the Perplexed*, 1:58, 135–36.

9. Buber wrote *I and Thou* in German, so the original terms were actually *ich-du* (I-Thou) and *ich-es* (I-It). He used the informal second-person pronoun *du* (meaning "thou"—which, some time ago, in English, had been the pronoun used with close friends and family) rather than the formal second-person pronoun, *Sie* (meaning "you"—which in English had been the pronoun used in formal address). For this reason, some translators have used *thou* to render *du* when translating his work into English. But *thou* has fallen out of use, and thereby has lost all of the informal intimacy that *du* still has in German. Our translation, while retaining the classic title, uses the colloquial *you* in the text itself.

10. Buber, *I and Thou*, 60.

11. Buber, *I and Thou*, 57–58, 64.

12. Buber, *I and Thou*, 69.

13. Buber, *I and Thou*, 150.

14. Buber, *I and Thou*, 160–61.

15. Buber, *Moses*, 154–55.

16. Green, *Seek My Face*, 12.

17. Green, *Seek My Face*, 14.

18. Wyschogrod, *Body of Faith*, 101.

4. DOES GOD HAVE A GENDER?

1. Sacks, *Koren Rosh Hashana Mahzor*, 452.

2. Goldberg et al., *Mishkan Hanefesh*, 2:663.

3. Goldberg et al., *Mishkan Hanefesh* 2:644.

4. Bialik and Ravnitzky, *Book of Legends*, 505.

5. Jacobs, *Jewish Religion*, 444.

6. Scholem, *On the Mystical Shape*, 159–60. The brackets in this passage are mine; the parentheses are Scholem's.

7. Scholem, *On the Mystical Shape*, 102.

8. Scholem, *On the Mystical Shape*, 177–78.

9. Scholem, *On the Mystical Shape*, 103.

10. Scholem, *On the Mystical Shape*, 103.

11. Scholem, *On the Mystical Shape*, 177–78.

12. Meyer, *Response to Modernity*, 370.

13. Meyer, *Response to Modernity*, 373.

14. Stern, *Gates of Prayer*, 37, 286

15. Plaskow, *Standing Again at Sinai*, 123.

16. Plaskow, "Jewish Theology in Feminist Perspective," 74-75. Janowitz and Wenig's cocreated *Siddur Nashim: A Book of Sabbath Prayers for Women* was the first Shabbat prayer book to refer to God using female pronouns and imagery.

17. Plaskow, "Jewish Theology in Feminist Perspective," 74–75.

18. Plaskow, "Jewish Theology in Feminist Perspective," 76.

19. Christ and Plaskow, *Goddess and God*, 127.

20. Adler, *Engendering Judaism*, 83.

21. Hammer, *Or Hadash*, 311.

22. Falk, *Days In Between*, 9.

23. Falk, *Book of Blessings*, 464.

24. Frymer-Kensky, *In the Wake*, viii.

25. Frymer-Kensky, *In the Wake*, 118.

26. Frymer-Kensky, *In the Wake*, 140.

27. Frymer-Kensky, *In the Wake*, 203.

28. Frymer-Kensky, *In the Wake*, 211.

29. Trible, *Texts of Terror*, 3.

30. Tuling, "Shifting the Focus," 385.

31. Plaskow, *Standing Again at Sinai*, 123.

32. Raphael, *Introducing Thealogy*, 22.

33. Frymer-Kensky, *In the Wake*, vii.

5. GOD IS ONE

1. Sacks, *Koren Siddur*, 98–100.

2. I. Klein, *Guide to Jewish Religious Practice*, 18.

3. Friedland, "Were Our Mouths," 245, 261.

4. Brackets mine.

5. Brackets mine.

6. Epstein, *Babylonian Talmud: Pesachim*, 56a.

7. Maimonides, *Guide of the Perplexed*, 3:51, 622–23.

8. Maimonides, *Guide of the Perplexed*, 3:32, 529–30.

9. Schneerson, *Tract on Prayer*, 49–50.

10. Horowitz, *Kabbalah and Jewish Mysticism*, 99.

11. Zank and Anderson, *Value of the Particular*, 197.

12. The Soloveitchik family is a Lithuanian rabbinic family. Its influential members extended from early in the nineteenth century and continued through the twentieth. See Jacobs, *Jewish Religion*, 474.

13. Soloveitchick, *Worship of the Heart*, 96–97.

14. Singer, *Paradigm Shift*, 251.

15. Schachter-Shalomi, *Gate to the Heart*, 57–59.

16. Lamm, *Shema*, 3.

17. Jacobs, *Jewish Religion*, 204.

18. Green, *Seek My Face*, 17.

6. DOES GOD INTERVENE IN OUR LIVES?

1. E. Klein, *Comprehensive Etymological Dictionary*, 584.

2. E. Klein, *Comprehensive Etymological Dictionary*, 223–24.

3. E. Klein, *Comprehensive Etymological Dictionary*, 514.

4. Aschkenasy, *Woman at the Window*, 139.

5. Aschkenasy, *Woman at the Window*, 139.

6. Kay, *Seyder Tkhines*, 5.

7. Kay, *Seyder Tkhines*, 8.

8. Kay, *Seyder Tkhines*, 8.

9. Kay, *Seyder Tkhines*, 6.

10. Kay, *Seyder Tkhines*, 209–10.

11. Kay, *Seyder Tkhines*, 212.

12. Bialik and Ravnitzky, *Book of Legends*, 113.

13. E. Klein, *Comprehensive Etymological Dictionary*, 539.

14. In the biblical narratives, the name *tzevaot* is normally understood to refer to the angels who praise God continuously. The word also has a sense of multitudes: thousands upon thousands of angels are attending to God.

15. Ibn Pakuda, *Book of Direction*, 236–37.

16. Heschel, *Moral Grandeur*, vii.

17. Heschel, *God in Search of Man*, 286.

18. Scult, *Radical American Judaism*, 1.

19. M. Kaplan, *Year with Mordecai Kaplan*, xx, 24.

20. M. Kaplan, *Not So Random Thoughts*, 147.

21. M. Kaplan, *Judaism without Supernaturalism*, 26–27.

22. For more information about Rav Kook's life and theology, see Mirsky, *Rav Kook*.

7. DOES GOD INTERVENE IN HISTORY?

1. Sacks, *Koren Yom Kippur Mahzor*, 928–31.

2. Sacks, *Koren Yom Kippur Mahzor*, 928–40.

3. Epstein, *Babylonian Talmud: Berakoth*, 5a.

4. Epstein, *Babylonian Talmud: Berakoth*, 5a.

5. Einbinder *Beautiful Death*, 74–75.

6. Einbinder, *Beautiful Death*, 76–78.

7. Einbinder, *Beautiful Death*, 70–72.

8. Einbinder, *Beautiful Death*, 89.

9. Einbinder, *Beautiful Death*, 89.

10. Cohen, *Religion of Reason*, 283–84.

11. Rubenstein, *After Auschwitz*, 294–98.

12. Pace, "Hans Jonas, Influential Philosopher."

13. Jonas, *Mortality and Morality*, 134–38.

14. Kleinberg, *Hybrid Judaism*, xxiv.

15. Greenberg, I., *For the Sake*, 25–28.

16. Bialik and Ravnitzky, *Book of Legends*, 197.

17. Katz, *Interpreters of Judaism*, 81.

18. Katz, *Interpreters of Judaism*, 83.

19. Rosenak, "Theological Reflections," 163–66.

20. Rosenak, "Theological Reflections," 166.

21. Rosenak, "Theological Reflections," 166–67.

22. Soloveitchik, *Kol Dodi Dofek*, 2.

23. Soloveitchik, *Kol Dodi Dofek*, 3.

24. Soloveitchik, *Kol Dodi Dofek*, 7. The bracketed insertion appeared as a footnote in the original text.

8. GOD AND ISRAEL

1. Scherman, *Complete ArtScroll Siddur*, 361.

2. Frishman, *Mishkan T'filah*, 123.

3. Falk, *Book of Blessings*, 128–29.

4. Frishman, *Mishkan T'filah*, 123.

5. Falk, *Book of Blessings*.

6. Frishman, *Mishkan T'filah*, 162.

7. Frishman, *Mishkan T'filah*, 123.

8. Bialik and Ravnitzky, *Book of Legends*, 336.

9. Korobkin, *Kuzari*, 41.

10. Korobkin, *Kuzari*, 211–13.

11. Soloveitchik, *Kol Dodi Dofek*, 54. Soloveitchik's position here undoubt-
    edly reflected the bitter experience of racial antisemitism: "So long as
    a person's physiognomy testifies to his birth, so long as Jewish blood
    flows in his veins, and so long as his flesh is Jewish, he is compelled to
    serve the God of the Hebrews." There is no escaping the covenant of
    fate; that was one of the lessons of the Holocaust.

12. Soloveitchik, *Kol Dodi Dofek*, 67.

13. Soloveitchik, *Halakhic Man*, 19–20.

14. Berger, "Rabbi Eugene Borowitz, Influential Reform Theologian,
    Dies at 91."

15. Borowitz, *Renewing the Covenant*, 294.

16. Beit-Halachmi, "Refining the Covenant," 99.

17. Tirosh-Samuelson and Hughes, *Michael Fishbane*, 1.

18. Tirosh-Samuelson and Hughes, *Michael Fishbane*, 14.

19. Fishbane, *Sacred Attunement*, 123–24.

20. Audi, *Cambridge Dictionary of Philosophy*, 1127.

21. Hartman, *Putting God Second*, 46.

22. Hartman, *Putting God Second*, 167.

23. Hartman, *Putting God Second*, 110.

24. Hartman, *Putting God Second*, 78–79.

9. IS IT A BINDING COVENANT?

1. E. Klein, *Comprehensive Etymological Dictionary*, 240.

2. E. Klein, *Comprehensive Etymological Dictionary*, 563.

3. Hammer, *Or Hadash*, 111.

4. Hammer, *Or Hadash*, 111.

5. Hammer, *Or Hadash*, 111.

6. Freedman and Epstein, *Babylonian Talmud: Shabbath*, vol. 2, 88a.

7. Ibn Pakuda, *Book of Direction*, 188–89.

8. Rosenzweig, *Star of Redemption*, 177–78.

9. Rosenzweig, *Star of Redemption*, 436.

10. Novak, *Jewish Social Contract*, 33–34.

11. Novak, *Jewish Social Contract*, 44.

12. Novak, "Religious Rights in Judaic Texts," 189.

13. Bialik and Ravnitzky, *Book of Legends*, 354.

10. HOW SHOULD THE LAW BE UNDERSTOOD?

1. Homolka and Panken, *Engaging Torah*, 68.
2. Hammer, *Or Hadash*, 146.
3. Bialik and Ravnitzky, *Book of Legends*, 441.
4. Steinsaltz, *Reference Guide to the Talmud*, 226–27.
5. Berman, *Talmud: Bava Metzia Part 3*, 234–40.
6. Epstein, *Babylonian Talmud: Menahoth*, 29b.
7. Epstein, *Babylonian Talmud: Berakoth*, 9a.
8. Steinsaltz, *Reference Guide to the Talmud*, 230.
9. Steinsaltz, *Reference Guide to the Talmud*, 227.
10. Jacobs, *Jewish Religion*, 433.
11. Frank, Leaman, and Manekin, *Jewish Philosophy Reader*, 175–76. The insertions in brackets are this author's additions for the purposes of avoiding the use of gendered terms such as "men" or "mankind" when "humanity" is intended.
12. Berman, *Talmud: Bava Metzia*, part 3, 234–40.
13. Steinberg, *Basic Judaism*, 68–70.
14. Heschel, *Between God and Man*, 77.
15. Batnitzky, *How Judaism Became a Religion*, 32.
16. Batnitzky, *How Judaism Became a Religion*, 36–38.
17. Batnitzky, *How Judaism Became a Religion*, 40.
18. Batnitzky, *How Judaism Became a Religion*, 42.
19. Blackman, *Mishnayoth: Nezikin*, 489.
20. Blackman, *Mishnayoth: Nezikin*, 489.

CONCLUSION

1. Bialik and Ravnitzky, *Book of Legends*, 73.

Bibliography

Adler, Rachel. *Engendering Judaism*. Boston: Beacon Press, 1999.

Aschkenasy, Nehama. *Woman at the Window: Biblical Tales of Oppression and Escape*. Detroit: Wayne State University Press, 1998.

Audi, Robert. *The Cambridge Dictionary of Philosophy*. Cambridge: Cambridge University Press, 2015.

Batnitzky, Leora. *How Judaism Became a Religion: An Introduction to Modern Jewish Thought*. Princeton NJ: Princeton University Press, 2011.

Beit-Halachmi, Rachel Sabath. "Refining the Covenant." In *A Life of Meaning: Embracing Reform Judaism's Sacred Path*, edited by Dana Evan Kaplan, 89–101. New York: CCAR Press, 2018.

Bell, Dean Phillip, ed. *The Bloomsbury Companion to Jewish Studies*. London and New York: Bloomsbury Academic, 2015.

Berger, Joseph. "Rabbi Eugene Borowitz, Influential Reform Theologian, Dies at 91." *New York Times*, January 30, 2016.

Berman, Israel V., trans. and ed. *The Talmud: The Steinsaltz Edition*. Vol. 3, *Tractate Bava Metzia*, part 3. New York: Random House, 1990.

Bialik, Hayim Nahman, and Yehoshua Hana Ravnitzky, eds. *The Book of Legends: Sefer Ha-Aggadah, Legends from the Talmud and Midrash*. Translated by William G. Braude. New York: Schocken Books, 1992.

Blackman, Philip. *Mishnayoth*. Vol. 3, *Nashim*. 2nd ed. New York : The Judaica Press, Inc., 1963.

———. *Mishnayoth*. Vol. 4, *Nezikin*. 2nd edition. New York: Judaica Press, 1963.

Blumenthal, David. *Facing the Abusing God: A Theology of Protest*. Louisville KY: Westminister/John Knox Press, 1993.

Borowitz, Eugene. *Renewing the Covenant: A Theology for the Postmodern Jew*. Philadelphia: The Jewish Publication Society, 1991.

Buber, Martin. *I and Thou*. Translated by Walter Kaufmann. New York: Touchstone, 1970.

————. *Moses: The Revelation and the Covenant*. Amherst NY: Humanity Books, 1988.

Christ, Carol, and Judith Plaskow. *Goddess and God in the World*. Minneapolis MN: Fortress Press, 2016.

Cohen, Hermann. *Religion of Reason out of the Sources of Judaism*. Translated by Simon Kaplan. Oxford: Oxford University Press, 1995.

Davidman, Lynn, and Shelly Tenenbaum. *Feminist Perspectives on Jewish Studies*. New Haven CT: Yale University Press, 1994.

Einbinder, Susan. *A Beautiful Death: Jewish Poetry and Martyrdom in Medieval France*. Princeton NJ: Princeton University Press, 2002.

Elbogen, Ismar. *Jewish Liturgy: A Comprehensive History*. Translated by Raymond P. Scheindlin. Philadelphia: The Jewish Publication Society, 1993.

Epstein, I., ed. *Hebrew-English Edition of the Babylonian Talmud: Tractate Berakoth*. Translated by Maurice Simon. London: Soncino Press, 1990.

————. *Hebrew-English Edition of the Babylonian Talmud: Tractate Menahoth*. Translated by Eli Cashdan. London: Soncino Press, 1989.

————. *Hebrew-English Edition of the Babylonian Talmud: Tractate Pesachim*. Translated by H. Freedman. London: Soncino Press, 1990.

————. *Hebrew-English Edition of the Babylonian Talmud: Tractate Rosh Hashanah*. Translated by Maurice Simon. London: Soncino Press, 1994.

————. *Hebrew-English Edition of the Babylonian Talmud: Tractate Yebamoth*. Translated by Israel W. Slotki. London: Soncino Press, 1990.

Falk, Marcia. *The Book of Blessings: New Jewish Prayers for Daily Life, the Sabbath, and the New Moon Festival*. Boston: Beacon Press, 1996.

————. *The Days In Between: Blessings, Poems, and Directions of the Heart for the Jewish High Holiday Season*. Boston: Brandeis University Press, 2014.

Fishbane, Michael. *Sacred Attunement: A Jewish Theology*. Chicago: University of Chicago Press, 2008.

Frank, Daniel H., Oliver Leaman, and Charles H. Manekin, eds. *The Jewish Philosophy Reader*. New York: Routledge, 2000.

Freedman, H., and I. Epstein, eds. *Hebrew-English Edition of the Babylonian Talmud: Tractate Shabbath*. Vol. 2. New York: Traditional Press, 1938.

Friedland, Eric L. *"Were Our Mouths Filled with Song": Studies in Liberal Jewish Liturgy*. Cincinnati OH: Hebrew Union College Press, 1997.

Frishman, Elyse, ed. *Mishkan T'filah: A Reform Siddur Complete: Shabbat Weekdays, and Festivals*. Transliterated. New York: CCAR Press, 2007.

Frymer-Kensky, Tikva. *In the Wake of the Goddesses: Women, Culture, and the Biblical Transformation of Pagan Myth*. New York: Ballantine Books, 1992.

Goldberg, Edwin, Janet Marder, Sheldon Marder, and Leon Morris, eds. *Mishkan Hanefesh: Machzor for the Days of Awe*. Vols. 1 and 2. New York: CCAR Press, 2015.

Green, Arthur. *Seek My Face: A Jewish Mystical Theology*. Woodstock VT: Jewish Lights, 2003.

Greenberg, Blu. *On Women and Judaism: A View from Tradition*. Philadelphia: The Jewish Publication Society, 1998.

Greenberg, Irving. *For the Sake of Heaven and Earth: The New Encounter between Judaism and Christianity*. Philadelphia: The Jewish Publication Society, 2004.

Hammer, Reuven. *Or Hadash: A Commentary on Siddur Sim Shalom for Shabbat and Festivals*. New York: Rabbinical Assembly and United Synagogue of Conservative Judaism, 2003.

Harlow, Jules, ed. and trans. *Siddur Sim Shalom*. New York: Rabbinical Assembly and United Synagogue of Conservative Judaism, 1985.

Hartman, Donniel. *Putting God Second: How to Save Religion from Itself*. Boston: Beacon Press, 2016.

Heschel, Abraham Joshua. *Between God and Man: An Interpretation of Judaism*. Edited by Fritz A. Rothschild. New York: Free Press, 1959.

———. *God in Search of Man: A Philosophy of Judaism*. New York: Farrar, Straus, and Giroux, 1993.

———. *Man Is Not Alone*. New York: Noonday Press, 1994.

———. *Moral Grandeur and Spiritual Audacity: Essays*. Edited by Susannah Heschel. New York: Farrar, Straus, and Giroux, 1996.

Homolka, Walter, and Aaron Panken. *Engaging Torah: Modern Perspectives on the Hebrew Bible*. Cincinnati OH: Hebrew Union College Press, 2018.

Horowitz, Daniel M. *A Kabbalah and Jewish Mysticism Reader*. Philadelphia: The Jewish Publication Society, 2016.

Ibn Pakuda, Bahya Ben Joseph. *The Book of Direction to the Duties of the Heart*. Translated by Menahem Mansoor. Oxford and Portland OR: Littman Library of Jewish Civilization, 2004.

Jacobs, Louis. *The Jewish Religion: A Companion*. Oxford: Oxford University Press, 1995.

The Jewish Publication Society. *JPS Hebrew-English TANAKH*. 2nd ed. Philadelphia: The Jewish Publication Society, 1999.

Jonas, Hans. *Mortality and Morality: A Search for the Good after Auschwitz.* Evanston IL: Northwestern University Press, 1996.

Kadushin, Max. *Worship and Ethics: A Study in Rabbinic Judaism.* New York: Bloch, 1963.

Kaplan, Dana Evan, ed. *A Life of Meaning: Embracing Reform Judaism's Sacred Path.* New York: CCAR Press, 2018.

Kaplan, Mordecai M. *Judaism without Supernaturalism.* New York: Reconstructionist Press, 1967.

———. *Not So Random Thoughts.* Wyncote PA: Reconstructionist Press, 1966.

———. *A Year with Mordecai Kaplan.* Edited by Steven Carr Reuben. Philadelphia: The Jewish Publication Society, 2019.

Katz, Steven T., ed. *Interpreters of Judaism in the Late Twentieth Century.* Washington DC: B'nai B'rith Books, 1993.

Kay, Devra. *Seyder Tkhines: The Forgotten Book of Common Prayer for Jewish Women.* Philadelphia: The Jewish Publication Society, 2004.

Klein, Ernest. *A Comprehensive Etymological Dictionary of the Hebrew Language for Readers of English.* Jerusalem and Tel Aviv: Carta, 1987.

Klein, Isaac. *A Guide to Jewish Religious Practice.* New York: Jewish Theological Seminary of America, 1992.

Kleinberg, Darren. *Hybrid Judaism: Irving Greenberg, Encounter, and the Changing Nature of American Jewish Identity.* Boston: Academic Studies Press, 2016.

Korobkin, Daniel, ed. and trans. *The Kuzari: In Defense of the Despised Faith.* Jerusalem: Feldheim, 2009.

Kushner, Harold. *When Bad Things Happen to Good People.* New York: Anchor, 2004.

Kushner, Lawrence. *Eyes Remade for Wonder: A Lawrence Kushner Reader.* Woodstock VT: Jewish Lights, 1998.

Lamm, Norman. *The Shema: Spirituality and Law in Judaism.* Philadelphia: The Jewish Publication Society, 2000.

Levy, Steven, and Sarah Levy. *The JPS Rashi Discussion Torah Commentary.* Philadelphia: The Jewish Publication Society, 2017.

Maimonides, Moses. *Guide of the Perplexed.* Vols. 1 and 2. Translated by Shlomo Pines. Chicago: University of Chicago Press, 1963.

Meyer, Michael. *Response to Modernity: History of the Reform Movement in Judaism.* Detroit: Wayne State University Press, 1988.

Mirsky, Yehudah. *Rav Kook: Mystic in a Time of Revolution.* New Haven: Yale University Press, 2019.

Novak, David. *The Jewish Social Contract: An Essay in Political Theology*. Princeton NJ: Princeton University Press, 2005.

———. "Religious Human Rights in Judaic Texts." In *Religious Human Rights in Global Perspective*, edited by J. Whittle and J. van der Vyner, 175–201. Leiden: Nijhoff, 1996.

Pace, Eric. "Hans Jonas, Influential Philosopher, Is Dead at 89." *New York Times*, February 6, 1993.

Plaskow, Judith. "Jewish Theology in Feminist Perspective." In *Feminist Perspectives on Jewish Studies*, edited by Lynn Davidman and Shelly Tenenbaum, 62–84. New Haven CT: Yale University Press, 1994.

———. *Standing Again at Sinai*. San Francisco: HarperOne, 1991.

Raphael, Melissa, *Introducing Thealogy: Discourse on the Goddess*. Sheffield, UK: Sheffield Academic Press, 1999.

Reuben, Steven Carr. *A Year with Mordecai Kaplan: Wisdom on the Weekly Torah Portion*. Philadelphia: The Jewish Publication Society, 2019.

Rosenak, Michael. "Theological Reflections on the Holocaust: Between Unity and Controversy." In *The Impact of the Holocaust on Jewish Theology*, edited by Steven T. Katz, 161–74. New York and London: New York University Press, 2005.

Rosenzweig, Franz. *The Star of Redemption*, trans. Barbara E. Galli. Madison: University of Wisconsin Press, 2005.

Rubenstein, Richard L. *After Auschwitz: History, Theology, and Contemporary Judaism*, 2nd ed. Baltimore and London: Johns Hopkins University Press, 1992.

Sacks, Jonathan, trans. *The Koren Rosh Hashana Mahzor*. Jerusalem: Koren, 2010.

———, trans. *The Koren Siddur, Nusah Ashkenaz*. Jerusalem: Koren, 2015.

———, trans. *The Koren Yom Kippur Mahzor*. Jerusalem: Koren, 2011.

Schachter-Shalomi, Zalman. *Gate to the Heart: A Manual of Contemplative Jewish Practice*. Boulder CO: Albion-Andalus Books, 2013.

Scherman, Nosson, trans. *The Complete ArtScroll Siddur: Nusach Ashkenaz*. Brooklyn: Mesorah Publications, 1990.

Schneerson, Sholom Dovber. *Tract on Prayer: Kuntres Hatefillah*. Brooklyn: Kehot Publishing Society, 1992.

Scholem, Gershom. *On the Mystical Shape of the Godhead*. New York: Schocken Books, 1991.

Schorr, Rebecca Einstein, and Alysa Mendelson Graf, eds. *The Sacred Calling: Four Decades of Women in the Rabbinate*. New York: CCAR Press, 2016.

Scult, Mel. *The Radical American Judaism of Mordecai M. Kaplan*. Bloomington and Indianapolis: Indiana University Press, 2013.

Singer, Ellen, ed. *Paradigm Shift: From the Jewish Renewal Teachings of Reb Zalman Schachter-Shalomi*. Northvale NJ and Jerusalem: Jason Aronson, 1993.

Soloveitchick, Joseph B. *Halakhic Man*. Philadelphia: The Jewish Publication Society, 1983.

———. *Kol Dodi Dofek: Listen—My Beloved Knocks*. Edited by Jefferey R. Woolf. Translated by David Z. Gordon. New York: Yeshiva University, 2006.

———. *Worship of the Heart: Essays on Jewish Prayer*. Brooklyn: KTAV, 2003.

Spinoza, Benedict. *Theologico-Political Treatise*. Translated by Martin D. Yaffe. Newburyport MA: Focus, 2004.

Stein, David E. S. *The Contemporary Torah: A Gender-Sensitive Adaptation of the JPS Translation*. Philadelphia: The Jewish Publication Society, 2006.

Steinberg, Milton. *Basic Judaism*. San Diego and New York: Harcourt, 1975.

Steinsaltz, Adin. *Reference Guide to the Talmud*. Jerusalem: Koren, 2014.

Stern, Chaim. *Gates of Prayer: The New Union Prayerbook*. New York: CCAR Press, 1975.

Tirosh-Samuelson, Hava, and Aaron W. Hughes, eds. *Michael Fishbane: Jewish Hermeneutical Theology*. Leiden and Boston: Brill, 2015.

Trible, Phyllis. *Texts of Terror: Jewish-Feminist Readings of Biblical Narratives*. Overtures to Biblical Theology. Minneapolis MN: Fortress Press, 1984.

Tuling, Kari Hofmaister. "Shifting the Focus: Women Rabbis and Developments in Feminist Theology." In *The Sacred Calling: Four Decades of Women in the Rabbinate*, edited by Rebecca Schorr, Rebecca Einstein, and Alysa Mendelson Graf, 379–90. New York: CCAR Press, 2016.

Waskow, Arthur. *Down-to-Earth Judaism: Food, Money, Sex, and the Rest of Life*. New York: William Morrow, 1995.

Whittle, J., and J. van der Vyner, eds. *Religious Human Rights in Global Perspective*. Leiden: Nijhoff, 1996.

Wyschogrod, Michael. *The Body of Faith: God in the People Israel*. Northvale NJ and London: Jason Aronson, 1996.

Zank, Michael, and Ingrid Anderson, eds. *The Value of the Particular: Lessons from Judaism and the Modern Jewish Experience*. Leiden: Brill Academic, 2015.

Index

Borowitz, Eugene, 265–68, 277, 349, 357

Buber, Martin, xxvii, 83–86, 88, 157, 264, 302, 364ch3n9

Cain (biblical figure), 54–56, 59–60

cake, 118–19, 200–207, 246–47, 279

Chabad. *See* Lubavitch Hasidism (Chabad)

chaos, xxiv, xxv, 8, 63, 135, 225, 237, 278

chosenness, 214, 217–18, 232, 253–55, 257, 285, 287–89, 300–301, 309

Christianity: in Cohen's thought, 217–20, 233; compared to Judaism, 35–36, 40–43, 58, 71, 74, 110, 203–4, 213–15, 257, 276; in dialogue with Judaism after Holocaust, 226–32; medieval, 203–4, 210–17; in Rosenzweig's thought, 297–302. *See also* Jesus (of Christian Bible)

Cohen, Hermann, xx, xxvii; and Enlightenment, 217; and ethics, 312; and evil, 53–56, 59; and Garden of Eden, 55; influence on Rosenzweig, 297; influence on Soloveitchik, 262; as interpreter of Kant, 54, 56; and monotheism, 54, 356; and suffering, 216–20, 233, 235, 356

collective guilt, 200, 204, 232

commandment, 31, 78, 277; bonding humans to God, 269–72; and commandedness, xxiv, 158, 187, 223, 234–35, 268, 357–58; and dogmatism, 275; as evidence of God's love, 249–51, 260, 262, 279–80, 285–89, 302, 309, 310;

and fertility, 6; and food, 33; and Garden of Eden, 32; as guideline, 265–66, 277; and holiness, 53, 55; and intellect, 48–49; and kingship, 114; and obedience, 207, 249, 295, 316–19, 342, 357; and pluralism, 312–13; received under duress, 289–90, 310; and redemption, 309; and revelation, 281–85; and Sabbath, 249–51, 257–60, 276; and *Shema*, 134–35, 137, 138–41, 164; as source of ethics, 297, 307–8, 310; Ten Commandments, 67, 69, 290, 322; and transcendence, xx, 33, 99, 271

concrescence, 269, 271

Conservative Judaism, 112, 140, 268, 286, 320, 333

covenant, xxvi, 9, 118, 120, 251–52, 256, 257–80, 281–314, 317; between Abraham and God, 244–49, 304; in ancient Israel, xxviii, 209, 241–80, 285, 302–12, 315–20, 357; as basis of human rights, 302–9; and circumcision, 109; and Holocaust, 220–23, 226–31, 234, 236; between Jacob and Laban, 243–44; as metaphor, xxviii, 241, 260, 265–68, 275, 279–80, 357–58; rituals to enact, 241–49

creation of the world, xxvi–xxvii, 3–34, 224–26, 293; and evil, 14, 26, 35–66, 237, 351–52; *ex nihilo*, 17–20, 257–60; and humanity, 3–7, 12–16, 21–24, 31–34, 35–40, 43–47; and predetermination, 182–84; in Rosenzweig's thought, 297–302, 310; for sake of covenant,

259; and Shabbat, 249, 251–53; and speculation about origins, 30–31. *See also* Ancient Near East: creation stories; first cause; mysticism: and creation

death, 184, 186, 210, 212–14, 233, 292, 298–301, 355–56; and book of life, 72; in childbirth, 176, 192; and choosing life, xxix, 141, 316–17, 319, 342; and corpses, 42, 58, 283; and deathbed, 142–45, 159, 162, 164; of God, 220–23, 236; and Holocaust, 210; as illusion, 163; imagining one's own, 159, 161–63; of Jacob, 142–45, 164; of Jesus, 71, 74, 110, 204; in Joseph story, 198, 200–205; and *Kaddish* prayer, 117; of Kushner's son, 57; and martyrdom, 205; of Moses, 134, 321; as punishment, 200–205, 282, 284; of Rav Kook, 195
deism, 10
determinism, xxi
dualism, xix, 86–87, 101, 115–16, 127, 137

"Eileh Ezkarah" ("These I remember") prayer, 199–205, 232
Einbinder, Susan, 210–16
'Ein-Sof ("without end"), 105–6, 151, 153, 154
Elijah the prophet (biblical figure), 100–104, 137, 324–27
Elohim. See under Tetragrammaton
Emancipation of the Jews, 216–17, 236, 344
Enlightenment, 24–25, 97, 216–17, 236, 311, 344

Enuma Elish. See Ancient Near East: creation stories
essence, 79–82, 105–6, 205, 237, 261, 263, 274, 341, 344, 352
essentialism. *See under* gender
Esther (biblical figure), 290–92. *See also* Purim story
ethics: and Bible, 54, 187, 307–8, 311–12; and Kant, 267, 310–11; and law, xxviii, 237, 294–97, 308, 310, 349; refinement of, 54–56, 59, 308; and religion, 272, 275, 278, 297, 312; and revelation, 331–32; universal, 294–95, 310, 312
Eve (biblical figure), xxvii, 5, 35–40, 47, 53, 54–55, 58–59, 109. *See also* Adam (biblical figure); creation of the world: and humanity
evil, xxvi–xxvii, 351–52, 356; as choice, 14, 43, 46–47, 55–56, 58–60, 63, 187, 189–91, 193; and forgiveness, 73; and Holocaust, 227–31, 236–37; as illusion, 62, 163, 355; as imbalance in God, 41; and impulse to do good, 43–47, 53–56, 58, 60; in Joseph's theology, xviii, 197–99; and the Original Sin, 35–36, 40–41, 58–59; and persecution, 200–204, 211, 232; and politics, 185; as predisposition, 53–54, 59; and reason, 330–31; as socially constructed, 47–53; and theodicy, 60–62, 103, 210, 225; types of, 50–51, 63. *See also* creation of the world: and evil
exile, 62, 194–95, 258, 288, 293, 347
ex nihilo. See under creation of the world

Ezra the scribe (biblical figure), 293, 347

Falk, Marcia, 121–25, 251–54
fatherhood: in Bible, xviii, 95, 143–44, 173, 197–98, 244–48, 293, 316, 319, 328–29; in blessings and prayers, 96–99, 112, 114, 122, 124, 129, 177, 244; and God, xxi, 95, 96–99, 114, 116, 124, 129, 208, 293, 298–99; as metaphor, xviii, 155, 185, 297, 335; and patriarchs, 112; and priesthood, 296
feminism, 90, 96, 103, 111–25, 128–30, 159, 174, 349, 353
fire, 33, 79, 82, 97–98, 202, 210–13, 232, 333; in Bible, 92, 95–96, 100, 102, 258–59; and God's chariot, 92, 95–96; as punishment, 12, 14, 101, 103–4, 115; in ritual, 246; and Torah, 213
first cause, xxvi, 17–20, 28, 81, 182
Fishbane, Michael, 268–72, 277–78
forgiveness, xvii–xix, 70–74, 87, 198–99, 200–205, 232
free will, xxi, 35, 56, 59–60, 63, 187–88, 189–91, 236, 352
Frymer-Kensky, Tikva, 125–31

G-d. See under Tetragrammaton
Geiger, Abraham, 344–46
Gemara, 26, 254–56, 289
gender, xxviii–xxix, 11, 91–132, 175, 352–53; essentialism, 95–96, 99, 115–17, 124; in Hebrew language, 93; in Talmud, 122; in Torah blessings, 121–25
Gikatilla, R. Joseph, 108–11

Goddess worship, 125–28, 130
Greco-Roman world. See Hellenism and the Greco-Roman world
Green, Arthur, 21–24, 28, 86–88, 166, 269
Greenberg, Irving (Yitz), 226–33, 236, 271, 279, 356

Haggadah. See under Passover
halakhah, 12, 118–19, 237–38, 261–68, 277, 312–13, 322–29, 342–43, 349, 358
Halevi, Judah, 257–60, 262, 276
Hannah (biblical figure), 171–93
Hartman, Donniel, 272–75, 278
Hashem. See under Tetragrammaton
Hasidism, xx, 21, 23, 62, 83, 150–54, 162, 165, 185, 187, 265, 353
Hebrew Bible. See Torah
Heidegger, Martin, 223, 268
Hellenism and the Greco-Roman world, 43, 104, 126–28
Heschel, Abraham Joshua, xxi–xxiii, 33–34, 184–88, 193, 302, 338–43, 358
hierarchical relationships, 90, 115–17, 123, 317, 353. See also feminism
High Holy Days, 70, 87, 96–98. See also Rosh Hashanah; Yom Kippur
Hirsch, Samson Raphael, 345–46, 349
holiness, 188; of angels, 9, 11–12; in Cohen's thought, 53–56; and God, xx, 97–98; and Hebrew root, 284; as name of God, 12–13, 31, 60, 71–72, 74–78, 101–2, 179, 181, 206, 208, 229, 254–55, 290, 322, 324, 326–27, 354; of places, 181, 286, 288; and purity, 284–85;

of sacrifices, 177; of Shabbat, 8,
249–53, 276; of texts, 200, 202,
214, 232
Holocaust, xxiii, xxviii, 62, 186, 203,
205, 210, 217, 219–34, 271, 279,
356; and God's silence, 197, 234–
35; and morality, 236, 356
hypostasis, 81, 105–6

Ibn Pakuda, Bachya, xxvi, 16–20, 21,
27–28, 182–84, 193, 293–97, 310, 357
immanence, xx, 86, 98, 166, 189, 191,
221–25, 250, 269–72, 277–78, 302
ineffable, xxiii, 338–42
infertility, 171, 191
intelligent design, 20
Isaac (biblical figure), 62, 108–12,
143–44, 197–98, 244, 284, 293,
316, 319
Islam, 16, 258, 276, 293, 313–14
Israel: and Cohen's thought, 218–19;
and Greenberg's thought, 226–
31; land of, 8, 31, 71, 94, 133–37,
139, 141, 194–95, 281, 288, 293,
296; modern nation-state of,
xxviii, 112, 141, 171, 194–95, 288;
and mysticism, 108, 111; and Novak's thought, 302–9, 312; people
of, 195, 201, 204, 211–14, 281,
320; and pluralism, 312–13; and
rabbinic literature, 31, 72, 143–44,
179, 181, 322, 335, 354; referenced
in prayer, 133–37, 201, 204, 249–
54, 285–89, 309, 320; and *Shema*,
133–37, 138–39, 143–44, 151–52,
157–61, 163, 165; and suffering,
354–56; and women, 116, 127–28.
See also chosenness; covenant:

in ancient Israel; Israelites: in
biblical era; Jacob (biblical figure
also known as Israel)
Israelites: in biblical era, 69–70,
92–95, 135–37, 172, 194, 207, 241–
43, 281–85, 292, 315–18, 321; and
Hellenism, 43; and obedience to
commands, 136–37, 141, 164, 207;
and relationship with God, 4–5,
29–30, 134, 253, 264, 277, 289–92,
313, 354–57; and relationship to
land, 32, 92–95, 141, 164; and sale
of property, 241–43; in Spinoza's
thought, 29; and worship, 8, 70,
136, 141. *See also* chosenness;
covenant: in ancient Israel
I-Thou. See I-You relation
I-You relation, 83–86, 157

Jacob (biblical figure also known as
Israel), 108–12, 164, 243–44, 293,
316, 319; on deathbed, 142–45
James, William, 21
Jerusalem, 4, 8, 62, 91–96, 194–95,
229, 293, 322, 335–36
Jesus (of Christian Bible), 41, 71, 74,
110, 204, 211, 217, 219, 233, 301. *See
also* Christianity
Jewish Renewal Movement, 158
Jonas, Hans, 61, 223–26, 228–30, 233
Joseph (biblical figure), xvii–xix,
197–200, 232, 248; in Bible,
xvii–xix, 197–99, 232; in liturgy,
199–205, 232
Joshua (biblical figure), 259, 347

Kabbalah, xx, 104–11, 152–53, 160,
163, 224, 363ch3n5

Moses (biblical figure): beholding God's presence, 67–70, 82, 85–88; as gifted, 89, 262; in Haggadah, 194; as lawgiver, 29, 72, 134, 143–45, 259, 277, 281–85, 311, 313, 315–22, 332; on Mount Sinai, xxvii, 67–68, 70, 85, 88, 212, 281–85, 322, 339, 343, 346–48, 358; and mysticism, 108–11; in poetry, 212–14; and prayer, 72; in rabbinic literature, 74–78, 322, 327–29; and revelation, 52, 248, 259, 261–62, 277, 281–85, 332, 342–43, 358

motherhood, xxiii, 91–96, 107, 122–23, 186, 197; and childbirth, 114–16, 124, 130, 178, 184; imagery in prayer, 114–17, 130, 171–93; and infertility, 171–93; and *Shekhinah*, 107

Mourner's Kaddish, 117–18, 120

mysticism: and Borowitz, 265; in Buber's thought, 83; and creation, 26, 40, 108–9, 111, 151, 153; definition, xx, 21; and evil, 40–41; in Green's thought, 87–88; and Hasidism, xx, 83, 150–54, 158–63, 165, 187, 265; in Heschel's thought, 184–88; in Jonas's thought, 223–26; and Kabbalah, xx, 104–11; and panentheism, 23; and partnership with God, 33–34; in prayer, 288, 309, 363ch3n5; and Rubenstein, 221; in Schachter-Shalomi's thought, 158–63; and *shefa*, 166–67, 187; and *Shekhinah*, 104–11, 124; and *Shema*, 139, 150–54, 156, 158–63

name of God. *See* Tetragrammaton

naturalism. *See* supernaturalism versus naturalism

negative limits, 306–9

Noah (biblical figure), 56, 186, 295, 303–10, 341

Noahide commandments, 295; as covenant, 302–10

Novak, David, 302–12, 357

omnipotence, 26, 58, 61–62, 183, 355

Original sin. *See* sin: Original

Orthodox Judaism, xx, 89, 155, 226, 269, 315; ultra-, xxviii–xxix, 275, 315, 344–46, 349

panentheism, xix, 23, 76, 161

pantheism, xix, 22–23, 28, 161, 223

Parsee. *See* Zoroastrianism

partnership with God, 22, 24, 90, 174, 357; in covenant, xxvi, 237–80; in Greenberg, 226–32, 234; in Heschel, 33–34, 184–88, 193

Passover, 307, 314, 354; Haggadah, 194; seder, 193–94, 307, 355

Plaskow, Judith, 111–17, 124, 130

pragmatism, 190, 264

prayer, xxii–xxiii, xxv, 34, 41–42, 58, 73, 86, 87, 210, 276, 310, 352–53, 363ch2n4; affects God, 174–75, 180–81, 188, 191–93; forms, 8–9, 11, 12, 27, 43, 71, 89, 137, 147, 270, 280, 330–33, 338; and gender, 96–100, 111–25, 129, 174–79, 180–82, 191–93; and meditation, 145–50, 153–54, 159; and prayer books, 72–73, 111–24, 175–79, 215, 286–89, 309, 321, 338, 362n5, 365n16; and sacrificial system,

Schachter-Shalomi, Zalman, 158–63, 165, 353

Schneerson, Sholom DovBer, 150–54, 155, 165, 353

Scholem, Gershom, 104–11

Second Temple. *See* Temple: in Jerusalem, destruction of

seder. *See under* Passover

sefer Torah. See Torah

Sefirot (Sefiroth, sing., *Sefirah),* 105–11, 124, 152–53

Shabbat, 111, 259–60, 286, 320, 365n16; and blessing children, 121–25; and *Kiddush* prayer, 249–54; origins, 7–8, 27; sacrificial offerings, 9; sanctification of, 7–8, 249–54, 276

Shavuot, 307

shefa, 166–67, 187

Shekhinah, 104–11, 124, 143

Shema, 353; recitation of, 137–67

Shoah. See Holocaust

sin, 96, 178; and Adam, xxvii, 40, 47–53, 58; and angels, 14–15; in Cohen's thought, xxvii, 53–56, 59; communal, 200–205, 232, 356; and God Manipulation, 273; of Golden Calf, 70; in H. Kushner's thought, 57; and mysticism, 108–9; Original, 35–36, 40–43, 54, 58, 110; in rabbinic literature, 43–47, 58, 60, 71–73, 101, 103, 207, 210, 232, 235, 255, 297, 356; and sacrificial system, 147, 164. *See also* retribution and punishment: for sin

Sinai, 112, 116, 124, 268, 309, 320–21, 337–38, 342, 346; in Heschel's thought, 339, 341, 343, 358; in medieval literature, 212–14; in Novak's thought, 303–6, 310; in rabbinic literature, 102, 289–90, 324, 326–27, 347–48, 358; in Soloveitchik's thought, 260–61, 264, 277, 357. *See also* Moses (biblical figure): on Mount Sinai

Soloveitchik, Joseph, xx, 155–58, 165, 236–38, 260–64, 266–67, 277, 280, 353, 357, 366ch5n12, 368ch8n11

soul, 33, 99, 200–201, 257–58; and purity, 40–43, 58, 283; in rabbinic literature, 206, 209, 229; in Rosenzweig's thought, 298–99; and *Shema,* 134, 136, 138, 140–41, 146–49

Spinoza, Benedict, 28–29, 161, 223, 311

Steinberg, Milton, 333–38, 343, 358

Steinsaltz, Adin, 322, 329

suffering, 172, 186, 273–74, 354–56; in Cohen's thought, 216–19, 233; of God, 62–63; in Greenberg's thought, 226–30; and health, 50–51; of Joseph, 199; in medieval texts, 215–16; and punishment, 55; in rabbinic texts, 205–9, 232; and relationship to God, xxviii, 57, 194, 197, 235–38; of righteous, 205–9, 232; and Rubenstein, 220; and Soloveitchik, 237–38; and Suffering Servant, 208–10, 216–20, 226–31, 233

supernaturalism versus naturalism, 63, 183, 335; and Green, 21; and Halevi, 258–59; in Kaplan's thought, 188–93; and Plaskow, 117; and Spinoza, 28–29

In the JPS Essential Judaism Series

Thinking about the Torah:
A Philosopher Reads the Bible
Kenneth Seeskin

Thinking about God: Jewish Views
Rabbi Kari H. Tuling

Justice for All: How the Jewish
Bible Revolutionized Ethics
Jeremiah Unterman

To order or obtain more information
on these or other Jewish Publication
Society titles, visit jps.org.